D0207819

Surveillance Society

The Rise of Antichrist

Dr. Grant R. Jeffrey

Frontier Research Publications, Inc.
P.O. Box 129, Station "U", Toronto, Ontario M8Z 5M4

Surveillance Society

Copyright © 2000 by Dr. Grant R. Jeffrey

Library of Congress Cataloging in Publication Data:
Jeffrey, Dr. Grant R.
Surveillance Society
1. Prophecy   2. Big Brother Surveillance   3. Antichrist
1. Title

July 2000 Frontier Research Publications, Inc.

ISBN 0-921714-62-9

Second Printing: September 2000

Unless otherwise indicated, Scripture quotations are from the Authorized King James Version.

Cover design: The Riordon Design Group
Printed in Canada: Harmony Printing Limited

Table of Contents

Acknowledgments

Surveillance Society — Rise of Antichrist is an exploration of the growing dangers to our privacy and freedom from the relentless development of surveillance technologies and the willingness of governments to exercise that power against citizens. In addition, the book explores how these trends and technological capabilities are setting the stage for the rise of the Antichrist in this generation. For the first time in history it is possible to understand how such developments as examined in this book would make it possible for a future dictator to achieve totalitarian control of the world's population and implement the Mark of the Beast system.

This book is the result of over thirty-five years of research involving thousands of books, articles, interviews with experts in intelligence, military surveillance, and study of the Scriptures. As this book demonstrates, while these trends are dangerous, our faith and hope for the future is grounded upon a strong conviction in the promise of Jesus Christ: "And when these things begin to come to pass, then look up, and lift up your heads; for your redemption draweth nigh" (Luke 21:28).

My parents, Lyle and Florence Jeffrey, have continuously inspired in me a profound love for Jesus Christ and the prophetic truth found in the Word of God. They have constantly encouraged me to share my research on prophecy with others through these books. I am especially thankful to my editorial assistant, Adrienne Jeffrey Tigchelaar, who has provided valuable research and editorial services to make this project possible.

I dedicate *Surveillance Society* to my wife Kaye. She is a continuing inspiration to my work and a faithful partner in the ministry of Frontier Research Publications, Inc. Without her support and assistance this book could not have been completed. I trust that the information revealed in the following pages will encourage you to personally study the Bible's prophecies about the last days and the triumphant return of Jesus Christ to set up His kingdom on earth.

Dr. Grant R. Jeffrey
Toronto, Ontario
July 2000

1

Introduction

The world is on the verge of the greatest crisis in history. The development of revolutionary new military weapons, information warfare, and surveillance technologies are transforming our world. Jesus Christ warned that humanity would experience a tremendous historical crisis just before He returned to establish His Kingdom. This crisis, He indicated, would produce an unprecedented "great tribulation, such as was not since the beginning of the world to this time, no, nor ever shall be" (Matthew 24:21). The prophet Daniel foretold that the terrible "time of tribulation" will last seven years and conclude with the return of the Messiah at the cataclysmic Battle of Armageddon. The prophets also warned that the most evil man in history would arise during this last generation and would be satanically empowered to seize political, economic, military, and religious control of the entire world's population. This man is identified by a number of names throughout the Scriptures, including the "lawless one," "the man of sin," "the Wicked," and even "the abomination of desolation." Yet most people know him by the name given to him by the prophet John in his second epistle — the "Antichrist." This man will embody Satan's age long passion to set himself up as "god" to be worshipped by all of mankind.

For thousands of years millions of Jews, Christians, and even Muslims have been fascinated by the Bible's prophecy that the most wicked dictator in history will arise in the final years of this age, just before the return of Jesus Christ to establish His kingdom on earth. This mysterious person will embody pure evil, satanic possession, and he will demand that humanity worship him as their only true "god" or die during the coming apocalypse. However, in previous times it was very difficult to understand how the Bible's prophecies could ever be fulfilled literally. The book of Revelation describes devastating military attacks from the air, the deliberate poisoning of one-third of the planet's water, and the destruction of a large portion of the planet's population. Serious students of the Bible naturally wondered how these predictions could ever be fulfilled in reality. Did the Scriptural prophecies speak of actual events or were they only a spiritual symbol referring to a symbolic apocalyptic war at the end of the age between good and evil? However, since World War II we have experienced the terrible danger of thermonuclear weapons, biological and chemical warfare, as well as the totalitarian control over billions of people. For the first time in history it is possible to contemplate the destruction of life on this planet. These new technologies have changed history forever. Some scientists fear that these "doomsday" technologies will put an end to human history altogether. Ominously, throughout history every single weapon system, regardless of its power or horror, has ultimately been used in military conflict.

In this book we will explore the detailed prophecies that describe the Antichrist's rise to power, and the nature of the oppressive global government that he will use to enslave humanity until Jesus Christ returns to destroy him. The Scriptures reveal that the Antichrist will rapidly rise in the last days to become the leading political, military, and religious figure in the world. It is important that everyone understand the prophecies about the coming "Wicked One" because God revealed these prophetic truths to us to awaken Christians to the signs of His near return to take His Church to Heaven.

All of those who previously rejected Christ's offer of salvation will be left behind to face the seven years of global cataclysm known as the Tribulation period. During this final great crisis of humanity in the last three and a half years of his dictatorial global government before Armageddon, everyone on earth will face a desperate life-and-death decision. The Antichrist will claim to be "god on earth" and his partner the False Prophet will demand that everyone worship him as "god" and openly declare their allegiance to him by accepting the Mark of the Beast — 666. The Scriptures warn that anyone who chooses to accept the Mark will be damned forever to the lake of fire. However, the Bible promises that anyone who rejects the Antichrist and worships Christ will be saved. If we are to understand the implications of the rush to global government and the astonishing new developments in surveillance technology that will allow the totalitarian government of the Antichrist to quickly introduce his dreaded "Mark of the Beast," it is essential that we understand the warnings of the prophets about the coming world dictator — the Antichrist.

This book will examine the rapid development of a powerful world government that is eroding our national sovereignty and our cherished democratic values. We will investigate the development of a web of international treaties that is preparing the way for the virtual surrender of own national control over our environment, our economy, our currency, our education, and immigration. Step by step, in the name of globalization and the demand of various United Nations' agencies to harmonize our laws with other nations, our national sovereignty is being eroded. The proud national sovereignty of western nations that allowed us to create a free enterprise economy with political and religious freedom is being surrendered by our modern political leaders. These new leaders no longer believe in the patriotic love of their sovereign nation; they have adopted a philosophy of globalism and share the desire to become citizens of the world.

Today we face an unprecedented assault on our precious freedom and privacy due to the remarkable advances in surveillance technology and the increasing desire of national governments throughout the world to spy on their population and collect massive amounts of data about every citizen. The technological advancement in surveillance equipment, including the global spy system known as Project Echelon that can listen to every phone call and Internet communication on earth, is destroying every vestige of our privacy. The creation of a total surveillance society throughout the world is setting the stage for the totalitarian police state described two thousand years ago by the prophet John. An examination of the explosive growth of the Internet and its pervasive influence on modern society reveals that it is transforming our communications and economy while opening the door to the government's complete surveillance of our lives, finances, and actions. In the book of Revelation, John prophesied that the "Mark of the Beast" system would be utilized in the last days to force everyone in society to worship the Antichrist as "god."

The research examined in this book will demonstrate that the technology for implanting computer chips beneath the skin may lay the groundwork for the fulfillment of John's prophecy about the totalitarian police state during the last seven years of this age. The development of sophisticated and revolutionary new weapons systems, neutron bombs including suitcase-sized tactical nuclear weapons, biological, and chemical weapons of mass destruction, and computerized information warfare can neutralize an enemy's economy and infrastructure. The production of revolutionary new weapons using remarkable electromagnetic forces to control the weather, destroy another nation's computer systems, or remotely influence the mind of a human explains how the kingdom of the Antichrist may quickly establish global domination. Finally, we will explore the geopolitical situation that is developing in the shifting power alliances between America, Russia, China, the Arab states, and Israel. This shift in power is laying the groundwork for the dramatic battles that will lead to the establishment and the eventual destruction of the global kingdom of the Antichrist.

A number of biblical prophecies specifically teach that Jesus Christ will return to take His Church to Heaven immediately before the Tribulation period begins. The goal of Christians is the Resurrection, the "blessed hope." For the last two thousand years Christians have longed for the "blessed hope, the appearing of our Savior Jesus Christ." We are commanded by the Lord to rejoice in the constant expectation that "when he who is our life shall appear, then shall we also appear with Him in glory." Therefore the message of prophecy is not one of "doom and gloom" as some have suggested. Rather, Jesus commanded that His followers should respond to the beginning of the fulfillment of the prophecies with joyful anticipation because the prophecy of His return promises redemption for all those who have faith in Him. Jesus said, "And when these things begin to come to pass, then look up, and lift up your heads; for your redemption draweth nigh" (Luke 21:28).

The book of Revelation promises a special blessing to anyone who reads and studies it. "Blessed is he who reads and those who hear the words of this prophecy, and keep those things which are written in it; for the time is near" (Revelation 1:3). Yet, there is no other book in the Bible that is studied less than the book of Revelation. Our Lord Jesus Christ spoke of those who would ignore the prophecies about His return. He said, "O fools, and slow of heart to believe all that the prophets have spoken" (Luke 24:25).

Many Christian lay people and some pastors now believe that the prophetic message of the Scriptures is both controversial and uncertain. After listening to their seminary professors explain a variety of alternative prophetic interpretations about the events of the last days many pastors concluded that it was wiser to avoid the topic entirely. Some Christian commentators have publicly declared that most prophecy teachers and authors, such as myself, are "sensationalists" because we take the Lord's prophecies seriously enough to investigate and discuss whether these predictions are being fulfilled in our generation. However, the Word of God clearly commands Christian believers to pay attention to the prophetic portions of the Scriptures. The apostle Peter assures us that "We have a more sure word of prophecy; whereunto ye do well that ye take heed, as unto a light that shineth in a dark place, until the day dawn, and the day star arise in your hearts" (2 Peter 1:19). There are 31,124 verses in the Bible, of which 27 percent focus on the topic of prophecy. The fact that one-quarter of the Bible is prophecy indicates to us the tremendous importance of the prophetic message in the plan of God.

The Bible declares that "All scripture is given by inspiration of God, and is profitable for doctrine, for reproof, for correction, for instruction in righteousness: That the man of God may be perfect, thoroughly furnished unto all good works" (2 Timothy 3:16,17). An appreciation of the prophecies allows a Christian to fully understand the other great doctrines of the Word of God. The prophecies reprove and correct us, reminding each of us that we will all someday stand before our Lord in Heaven to give an account of our Christian life and our obedience to His commands. The great prophetic truths about the imminent return of Christ encourage believers to live in righteousness by reminding us that our actions will be measured against the eternal standards of God, as opposed to the transitory standards of daily life and the rapidly changing moral values of modern society.

Sir Isaac Newton and the Importance of Prophecy

The great scientist Sir Isaac Newton was also fascinated with Bible prophecy. He wrote many manuscripts about the prophets, and a book called *Observations on the Prophecies of Daniel and the Apocalypse of St. John*. He wrote, "And the giving ear to the prophets is a fundamental character of the true Church. For God has so ordered the prophecies that in the latter days 'the wise may understand, but the wicked shall do wickedly, and none of the wicked shall understand' (Daniel 12:9–10)."

Newton commented on the tremendous importance of prophecy in his book:

> The authority of the Prophets is divine, and comprehends the sum of religion. . . . Their writings contain the covenant between God and His people, with instructions for keeping this covenant, instances of God's judgments upon them that break it: and predictions of things to come. . . .

> For it is a part of this prophecy [Revelation] that it should

not be understood before the last age of this world; and therefore it makes for the credit of this prophecy that it is not yet understood. But if the last age, the age of opening these things, be now approaching, as by the great successes of late Interpreters it seems to be, we have more encouragement than ever to look into these things. . . .

He gave this, and the prophecies of the Old Testament, not to gratify man's curiosities by enabling them to foreknow things, but so that after that they were fulfilled they might be interpreted by the event; and His own providence, not the interpreter's, be then manifested thereby to the world. For the event of things, predicted many ages before, will then be a convincing argument that the world is governed by providence. . . .

The event will prove the Apocalypse; and this prophecy, thus proved and understood, will open the old prophets, and all together will make known the true religion and establish it. . . .

There is already so much of the prophecy fulfilled, that as many will take pains in this study may see sufficient instances of God's providence; but then, the signal revolutions predicted by all the holy prophets, will at once both turn men's eyes upon considering the predictions and plainly interpret them.[1]

Bishop Thomas Newton on the Prophecies

Bishop Thomas Newton, one of the wisest commentators on Bible prophecy in the seventeenth century, declared in his book *Dissertations on the Prophecies* that history was the great interpreter of prophecy. In other words, the fulfillment of the ancient biblical prophecies in our times provides proof of their inspiration and is a warning of events to be fulfilled in the last days when the Messiah will return to establish His kingdom.

Prophecy is, as I may say, history anticipated and contracted; history is prophecy accomplished and dilated, and the prophecies contain the fate of the most considerable nations, and the substance of the most memorable transactions in the world, from the earliest to the latest times. Daniel and St. John with regard to those latter times, are more copious and particular than the other prophets. They exhibit a series and succession of the most important events from the first of the four great empires to the consummation of all things. Their prophecies may really be said to be a summary of the world; and the history of the world is the best comment upon their prophecies. And the more you know of ancient and modern times, and the further you search into the truth of history, the more you will be satisfied of the truth of prophecy.

An understanding of the prophecies strengthens our faith and produces a strong confidence and hope in a world that appears hopeless. These prophetic truths teach those who follow Jesus Christ "to look for a city which hath foundations, whose builder and maker is God." On the basis of this declaration we can be confident that the one quarter of Scripture that is prophetic is absolutely vital in the spiritual life of the individual Christian as well as the Church. The Lord commands His Church to teach "the whole counsel of God."[2]

The first prophetic warning in history was given to Noah before the worldwide flood that destroyed virtually all life on this planet. For one hundred and twenty years Noah and Enoch, "the preacher of righteousness," taught the need for righteousness and warned their evil generation of the coming judgment of God. However, despite the fact that Noah spent over a century building a huge ark, demonstrating his faith in God's prophecy of the coming flood, the whole population rejected the warning. Even when Noah and his family actually entered the huge ark, that generation refused to believe the prophetic warnings until it was too late. When the rain began to fall and the flood waters began to rise, they finally realized that disaster was at hand. However, the doors to the ark were shut. Noah's generation had knowingly rejected God's message. Tragically, that entire generation died.

The message of prophecy is important to the Church in these last days for four basic reasons. The first is that the accuracy of the prophetic message absolutely proves the inspiration of the Scriptures and validates the message of Jesus Christ as the inspired Word of God. Secondly, the prophecies call upon Christians to live in holiness in an immoral world. The New Testament tells us that the hope of the second coming of Christ reminds Christians to live in holiness while awaiting His return, "And every man that hath this hope in him purifieth himself, even as he is pure" (I John 3:3). The third reason prophecy is vital in that it encourages Christians to witness to their friends and family. The apostle John warns us that we have limited time to share our faith with our neighbors. Jesus said, "I must work the works of him that sent me, while it is day: the night cometh, when no man can work" (John 9:4). In the same manner that Jesus urgently witnessed to His generation, because He knew that it was rapidly coming to judgment with the destruction of Israel in 70 AD, the message of prophecy now indicates that our generation is approaching the Second Coming of Jesus Christ. As our Lord Himself warned, our time to witness to those around us is limited. In light of the soon return of our Lord Jesus Christ we need to witness to our generation while we have the opportunity. The fourth and final reason is that prophecy is the most effective way to witness to those who have not yet found faith in Christ. Even those who have never before expressed interest in the Christian faith are often fascinated by the fulfillment of prophecy in our generation that points to the truthfulness of the Word of God.

In 1 Chronicles 12:32 we read, "And of the children of Issachar, which were men that had understanding of the times, to know what Israel ought to do." The tribe of Issachar was noted for their interest in prophecy in "understanding of the times." However, that knowledge was not academic; it was practical. They understood their times so that they would "know what Israel ought to do." Our understanding of the biblical prophecies about our generation and the rise of Antichrist's kingdom should motivate us to become a beacon of light in a dark time when many are looking for a reason to hope. Our hope is in the soon return of Jesus Christ.

Notes

1. Isaac Newton, *Observations on the Prophecies of Daniel and the Apocalypse of St. John* (London: J. Darby and T. Brown, 1733).
2. Thomas Newton, *Dissertations on the Prophecies* (London: R. & B. Gilbert, 1817).

2

Setting the Stage for World Government

Thousands of years ago the prophets Daniel and John foretold that a world government, led by the Antichrist, would seize global power in the last days (Daniel 7:14).

And it was given unto him to make war with the saints, and to overcome them: and power was given him over all kindreds, and tongues, and nations. And all that dwell upon the earth shall worship him (Revelation 13:7–8).

This prophecy by John, and parallel predictions in the book of Daniel, reveal that the population of earth will be placed under the control of a single government in the last days. For the first time in history, one man, the future Antichrist, will have power "over all kindreds, and tongues, and nations." Despite the rise and fall of countless empires throughout history, there has never been a true world government. However, as we begin the new millennium, the elite are moving behind the scenes to create one. The rising power of the United Nations, the International Monetary Fund, World Bank, the World Trade Organization, and the World Court are moving us quickly beyond the days of national sovereignty and politically independent nations.

One of the most effective arguments of globalists in favor of world government is their claim that the hundreds of millions of deaths due to the horrific conflicts of two World Wars and the history of international warfare over the last several centuries shows the absolute necessity of eliminating the nation states that have fought these wars. They argue that if there were no nations then war will become almost impossible. While this sounds reasonable, a closer examination reveals the flaw in such thinking. There are at present far more violent and deadly civil wars that are being fought today *within* the borders of nations than international wars.

For example, numerous sub-national wars between regions, tribes, ethnic, and religious groups have killed many more soldiers and civilians in Rwanda, Burundi, Congo, Sudan, Algeria, and the former Yugoslavia than were ever killed in national wars such as the present conflict between India and Pakistan. If traditional patriotism and national loyalty are destroyed through the creation of world government, then we will certainly witness more outbreaks of internal civil wars. History reveals that civil wars are much more likely to result in atrocities and massacres than traditional national wars. In addition, the history of the past hundred years reveals that civil wars are much more difficult to stop and to reconcile the belligerents.

The Report of the Commission on Global Governance

In 1991, a meeting of elite globalists in Stockholm, Sweden produced a manifesto entitled *Common Responsibility in the 1990s: The Stockholm Initiative on Global Security and Governance.* Many world leaders, including Dr. Boutros Boutros-Ghali (appointed as the Secretary General of the United Nations in 1992), endorsed this key planning document for the coming world government. Another report entitled *Our Global Neighborhood, The Report of the*

Commission on Global Governance, by an independent group of 28 global leaders, describes both the philosophy and the strategy to replace the present situation of fragmented and uncoordinated national governments with a true world government. Since 1992 this advisory group has suggested various ways that the world community of nations could better govern the earth's population. This document illustrates the plans of those who wish to replace our present system of national sovereignty with a new world order under the popular catch phrase of "global governance."

The report *Our Global Neighborhood* claims that the international system that the UN Charter put in place at the end of World War II needs to be renewed. The writers declare that the inadequacies of existing institutions must be overcome. A continuing theme in the document is that the UN needs to create a group of interlocking international norms, while expanding the rule of global law, and the need to find ways of enabling citizens to democratically exert their influence on global processes.[1]

On September 11, 1991, former President George Bush announced to Congress that he was working to create a "New World Order." Bush subsequently used the term "New World Order" more than 200 times in his speeches. However, noting the growing opposition to world government from patriotic citizens who began to realize the true implications for American democracy, Bush's National Security Advisor, Brent Scowcroft, persuaded Bush to refrain from alerting the public about what the New World Order really meant.

The powerful Democratic Senator, Alan Cranston, from California, was at one time the President of United World Federalists. Cranston declared, "I believe deeply in the need for world law. . . . I believe in the concept of federalism on the world scale." However, Senator Cranston also realized they could only achieve their goals of world government by stealth, rather than through open debate and democracy. In an interview to *Transition* magazine, published by the Institute For World Order, Senator Cranston admitted, "The more talk about world government, the less chance of achieving it, because it frightens people who would accept the concept of world laws." The truth is that "the new world order" encompasses the creation of a global government under the United Nations with a joint American and Russian superpower partnership. Tragically, a New World Order will ultimately and inexorably lead to political, economic, and religious slavery for us all.

Former British Prime Minister, Margaret Thatcher, revealed this terrible truth about the coming political merger in Western Europe. Thatcher declared that "it would be the greatest abdication of national and political sovereignty in history." Unfortunately, most people will not listen to the warnings until it is too late — until hundreds of millions have yielded their freedom to the socialist rulers of a new global super state. Sir Geoffrey Howe, the Deputy Prime Minister of the United Kingdom, planned the overthrow of Prime Minister Thatcher because her patriotic pro-British stance stood in the way of the UK's enthusiastic entry into the European Union. Howe admitted that the plans for the formation of the European super state were originally created following the end of World War II.

The ultimate purpose of the New World Order will involve two major goals. The first and most obvious is the consolidation of military and political power. The active military involvement of all the national states of Western Europe, Canada, and the USA, in Operation Desert Storm, was the New World Order's most public revelation of their growing military cooperation. The economic convergence will ultimately affect our lives far more than sporadic military exercises in countries like Iraq and Kosovo. The economic implications of the new global super state will be explored in a later chapter.

The Trilateral Commission

The Council on Foreign Relations was established following World War I in an attempt by the elite groups controlling the financial and political life in the United States to make sure that the future foreign policy of America followed their interests. With more than two thousand current members they commissioned studies, networked their people into the State Department, and built relationships with similar one world government groups in Britain and Europe.

The list of major well-known media personnel that are members of the Council on Foreign Relations is staggering. Many of the well-known major American media people have been members of this secret group for decades. There is an interlocking membership involving key players of the Trilateral Commission (TC), the Council on Foreign Relations (CFR), international banking and manufacturing corporations, high military positions, powerful State Department diplomats, and White House cabinet officials. Very few people make it into the inner circles of true power in Washington unless they have first served as members of the CFR or the Trilateral Commission.

The leader of the powerful Chase Manhattan Bank, David Rockefeller, is the Chairman of the Council on Foreign Relations and is also the Chairman of the North American division of the Trilateral Commission. It has been publicly reported that Presidents Richard Nixon, Gerald Ford, Jimmy Carter, George Bush, and William Clinton were members of the Council on Foreign Relations and most also joined the Trilateral Commission. President Reagan was the only recent president who was not a member of this organization, however, his vice president, George Bush, was a long standing member. The presidential elections have been reduced to popularity polls because citizens are given only two real choices: Team A or Team B. The teams wear different colored sweaters, but the hidden management, ownership, and players are virtually identical. Most cabinet members, senior military staff, and State Department officials in every administration are also involved in the CFR or the Trilateral Commission.

The *Manchester Union Leader* ran an editorial during the 1979 presidential primaries that warned about the Trilateral Commission: "It is quite clear that this group of extremely powerful men is out to control the world." President Ronald Reagan's administration had at least 225 CFR and TC members. George Bush's administration was overwhelmingly represented by CFR and Trilateral members, including almost every member of the White House cabinet. When President Bill Clinton took office, every single officer of his new cabinet and sub-cabinet were drawn exclusively from the members of the CFR and TC.

The Council on Foreign Relations is committed to the elimination of existing national boundaries and the merging of all nation states into a powerful world government. Members of the CFR and their globalist allies in other key nations have shaped the economic, foreign, and defense policies of the United States of America, Britain, France, Canada, Japan, and Germany for the last fifty years. The move towards a New World Order is no accident. Every single move has been meticulously planned by these secret groups. It's time to wake up and realize where they are taking our nations, our democratic rights, and our freedom. The purpose of the Trilateral Commission and the Council on Foreign Relations is to quietly infiltrate the decision-making bodies of government, education, business, the military, and the media, to consciously influence the key leaders to adopt the globalist philosophy of the New World Order. The whole process depends on networking at the most sophisticated level.

The Council on Foreign Relations described its methods and goals as follows:

> In speaking of public enlightenment, it is well to bear in mind that the Council has chosen as its function the enlightenment of the leaders of opinion. These, in turn, each in his own sphere, spread the knowledge gained here in ever-widening circles.

The National Security advisor to former President Jimmy Carter, Zbigniew Brzezinski, and David Rockefeller, as key members of the secretive CFR, formed the Trilateral Commission in 1973. The Trilateral Commission brought together the elite power brokers from the areas of the military, politics, and business from the three vital geographical spheres that now control the world. The United States, Japan, and the European Union are the dominant superpowers in the key globalist groups (the United Nations, NATO, and the World Trade Organization).

Initially the Trilateral Commission membership included three hundred of the most elite leadership of the three great regions that now control the planet. The Trilateral Commission described their purpose as follows:

> The founders of the Commission believed it important that cooperation among Western Europe, North America (including Canada) and Japan be sustained and strengthened — not only on issues among these regions but in a global framework as well.

The declared political purpose of the Trilateral Commission is to achieve "close trilateral cooperation in keeping the peace, in managing the world economy, in fostering economic redevelopment and alleviating world poverty which will improve the chances of a smooth and peaceful evolution of the global system" (*The Trilateral Commission: Questions and Answers*, 1980).

The plan required that each of the three geopolitical superpowers must create a political, military, and economic alliance to dominate neighboring countries in their respective hemisphere. Once they were able to consolidate geopolitical and military control in their own sphere, their final step will be to merge the three great spheres of power into a true one-world government.

The Trilateral Commission became publicly known during President Carter's administration. The press realized that twenty of Carter's highest officials and cabinet members belonged to the secret group, including President Carter, Vice President Mondale, and the head of the CIA. An article in the *Atlantic Monthly* reported, "Although the Commission's primary concern is economic, the Trilateralists pinpointed a vital political objective: to gain control of the American presidency." Craig Karpel wrote a fascinating book about the inner workings of the Carter presidency entitled *Cartergate: The Death of Democracy* in which he stated:

> The presidency of the United States and the key cabinet departments of the federal government have been taken over by a private organization dedicated to the subordination of the domestic interests of the United States to the international interests of the multinational banks and corporations. It would be unfair to say that the Trilateral

Commission dominates the Carter Administration. The Trilateral Commission *is* the Carter Administration.

Regardless of whether the White House administration is in the hands of the Republicans or the Democrats, the true power that rules America is concentrated in the hands of the several thousand individuals from every key area of American society who have been nominated to join this globalist elite.

There is a third secretive globalist group that is centered in Europe. It has now attracted elite members from every key nation on earth. It is by far the most secretive of the private international councils working to achieve world government. It is known as the Bilderbergers. In the early 1950s the political and financial leadership of war-torn Europe gathered at the Hotel de Bilderberg in Oosterbeek, Holland, to create the essential plans and relationships to unify the nations of Europe for the first time since the days of Rome. During the last five decades they have held top-secret meetings totally closed to the press. Although they are publicly known as the Bilderbergers, the members call their group "The Alliance." There are strict rules of censorship against members ever discussing plans and policies outside their secret meetings.

The Bilderberger group was initially financed by the US Central Intelligence Agency and organized by US General Walter Bedell Smith. Key members included Colin Gubbins, head of British intelligence, Stansfield Turner, director of the CIA, Henry Kissinger, Lord Rothschild, and Lawrence Rockefeller. They began to meet twice a year to consolidate their efforts to create the "United States of Europe" as well as their ultimate plans for world government. A four-day meeting of the Bilderberg group involved 111 members from twenty-four nations and occurred at Sintra, Portugal ending June 6, 1999.

During the last few decades the powerful members of the Council on Foreign Relations, the Trilateral Commission, and the extremely secretive international group, the Bilderbergers, have consolidated their control of the military, the economy, and the political arena throughout the governments of America, Canada, Europe, and Asia. The globalist planners admit that:

> "The public and leaders of most countries continue to live in a mental universe which no longer exists — a world of separate nations — and have great difficulties thinking in terms of global perspectives and interdependence."[2]

The globalist elite realize that people love their countries, and will not readily give up their beloved nation unless motivated by fear. President George Bush explained that global government could not be achieved unless some great public crisis motivated the population to abandon their national sovereignty. Bush warned, "From chaos will emerge the New World Order."

The great English historian, Arnold Toynbee, observing the terrible devastation caused by the great wars in the last century, concluded in his book *Surviving the Future* that it was essential for a world government to be formed to prevent the total extinction of humanity in a future war between the world's super powers. Toynbee wrote:

> We are approaching the point at which the only effective scale for operations of any importance will be the global scale. The local states ought to be deprived of their sovereignty and subordinated to the sovereignty of a global world government. I think the world state will still need an armed police [and the] world government will have to command sufficient force to be able to impose peace. . . . The people of each local sovereign state will have to renounce their state's sovereignty and subordinate it to the paramount sovereignty of a literally worldwide world government. . . . I want to see a world government established.[3]

These words about the need for world government are no longer considered revolutionary. Unfortunately, Toynbee's rejection of the value and need for a traditional sovereign nation state to preserve our democracy, freedom, and culture, is now shared by the financial, political, and media elite who see themselves as "world citizens" and are now confidently planning to create a true new world order.

The Bible revealed that in the ancient past, all the peoples on earth lived as one common community sharing one common language. However, the wicked men of that day joined together to defy God by creating an engineering feat — the Tower of Babel in ancient Mesopotamia. The Lord intervened and miraculously confused their language, preventing them from communicating or understanding one another. He destroyed their project by creating a multitude of new languages, forcing the population to separate into individual language groupings that have now continued for thousands of years. Through God's supernatural intervention at the Tower of Babel the first language groupings and nation-states were created. The nation state is part of God's long-term plan for humanity to preserve the cultural diversity of mankind. The prophecy of Revelation foretold that the nations will still continue to exist in the New Earth after the completion of the Millennium. "And the nations of those who are saved shall walk in its light, and the kings of the earth bring their glory and honor into it" (Revelation 21:24).

Now, after thousands of years of national independence, elite groups from around the world are planning to create a New World Order that will unite all of the nations on earth into a one-world government. Zbigniew Brzezinski, the former National Security Adviser to President Carter and a founding member of the globalist Trilateral Commission, wrote *Between Two Ages*, a book that strongly argued the case for world government. Brzezinski wrote that "national sovereignty is no longer a viable concept." Realizing that the natural patriotism of citizens of the United States, Canada, and many other nations would prove to be a serious obstacle to their globalist plans, Brzezinski suggested that world government could best be achieved through gradual "movement toward a larger community of developed nations . . . through a variety of indirect ties and already-developing limitations on national sovereignty."[4]

The United Nations and the Coming World Government

These elite groups have embarked on a long-range program to break down the sovereignty of all nation states, including the USA and Canada. Henry Morgenthau, a member of the globalist Council on Foreign Relations and a former Treasury Secretary for President Roosevelt, declared, "We can hardly expect the nation-state to make itself superfluous, at least not overnight. Rather, what we must aim for is recognition in the minds of all responsible statesmen that they are really nothing more than caretakers of a bankrupt international machine which will have to be transformed slowly into a new one."

A key element in this strategy is their plan to "financially bankrupt the international machine." Nations will be encouraged to turn to the International Monetary Fund (IMF) and World Bank for a financial bailout, but under the condition that borrowers must abandon their national sovereignty. The IMF and the World Bank are aware that a worldwide financial collapse is the key event that will allow them to seize control of the nations' currencies and economies in preparation for global governance.

In 1999, the Ford Foundation financed a provocative United Nations study called *Renewing the United Nations System*, written by two former UN officials, Sir Brian Urqhart and Erskine Childers. The study recommended significant changes to streamline and strengthen UN operations and suggests that the United Nations General Assembly, the Security Council, the International Monetary Fund, World Health Organization, and International Labor Organization be transferred to one central location, possibly Bonn or New York, to improve efficiency and centralize political control. The authors also recommended the abolition of the current weighted voting system of the International Monetary Fund that permits the superpowers to dictate policy in favor of a radical new voting system allowing impoverished third world nations to dictate where and when loans would be granted from rich countries to poorer ones.[5]

This proposal is obviously intended to lay the foundation for a one-world government. Consider this quotation: "While there is no question, *at present*, of the transformation of the UN system into a supranational authority, the organization is in a transitional phase, basically shaped and constrained by national sovereignty, but sometimes acting outside and beyond it."[6] Notice the provocative use of the phrase, *"at present."* This document, in its entirety, constantly refers to: "gradual limitation of sovereignty," "notable abridgements of national sovereignty," "chipping away at the edges of traditional sovereignty," and "small steps towards an eventual trans-sovereign society." The authors discuss their plan to progressively erode, and then replace, our nation's cherished sovereignty. However, they recommend that the transition proceed gradually, so as not to alarm citizens of Western democracies.

This UN report, *Renewing The United Nations System*, also recommends very significant steps toward world government. Throughout the document, the authors discuss interim steps that must be taken "until the world is ready for world government." The report suggests that the United Nations should independently raise funds for its own budget by assessing a global surcharge tax on "all arms sales," on "all transnational movement of currencies," on "all international trade: or on the production of such specific materials as petroleum," and "a United Nations levy on international air and sea travel."[7] Other recommendations include assessing a "one day" income tax on all people of the planet every year. Proposals to have the UN assess a global tax on the citizens of the world are a key indication of the planned gradual transformation from the existing international UN consultative body of member states toward the creation of a truly global super state. The United Nations has also called for a one-time global tax to be used to reduce government deficits and stimulate economic activity. This incredible precedent represents a major step toward the coming world government. If the UN was able to independently generate its own global revenue to fund its annual budgets then it would no longer depend on the political and financial support from its member states.

The study, *Renewing the United Nations System*, presents a series of political steps required to establish a powerful new world government. This is obviously a key strategy to build public support for the replacement of the historical sovereignty of our individual nations with a newly enhanced United Nations that will ultimately become the nucleus of a powerful world government. There is a huge difference between the present UN system, which is an assembly of representatives of national governments, and the recently proposed plan that would have parliamentarians directly elected by all citizens throughout the planet. Using the example of the directly elected European Parliament representing the citizens of the European Union, many globalists are now calling for a "world people's assembly."[8]

The former leader of the USSR, ex-President Mikhail Gorbachev, has now become an international senior statesman and is working behind the scenes as a public spokesperson for a number of world government groups. It is interesting that Gorbachev has called for the creation of regional UN security councils to work toward world government under a mandate from the United Nations. In May 1993, Gorbachev wrote an column for a United Kingdom newspaper, *The Daily Telegraph*, stating that there was an urgent need for:

> . . . a European Security Council, a Secretary General for Europe, structures that have authority and a collective mandate, plus military forces for prevention of future crises and for rapid deployment when necessary. . . . Obviously, the United States and Canada need to be associated with these structures, but these new organizations would take on regional functions directly. . . . Many of today's tragedies are born from the absolute ascendancy given to national sovereignty. People have the right to their identity, culture, and language. But to carry this principle beyond the bounds of reason mires us in problems that no one can solve.[9]

The European Union and its elected European Parliament is certainly the most advanced and sophisticated of the world's developing supranational organizations that are intended to ultimately replace the historic role of the nation state. While this organization of nation states is unique in the world today, it is a pattern that almost certainly will follow in the years ahead if the globalists have their way.

The New International Criminal Court

By the year 2002, the International Criminal Court (ICC) will be set up in The Hague, Netherlands. The purpose will be to try individual soldiers, anywhere in the world, who are accused of war crimes. The existing International Court of Justice, often called the World Court, is also at The Hague, but it only rules on cases or disputes between sovereign states. To date, 97 countries have signed the new global war crimes ICC treaty but it requires 60 nations to officially ratify the treaty before it comes into effect. So far 12 nations have ratified the treaty. This treaty is one more step toward the globalization of criminal law.

There is serious concern in the US Senate that the proposed statutes for the International Criminal Court will permit the trials of American soldiers and US civilians who are on active duty around the world. As a result of this concern, the American representatives have proposed that any prosecution must first be approved by the UN Security Council where the United States has a veto vote. However, the other nations have refused to accept this American proposal.[10]

The Totalitarianism of the New European Union

Christopher Booker, a British journalist, spoke to the Institute of Directors at a lecture in the United Kingdom in February 1995, on the topic: "Europe and Regulation — The New Totalitarianism." Booker warned that the new reality within the nations of the European Union was no longer a truly democratic one. For example, the people of the United Kingdom are now living under a new undemocratic system of European Union governmental power that does not appear to be responsive in any practical way to the input of the average citizen. Booker provided examples of the overwhelming flood of unnecessary regulations flowing from the bureaucrats serving the appointed members of the EU's executive in Brussels, the European Commission. Booker defended his position that Britain and all other member states within the

European Union are progressively becoming members of an undemocratic and totalitarian society by stating that, "the illusion is still given us . . . that our democratically-elected politicians are still somehow in charge, able to make decisions on our behalf."

However, Booker noted that "it is no longer the elected politicians who are even nominally in control. It is not even those shadowy armies of officials who, behind the scenes, at least go through the motions of formulating those decisions. . . . What is in control is the system itself. And, with rapidly accelerating momentum in the past few years, it has been turning into a very odd system indeed." Booker had noted that the useless and restrictive EU regulations were often so oppressive that when UK citizens wrote to their British MP requesting their personal intervention to solve their problem, they were given an eternal go-around involving self-justification letters from the very EU bureaucrat who originated the offending regulation in the first place. Booker also explained that the European Union system is not, "in any recognizable, traditional sense a democracy. It is a perfect example of a closed system, which has not touched reality at any point. Nothing at all has been achieved. The constituent is still in his awful mess. The only lesson he has learned, if he didn't know it already, is that the bureaucracy, the monster, is always right. Whatever it does."[11]

Christopher Booker pointed out that the European Union's new system of supranational government is a system basically out of control and without any meaningful political input from individual citizens. The reporter argued that such a system was, in reality, authoritarian. Unfortunately, in a super-state system like the European Union, the tendency is for the unelected bureaucrats to continue issuing regulations without responding to criticism. In addition, the democratic remedy for bad decisions is unlikely to work, because the regulators are so far away and are not subject to elections or to political pressure from locally elected MPs. As a result, the correction of bad EU decisions such as the disastrous European Common Agricultural Policy, is virtually impossible. Booker estimates that it might take 25 years or more for the nationally elected EU politicians to reverse this disastrous policy.[12]

It certainly seems that the world's first super-national experiment is not a promising example of successful world government for those who truly love their country, their freedom, and their democratic way of life. Despite the obvious trappings of democracy, the European Parliament does not possess the democratic political power to choose executives, set specific laws, or establish or alter taxation. Most of the real political power in the European Union still lies in the hands of the twenty-one appointed members of the EU Executive Commission. The directly elected European Parliament is little more than a showpiece "debating society" with no real political power or substantive influence compared to the powerful unelected Executive Commission.

The unwavering pattern displayed by all international organizations is that real political power is exercised secretly by key members of the elite group from behind locked boardroom doors. Subsequently, their private decisions are "sold" to the public through spin-doctors, public relations programs, and effective media manipulation. History suggests that meaningful representative democracy can only function effectively at the local or national level. Once we enter the arena of international politics between non-government organizations (NGOs) and nation states, true democratic government is quietly replaced by sophisticated bargaining and trade-offs negotiated behind the scenes between the little-known but key power brokers controlling these international organizations. The present situation in the Executive Commission of the European Union is but a preview of how true power will be exercised in a future world government. History suggests that a powerful individual will inevitably arise to seize political power and rule this future world government.

Enlarging the Powers of the United Nations

While UN spokesmen are usually quite discrete in discussing the approaching world government, occasionally a diplomat or a report will reveal their plans. Former British Foreign Secretary Douglas Hurd claimed in an interview that the United Nations needs to prepare itself to take on an "imperial role." He declared that the UN must usurp national sovereignty and take control of countries as the occupying military and political power when governments collapse, as in Kosovo, Somalia, Rwanda, and Sierra Leone. During an interview held at the UN in New York, Foreign Secretary Douglas Hurd drew attention to what he called "a new phase in the world's history." There is a need for the UN to intervene in crisis situations earlier to "prevent things getting to the stage where countries are run by corrupt war lords, as in Somalia," he said. Hurd warned that since the breakup of the former Soviet Union — leaving three or four crisis areas — the United States was the lone superpower but it had no wish to become the "policeman of the world." While the United States is demanding that we must create a more unified and efficient UN structure, US diplomats are arguing that there is an urgent need to organize the world body's peace-keeping forces to deal with global hot spots like Kosovo, Haiti, Rwanda, and Sierra Leone.

This is part of a trend of powerful European and North American politicians encouraging this new variation of neo-colonialism. Some propose that the UN must establish some kind of "trusteeship" over nations whose governments are collapsing in disarray due to drought, famine, or civil war, such as recently occurred in Somalia, the Congo, Rwanda, and Sierra Leone. These tragic situations in Africa, as displayed on CNN, provide ready-made propaganda for those who have an underlying goal to establish the United Nations as the nucleus for world government. It is difficult to observe the tragic collapse of governments, economies, and peace throughout Africa, the Balkans, and parts of Southeast Asia, without agreeing that some drastic intervention is necessary to save these people from an approaching apocalypse.

Plans for a United Nations Army

A key goal of the globalists is to create a permanent standing army of significant size that will allow the UN Security Council to enforce the will of the governing world body against any renegade nation or group of rogue nations opposing its political agenda. In the last decade, the UN engaged in far more peace-keeping operations than it did in its first forty years. In the 1990s, the UN's peace-keeping budget increased over 1000 percent, and their military personnel in UN police operations increased 7000 percent. In addition, one hundred times as many civilian personnel are now involved in UN peace-keeping operations. The UN Security Council has deployed troops in two dozen nations around the world at an annual cost of over $3 billion in the last few years. At present there are fifteen peace-keeping operations in Africa, Asia, Europe, Haiti, and the Middle East.

Significantly, an article in *Newsweek* in 1994 called for the creation of a powerful standing army for the New World Order to respond to future military crises anywhere in the world.

> The United Nations needs its own army, accountable not to national governments but to the United Nations itself. The rich nations would have to donate equipment to such an army; real live soldiers would be recruited from volunteers. Some would be trained mercenaries, like the Nepalese Gurkhas; others would be units from the armies of the western world.[13]

Many articles have also appeared in the *New York Times*, *TIME*, and *The Economist*, written by political, military, and foreign affairs specialists calling for the creation of a permanent standing army for the United Nations that would be under the control of the UN Security Council. The August 1994 issue of *The Economist* contained an article about the disasters in Somalia and Rwanda as the UN repeatedly tried but failed to create a professional international army from the disparate units of dozens of military forces provided by its member states. Often the donated ammunition was of a different caliber than the weapons, the troops were not trained for the supplied equipment, and the soldiers were often commanded by foreign officers unable to speak the language of the troops.

A recent study of the tragedy of Rwanda revealed that the United Nations saw disaster coming, but was paralyzed by competing political agendas and general indifference of the UN Security Council. When the UN finally acted, after the horrible pictures of genocide filled our television screens, it was a case of "too little too late." As one commentator noted,

> Never has intervention been needed more quickly than in Rwanda; never has it materialized more slowly. A prompt response when the slaughter began in April could not have saved all the victims, but it might have saved a great many. . . . Their foot-dragging over Rwanda is the best argument yet for the UN to have a small flexible peacekeeping force of its own. A standing force would respond to emergencies only when the Security Council told it to . . . it would be ready to try at once, not after UN officials had gone cap in hand to umpteen governments. The idea bristles with tricky questions: command, recruitment, training, pay, nationality, transport, supply, and support back-up. But it should be possible to create a brigade-sized force of this kind. And it is what the UN needs if it is to be a peacekeeper worthy of its name.[14]

The creation of a permanent United Nations rapid reaction armed force will be one of the key milestones on the road to world government. The UN Secretary-General Kofi Annan has repeatedly called for the creation of a permanent UN rapid deployment military force of sufficient size to defeat any foreseeable potential opponent. He wants member states to provide these trained soldiers with equipment and necessary funding on a permanent basis, to be supported by each member state's defense budget. Secretary-General Annan is committed wholeheartedly to the concept of the coming new world order that will replace national sovereignty with a world government led by the United Nations.

Despite all of the obvious problems, the global education of the new generation in favor of world government, has been very successful according to the results of a new poll taken by the University of Maryland. The study found that 61 percent of the respondents supported the process of globalization, while 35 percent felt that it should be stopped. Interestingly, a full 76 percent of respondents supported global free trade.[15]

Israel's Key Role in Plans for World Government

Israel plays a key role in the secret plans for world government because of its strategic position on the land bridge that links Europe, Asia, and Africa. Whatever major military power controls the land bridge between the three continents is in a position to dominate geopolitical world events. Israel is vital to any super power that has plans to dominate world events. Their strong army and powerful air force can militarily dominate the surrounding nations of the Middle East and exercise control over the Persian oil fields and the Suez Canal, both of which are essential for European, Middle Eastern, and African trade. Whoever can control the oil supply of the Middle East that fuels all of European, Asian, and North American industry is in a position to control the world. That is why both Russia and America are tremendously interested in the ultimate results of the Arab–Israeli Middle East Peace talks.

It also explains the tremendous financial support and enormous arms shipments by both super powers, as well as China, to that strategic area during the last five decades. Seven of the largest arms-importing nations in the world are found in the Middle East, surrounding the nation of Israel. Despite the fact that Israel is one of the smallest nations on the planet, composed mostly of empty desert, the largest nations of the world are very interested in the final outcome. Those elite groups that are planning to create a global government are working to coordinate with the Jewish socialist leaders of Israel's present Labor coalition to assure that the Jewish state plays its assigned part.

Israel possesses only 8,020 square miles of territory (only 3 percent the size of Texas) and its population of only six million citizens is less than one-tenth of one percent of the earth's present population of over six billion. The tiny Jewish state is surrounded and opposed by the thirty-five Muslim states composing the Islamic League. These Islamic nations possess 8,879,548 square miles of territory and have a combined population of 804 million. To put this in perspective, the surrounding Islamic nations are 1,107 times larger than the Jewish state. The Islamic and Arab countries possess vast uninhabited areas within the 8,879,548 square miles of their enormous territory (over 500 times larger than Israel and almost three times larger than the size of the continental United States). In addition, the Islamic nations own vast oil reserves that could easily provide the wealth to facilitate the building of Palestine.

Despite this incredible imbalance between the tiny Jewish state and the overwhelming power and territory of their Muslim opponents, many debates, conferences, and resolutions are passed every month against the nation of Israel by many international organizations, including the United Nations. The leaders of these nations recognize that if the prophesied Battle of Armageddon ever starts, it will almost certainly begin in Israel. Jerusalem, the spiritual home of three major religions, Judaism, Christianity, and Islam, captures the focus and attention of the world's governments and citizens. Twenty-five centuries ago, the prophet Zechariah foretold that the nations of the world would form a huge alliance and attack Jerusalem and Israel in the last days.

> Behold, I will make Jerusalem a cup of drunkenness to all the surrounding peoples, when they lay siege against Judah and Jerusalem. And it shall happen in that day that I will make Jerusalem a very heavy stone for all peoples; all who would heave it away will surely be cut in pieces, though all nations of the earth are gathered against it. (Zechariah 12:2–3)

Today humanity faces the greatest crisis in our history. One path leads toward an abyss of unimaginable destruction that could mean the end of human life on this planet; perhaps the end of history itself. The world is endangered by rampant nationalism and brutal ethnic hatreds that may in the near future be equipped with the devastating power of nuclear, chemical, biological, and electromagnetic weapons, and could easily lead to catastrophic horrors that may far exceed the worst terrors of World War II. Another path leads toward the New World Order that could quickly allow a future totalitarian government to extinguish human freedom forever. A century ago the British Lord Acton warned, "Absolute power corrupts absolutely." A strong argument can be made that human freedom and democratic choice can only prevail in a political system that permanently divides real power among different groups to create natural checks and balances between competing interests. However, current trends are leading us inexorably toward a totalitarian New World Order in which all political, military, and religious power will be exercised by one supranational global institution that will inevitably be led by one supreme leader.

The fundamental problem we face regarding New World Order is that, even if the first few leaders of the coming global government are benevolent in their intentions, history strongly suggests that eventually someone will rise to power who will have evil totalitarian intentions. According to the ancient prophecies of the Bible that future dictator, known as the Antichrist, will achieve absolute political power over the global government, enabling him to create a worldwide totalitarian dictatorship. In the coming New World Order there will be no opposing independent nation states left such as America or the United Kingdom to mount a military or political alliance against a totalitarian world government. Where would the suffering citizens of such a worldwide dictatorial government turn for relief from the long dark night of political and religious slavery? Our world would quickly descend into a black abyss of absolute totalitarian power beyond our darkest nightmares. The awesome new electromagnetic frequency, nuclear, and biological weapons together with the overwhelming new surveillance technologies of the coming "Big Brother" government will leave humanity without any realistic hope of revolution or political freedom. Unfortunately, this dreadful nightmare awaits humanity at the end of the road toward world government proposed by the globalist elite proponents of this "Brave New World Order." The prophecies of the Word of God provide the only hope for humanity faced with such overwhelming military and police powers. At the moment when it seems that no hope remains for human freedom, the Scriptures assure us that Jesus Christ, the Messiah, will return from Heaven with His army of angels and resurrected saints to utterly defeat the Antichrist and his evil forces forever. Then Christ will establish His eternal Kingdom of God on earth.

Notes

1. *Our Global Neighborhood, The Report of the Commission on Global Governance* (Oxford University Press, 1995).

2. Richard N. Cooper, Karl Kaiser, Masataka Kosaka, *Toward a Renovated International System*, Trilateral Task Force (1977).

3. Arnold Toynbee, *Surviving the Future*, 1971.

4. Zbigniew Brzezinski, *Between Two Ages* (New York: Greenwood Publishing Group, December, 1982).

5. Brian Urqhart and Erskine Childers, *Renewing the United Nations System* (Uppsala: Dag Hammarskjold Foundation, 1994).

6. Brian Urqhart and Erskine Childers, *Renewing the United Nations System* (Uppsala: Dag Hammarskjold Foundation, 1994).

7. Brian Urqhart and Erskine Childers, *Renewing the United Nations System* (Uppsala: Dag Hammarskjold Foundation, 1994).

8. Brian Urqhart and Erskine Childers, *Renewing the United Nations System* (Uppsala: Dag Hammarskjold Foundation, 1994).

9. Mikhail Gorbachev, *The Daily Telegraph*, May 1993.

10. Evelyn Leopold, "Washington Fights Battle to Change New Global Court," *Reuters*, 13 June, 2000).

11. Joe de Courcy, *Globlists vs The Nation State* (Brimpsfield: Intelligence International Ltd. 1995).

12. Joe de Courcy, *Globlists vs The Nation State* (Brimpsfield: Intelligence International Ltd. 1995).

13. *Newsweek*, 26 September, 1994.

14. *Economist*, August, 1994.

15. David Briscoe, *Associated Press*, 1 April, 2000.

3

NATO's Military Strategy in Support of World Government

The Growing Military Power of Europe

Following the close of the catastrophic and costly World War II, America and Canada strongly supported the creation of the North Atlantic Treaty Organization (NATO) in 1948 to prepare a powerful defensive alliance against the huge armies of Russia and the Warsaw Pact nations. A secondary goal of NATO was to create a powerful military alliance to prevent Germany from ever again becoming a strong independent military power in central Europe, threatening the peace of the world as it had, twice already, in that century. The Europeans and Americans both felt that it was safer to have Germany inside the alliance where they could closely monitor her activities. Most analysts and historians agree that NATO is the most successful military and strategic alliance in history.

Since the beginning of the political movement in the 1960s to create a "United States of Europe," there have been repeated negotiations and plans to develop a powerful European military force composed of the united armies of member nations, capable of providing an independent defense of the continent. However, a combination of factors prevented this. The Western European governments were reluctant to invest the necessary funds to create a world-class military force. But, more importantly, the United States was powerfully opposed to an independent European military force because it could greatly reduce America's ability to enlist Europe's political, economic, and military support in support of her own foreign policy goals.

However, during the last decade, America's citizens as well as her politicians, have become weary of paying more than $40 billion annually to provide the lion's share of the military forces necessary to protect Western Europe. Being the world's policeman, with the American taxpayer bearing the financial burden, became less and less acceptable to Washington. As a result, the United States began to pressure members of the European Union to increase their defense funding as well as to take steps toward creating a powerful military force for the independent defense of Europe. The weakness of Europe's individual military forces and uncoordinated political leadership was unfortunately demonstrated by their inability to assist appropriately during the recent air bombing campaign against Serbia. Within weeks of the start of that campaign, it became apparent that the various European NATO allies (with the exception of Britain) could not provide the essential high-technology military forces and massive air-lift capacity necessary to guarantee military success against sophisticated air defenses. As a consequence of their military deficiencies, the European allies were repeatedly forced to defer to US and British military leadership and strategy.

In 1999, following decades of failed efforts, the European Union met in Helsinki, Finland to create a pan-European armed force. Composed of elite soldiers from each of the European Union's member states, this rapid-reaction force, initially comprising 60,000 soldiers, will be prepared for any crisis within Europe. Over the years, this force is expected to be enlarged to become capable of independently defending Europe from any potential enemy force. Once this process has begun, it will almost certainly gather political momentum. One political consequence of this newly created European Union military force is that America is beginning to realize that the former political dependence of Europe upon US military leadership in NATO (characterizing their relationship since World War II) will probably decrease.

NATO's New Imperialistic Strategic Doctrine

The representatives of the member states of NATO met in Washington on April 23–24, 1999, to celebrate the 50th anniversary of the military alliance and to negotiate the basis for continuation and expansion of the alliance in the new millennium. Many of the members of NATO had raised concern over the necessity for the military alliance, since the former Soviet Union and communist Eastern European nations (composing the former Warsaw Pact) were no longer considered a serious military threat to Western Europe. Other important issues were raised regarding the growing requests of formerly communist Eastern European nations to become members in NATO despite the total opposition to this trend by Russia.

The most serious issue involved the role of NATO military forces in future conflicts anywhere in Europe. Prior to the Kosovo conflict, for example, NATO had resolutely refused to become involved in any military operations outside the geographic region of its member states because the NATO treaty specifically limited its role to defense of the national integrity of its member states. That is why, for example, NATO played no role in the British war to regain the Falkland Islands from Argentina or America's military action in Grenada. Even though members of NATO, such as Britain, Canada, Italy, and Turkey, contributed significantly to the Gulf War response to Iraq's invasion of Kuwait, they did so as individual nations and not under the military unified direction of NATO. However, the human rights abuses in Kosovo and the obvious danger to European stability in the Balkans caused by Serbia's military actions, forced NATO to change its rules and to intervene decisively in the three-month bombing campaign that finally ended the Kosovo conflict. The proximity of Kosovo to NATO's member states in Western Europe and its location between the member states of Greece and Hungary, provided some justification for this intervention outside of NATO'S territory.

However, the Washington NATO summit of 1999 agreed to a massive transformation in the role and purpose of the alliance. This has received little media scrutiny and almost no political debate. The summit produced a document announcing that NATO will no longer be bound to its fifty-year-old principle of providing only a defensive alliance for protection and defending the territorial integrity and sovereignty of its member states. This new strategic concept for the NATO alliance is a complete reversal of that defensive stance that effectively preserved the peace in Europe for five decades. Both President Bill Clinton and Prime Minister Tony Blair endorsed this revolutionary change in military doctrine that will set the stage for the coming world government.

I am indebted to my friend Joe de Courcy, editor of *Intelligence Digest,* the most important private intelligence analysis agency in the world, for first alerting me to the implications and political significance of this new NATO strategic doctrine. *Intelligence Digest* has provided very accurate as well as timely intelligence information and analysis of critical situations throughout the world since 1938. Its reports are read by more than seventy heads of state and numerous executives of multinational corporations throughout the world. For more than twelve years I have found his organization's intelligence research to be impeccably accurate, insightful and often far in advance of the major media in spotting significant trends.[1]

This new strategic doctrine begins by declaring that NATO's "essential and enduring purpose . . . is to safeguard the freedom and security of all its members by political and military means." While this language appears innocent, the phrase "by political and military means" opens the doors for NATO to move into areas and activities far beyond its traditional role of military defense of its member states. The word "political" opens the door to espionage activities, political pressure, and many other previously unthinkable activities.

The document also defines the new strategic doctrine that will govern future military or political intervention by NATO as follows:

> The security of the Alliance remains subject to a wide variety of military and non-military risks. . . . These risks include *uncertainty and instability in and around the Euro-Atlantic area* and the possibility of *regional crises at the periphery of the Alliance* which could evolve rapidly. Some countries in and around the Euro-Atlantic area face serious economic, social and political difficulties. *Ethnic and religious rivalries,* territorial disputes, inadequate or failed efforts at reform, the *abuse of human rights,* and the dissolution of states can lead to *local and even regional instability.* The resulting tensions could lead to crises affecting Euro-Atlantic stability, to human suffering, and to armed conflicts. Such conflicts could affect the security of the Alliance by spilling over into neighbouring countries, including NATO countries, or in other ways, and could also affect the security of other states. [Italics added] [2]

This new definition of military and non-military situations that could provoke NATO military intervention is astonishing in its length and variety. During its first fifty years, NATO refused to intervene unless one of its members' territory was attacked. Now the Western Alliance declares to other nations that *"uncertainty and instability in and around the Euro-Atlantic area"* or even *"at the periphery of the Alliance"* justifies military intervention in a future crisis. Situations that could provoke a NATO invasion include: *"ethnic and religious rivalries," "abuse of human rights,"* or *"local and even regional instability."*

NATO's new strategic doctrine justifies its right to intervene militarily or politically in virtually any surrounding nation or territory if the leaders of NATO conclude that any of the above conditions exist. This new policy permitting NATO to invade other nations for such reasons, reminds us of the eighteenth-century colonial imperialism whereby super-powers such as the British Empire or France justified their military intervention in any part of the world that they considered their "sphere of influence."

Incredibly, the new strategic concept adds even more reasons for NATO to justify an invasion of another nation and the violation of its sovereignty:

> Alliance security interests can be affected by other risks of a wider nature, including *acts of terrorism, sabotage and organized crime, and by the disruption of the flow of vital resources.* The uncontrolled movement of large numbers of people, particularly as a consequence of armed conflicts, can also pose problems for security and stability affecting the Alliance.[3] [Italics added]

It is astonishing that the western nations now believe they have the right to invade another sovereign nation because of the existence in that country of *"acts of terrorism, sabotage and organized crime, and by the disruption of the flow of vital resources."* This same document declares another justification for the alliance's military intervention that would include even the *attempt* by another nation within its declared security zone to acquire nuclear, biological, and chemical weapons and the means to deliver such weapons that "can pose a direct military threat to the Allies' populations, territory and forces."

It seems now that the justifications for NATO's military invasion of another country are so many and so vague that virtually any pretext could satisfy the rationale for the next war. General Klaus Naumann, chairman of the Alliance's military committee, in April 1999 defined the regions that NATO considered to be within her security zone as, "the nations resting on its periphery from Morocco to the Indian Ocean." In other words, NATO has declared that it is ready and willing to intervene anywhere from Morocco across North Africa through the Middle East, including the Arabian peninsula, and extending to the east as far as Iran.

The NATO document also refers to the enormous effort to integrate the new Alliance member's military structures, weapons, and tactics to "prevent the renationalization of defence policies." The key elements of the new NATO strategy include:

> collective force planning; common funding; common operational planning; multinational formations, headquarters and command arrangements; an integrated air defence system; a balance of roles and responsibilities among the Allies; the stationing and deployment of forces outside home territory when required; arrangements, including planning, for crisis management and reinforcement; common standards and procedures for equipment, training and logistics; joint and combined doctrines and exercises when appropriate; and infrastructure, armaments and logistics cooperation.[4]

Could this remarkable new strategy of NATO set the stage for future wars and the coming world government that will rise to power in the last days as described in the Book of Revelation? This new imperialist strategy of NATO is an attack on the sovereignty of all nations, both those within the military alliance and those states that oppose it. These developments may lead to the fulfillment of John's prophecy about the kingdom of the Antichrist that will initially be based on the territory of the ancient Roman Empire. A later chapter will describe in great detail the prophecy of the revival of the Roman Empire in the end times that will become the power base for the coming world dictator. After World War II the doctrine of respecting and protecting the sovereignty of individual nations became the fundamental founding principle of the United Nations.

Creating a strong international military force capable of enforcing the policies of the United Nations is a key goal of the globalists. This force must be a professionally trained, rapid reaction military force with its own air- and sea-lift capability. Only a permanent standing army of significant size could permit the UN Security Council to enforce the will of the world body against any nation or group of states opposing its political resolutions. In the last decade alone, the UN has engaged in twice as many peace-keeping operations as it did in its entire first forty years. The number of UN peace-keeping and peace-making operations has soared, but the results have often been politically embarrassing. Occasionally the UN operations were military disasters. During the Rwanda civil war a group of Belgian UN troops were massacred without retaliation. In recent days UN troops were massacred in Sierra Leone without any reprisal.

The UN commanders and soldiers serving in peace-keeping operations have often complained bitterly about the lack of cohesive leadership, lack of funds, poor planning, insufficient ammunition, and officers who cannot communicate with the troops they command because of an inability to speak the language of the soldiers. Since the UN presently has no troops of its own, it is forced to "rent" troops for each peace-keeping mission from nations like Nigeria or Kenya — whose weapons are sometimes incompatible with each other. As a result of these confounding factors, and the permanent under-funding of UN peacekeeping operations, there has been little or no improvement in the world body's military capabilities despite fifty years of debate, studies, and bitter experience. The underlying causes and the resulting problems are very likely to persist for the foreseeable future.

Consider the tragic and horrendous failures of the previous UN missions in Somalia, Rwanda, and Sierra Leone in comparison to the effective and successful military campaigns of the western-led armies and air forces during the Gulf War or the Kosovo bombing campaign that was directly under NATO leadership. This comparison makes it clear that the only way the UN will ever achieve the military power necessary to enforce the will of the Security Council is to utilize the existing professional and modern integrated military forces of NATO.

Under the original fifty-year-old NATO doctrine of defence of only the territory of its member states, it was impossible to conceive of NATO forces being used outside of Western Europe to support the UN's mission to achieve world government. However, the development of the new imperial strategic doctrine of NATO articulated in the document of the fiftieth anniversary Washington summit will allow NATO's military alliance to be used to support the globalist plan to achieve world government.

The Historical Response to an Imperialistic Alliance

Another fascinating aspect of this radical new imperialistic doctrine of NATO is that throughout history, whenever an aggressive imperialistic military alliance or power has arisen to threaten the sovereignty and integrity of their neighbors, the surrounding nations have formed their own military alliance to defend themselves from that potential aggression. This is precisely what occurred when the communist Soviet Union gathered together the Warsaw Pact nations of Eastern Europe in an ideologically driven military alliance dedicated to the conquest of the democratic and free enterprise nations of Western Europe. Naturally, the Western European nations joined in a defensive alliance with the United States and Canada to defend themselves against the obviously imperialistic military threat of the Warsaw Pact.

The Threat to National Sovereignty

During the debates in the United Nations' Security Council regarding NATO intervention in Kosovo, Russia, China, and many Third World nations strongly objected. Their objection was never primarily that they disagreed with the West's opinion that Serbia was flagrantly attacking the human rights of the Albanian minority within its territory, but rather that NATO's action in Kosovo represented a dangerous precedent and a very real threat to their own sovereignty and every other nation outside the NATO Alliance. It is not surprising that Russia, China, India, and many Third World nations issued statements denouncing NATO's declaration of intervention. One example cited by the *Intelligence Digest* is a thoughtful article in the *Jordan Times* in early 1999 stating:

> But the most important issue raised by the NATO Yugoslavia confrontation is the inviolability of a country's sovereignty, or more specifically under what circumstances is intervention in an independent state's internal affairs permissible and who should be allowed to intervene. Many of the states opposing the NATO action fear it will set a precedent of support for separatist movements which

could be used against China in Tibet, against Russia in Chechnya, and against India in Kashmir. Another concern is the bypassing of the UN by NATO. NATO is viewed as simply promoting US interests and in effect making the US a sort of world policeman.[5]

If even an Arab nation such as Jordan, which is friendly to the West, expresses such deep concerns about the threats to all other nation's sovereignty from the implications of NATO's new imperialistic policies, then you can imagine the fear and concern of anti-western nations such as Russia and China to the perceived threat from NATO's new imperialistic strategy to intervene wherever they desire "from Morocco to the Indian Ocean." It seems that the inevitable response to NATO's new imperialistic doctrine must be the ultimate creation of an anti-NATO military alliance that will form over the next few years, composed of Russia, China, India, and many nations of the Third World. They have good reason to fear what they perceive as a new wave of imperialism and neo-colonialism from the western powers led by America and Britain.

The prophets Daniel and John foretold that an extremely powerful military, economic, and political power will arise in the last days led by a revival of the ancient Roman Empire in Europe. The Scriptures describe the growing power of the revived Roman Empire, ultimately encompassing the nations of the entire world for a few years during the Tribulation Period described in Daniel 2 and Revelation 13. However, the prophet Daniel clearly prophesied that the nations of the East will rebel against the worldwide domination of the western alliance of the Antichrist. "And the sixth angel poured out his vial upon the great river Euphrates; and the water thereof was dried up, that the way of the kings of the east might be prepared" (Revelation 16:12). The nations of the orient will mobilize with an enormous army of two hundred million men from "the kings of the East" to go to war against the western nations under the military leadership of the Antichrist, "And the number of the army of the horsemen were two hundred thousand thousand: and I heard the number of them" (Revelation 9:16).

The new imperialistic political and military developments in NATO and the naturally defensive response of the nations of the East and their Third World allies are setting the stage for the events described in the Scriptures that will occur just before the return of the Messiah to establish His kingdom.

Notes

1. Joe de Courcy, "NATO's Recipe for War," *Intelligence Digest*, 30 April 1999.

2. Joe de Courcy, "NATO's Recipe for War," *Intelligence Digest*, 30 April 1999.

3. Joe de Courcy, "NATO's Recipef for War," *Intelligence Digest*, 30 April 1999.

4. Joe de Courcy, "NATO's Recipe for War," *Intelligence Digest*, 30 April 1999.

5. *Jordan Times*, April, 1999

4

Astonishing New Weapons of the New World Order

As we enter the new millennium we are confronted with the fact that there is literally a revolution taking place in the area of both military weapons as well as the weapons used by the police forces of many nations throughout the world. Weapons of astonishing power have been developed in the weapons labs of the nations that are producing a true Revolution in Military Affairs (RMA) that will transform the future of global warfare. At the same time, remarkable advances in the field of surveillance as well as "non-lethal" weapons are providing police forces throughout the world with overwhelming power to control citizens within their own countries. When we examine these threatening developments in light of the prophetic warnings of the Scriptures about the nature of the global government in the last days it is clear that we are witnessing the beginning of the events that will culminate in the rise of the Antichrist, his totalitarian government, and the final battle of this age.

Biological DNA Weapons

A recent report from London, England reveals that scientists from the University of Texas have created the world's first synthetic DNA genetic code. It was developed from the molecules that make up the DNA genetic blueprint for all living creatures from the simplest one-celled amoeba to the incredible complexity of the cells of humans. Within less than 24 months these British genetic researchers announced their intention to create the world's first synthetic and artificially constructed biological organism. Genetic scientists have mapped out the precise manner in which four types of molecules must be arranged to form base pairs of two molecules. These genetic base pairs are then joined into long chains of paired molecules in a ladder-like construction that twists to form the complex double-helix DNA structure containing the genetic code that determines the biological growth of any living creature. The researchers of the University of Texas Genome Science and Technology Center participated in the Genome Project to map out the complete genetic structure of human DNA containing all the complex instructions that determine the structure of every organ in the human body.

These scientists determined precisely how they can arrange the synthetic DNA to create a microscopic microbe, the world's first synthetic organism that would be known as SO1. According to an article in the *Toronto Star* newspaper, Professor Glen Evans, director of the university's genetic project, admitted that SO1 "will have no specific function but once it is alive we can customize it. We can go back to the computer and change a gene and create other new life forms by simply pressing a button."[1] Dr. Evans declared that the University of Texas researchers are hoping to create a series of specially designed biological entities, created with new efficient techniques, to kill the rapidly multiplying cells in the human body that cause cancer tumors. Another intriguing proposal is to create an enzyme allowing humans to manufacture Vitamin C within the body. Our bodies lack a single enzyme that would otherwise allow us to produce this extremely useful vitamin C to assist in numerous bodily functions relating to our lifelong health. Evans suggests that the benefits of this genetic alteration could be available to everyone. Scientists would have to produce an ingestible pill that could insert an artificial genetic organism into our digestive system, allowing our body to produce vitamin C "naturally" for the rest of our life.

However, many critics warn that the genetic scientists are in danger of attempting "to play God with human biology." One powerful critic of this type of advanced genetic DNA research is Tony Juniper, the policy director of Friends of the Earth, who warns about the potential danger to our health and global environment posed by these genetic alterations of biological life forms. Juniper warns, "Scientists have already unleashed genetically modified organisms and we are now seeing the damage they can do. Playing God by creating entirely new life forms could have very serious consequences which should be publicly and fully debated."

There is a very real danger of such genetic research creating a dangerous, deadly artificial biological organism for which there may be no natural defense in nature. Scientists in the future could innocently develop a synthetic genetic organism for a benign purpose and, without intention, create a monstrous new plague, virus, or germ that we may be unable to destroy. While this possibility may occur by accident in a scientific laboratory intending to create something helpful, other laboratories in many nations around the world, which are declared enemies of the Western nations, are using the same genetic techniques to purposely develop biological weapons. These weapons may have devastating consequences if released into the air or water supplies.

There is a growing concern that continuing research in the areas of genetic engineering and the human genome diversity may create the possibility of someone developing weapons that could be targeted specifically at a particular race.[2]

Sniper Bullet Tracking Device

Remarkably, a new police surveillance system makes it possible to track the path of a fired bullet! The backward-tracking super-fast photographs on television cameras enable the operator to track in "real time" the path of a bullet traveling up to 1400 feet per second from an enemy's sniper rifle to the target. Then the computer system backtracks the bullet's path to determine its precise point of origin. The police SWAT team sniper can then fire at the enemy sniper with a super-accurate telescope aimed at the exact hidden location used by the enemy terrorist.

Sound-Wave Weapons

New sound-wave weapons are launched by a special acoustic cannon against enemy targets that will totally disrupt the hearing and the body functions of the enemy in the target zone. Launched from a low-flying helicopter, a narrow beam of low-frequency sound will intersect with another sound-wave beam from another aircraft, creating tremendous bodily discomfort to those targeted and causing them to desist from any provocative activities until their arrest by security authorities.

Radio-Frequency Thermal Weapons

A new type of radio-frequency weapon has recently been developed by the US military labs. It has the capability to affect its human target at a considerable distance, even through a solid wall. One variation of this weapon will allow a counter-terrorist team to focus the radio-frequency weapon at a terrorist through a wall, causing his body temperature to rapidly rise as high as 107 degrees. The target would become sick and disoriented, and therefore disabled. If the weapon's radio-frequency radiation was not turned off quickly, the target would die. Decades of research have been completed on the effect on humans from exposure to radio frequency.[3]

Surveillance Devices That See Through Clothes

A remarkable new surveillance device was developed in 1995 by researchers at AT&T's Bell Labs in Baltimore. These devices measure variations in the natural electromagnetic field that surrounds a human body. This energy field is distorted by the presence of a metal object. Another device sends out a pulsed radiation field that is reflected back to the hand-held scanner. It generates terahertz- or trillion-cycle-a-second electromagnetic pulses (T-rays) that can be aimed at an object or human from a distance. When these rays reflect back to the device, they alter their frequency slightly, depending on the chemical makeup of the object scanner. A computer device on the mobile scanner can even detect the difference between a knife and a revolver. Police officers or customs agents can use these mobile devices (costing less than $10,000) to scan a group of people on a street corner, instantly determining if any of them are armed. The scanner can examine luggage on a conveyer belt in an airport, instantly detecting the presence of hidden explosives, drugs, or weapons. The security applications of this new system will allow security officers to detect bombs, contraband, or weapons at a safe distance.[4]

Electrical Interdiction Weapons

Special US planes flying over Baghdad during the Gulf War dropped clouds of carbon-based materials that landed on virtually all of the city's electrical equipment and high power wires. Almost immediately this carbon material triggered electrical short-circuits, seriously disrupting Iraq's electrical power systems. Later in the 1990s, American planes devastated the electrical power system of Belgrade and other key Serbian cities during the liberation of Kosovo.

Another interesting non-lethal weapon stores up a massive electrical charge in a battery that can be triggered whenever a target car drives over a long wire running across the highway. Immediately, the huge electrical charge overwhelms the car's ignition and the targeted car is disabled.

A variation of this electronic technology will permit authorities to utilize stored electrical power by sending it to a targeted building, shorting out all of the building's computers, lights, and electrical security systems. Still other new devices will allow authorities to send a wave of focused microwave power through the air to a targeted plane, railway car, or automobile to disable its electrical and ignition systems, forcing it to stop.

Strobe Lights

Strobe lights not only distract individuals, but they can also cause loss of co-ordination of bodily functions, enabling authorities to readily subdue individuals in a riot situation or civil disruption. Another technology utilizing special strobe-light cameras was developed by a European company to rapidly film traffic patterns at over 100 photos a second. The Chinese government purchased this system and used it during the Tian'anmen Square democracy demonstrations to produce enormous numbers of photographs that filmed the face of virtually every single demonstrator. Subsequently, the Chinese secret police used the thousands of high-tech photos to arrest and allegedly execute over ten thousand of the demonstrators throughout China through the broadcast of these incriminating photographs in both newspapers and television programs.

Slippery Foam

A new method to achieve crowd control is available through the use of "slippery foam." Volumes of foam bubbles can be shot from a cannon or large hose at an unruly crowd. The foam makes the surface super-slippery, making it impossible to walk or stand. The disabled participants at a demonstration can then be arrested. There is another variation that alters the chemical composition of the foam to make it sticky. When sprayed on an area it is almost impossible for the people to escape — their shoes, clothing, and even their flesh stick to the surface.

Psychotronic Weapons

There are reports that Russian military scientists have developed psychotronic weapons that use electromagnetic radiation to secretly attack the mind and nervous system of a human target at a distance. This has devastating results. A 1998 article in the *Bulletin of the Atomic Scientists* described these weapons:

> Russia's psychotronic weapons include a psychotronic generator which produces electromagnetic emanations that can be sent through telephone lines, TV, radio, or even

light bulbs; an 'infrasonic sound' generator that destroys all life forms; a 'nervous system generator' known, so far, to paralyze insects; 'ultrasound emanations,' which kill by attacking internal organs without leaving a mark on the skin; and 'noiseless cassettes' featuring voices too low to be heard, which are nevertheless detected by the subconscious.[5]

Information Warfare

Today we are faced with very different enemies than we faced in the past. These new enemies include amateur computer hackers, professional electronic warfare specialists from enemy nations, and enormously rich criminals as well as hackers employed by powerful drug cartels. These criminals attempt to elude authorities by transferring billions of illegally acquired dollars through money laundering. They are capable of hiring knowledgeable intelligence and computer specialists who will use their expertise to hide from and attack Western government.

The United States and other Western nations have set up sophisticated computer operations to specifically target drug cartels as well as numerous dictators who have accumulated billions of dollars of illegally acquired funds. Today the West's NSA elite computer specialists use the most sophisticated computer technology in the world in their attempt to break the secret codes and track the global transfer of more than $7 trillion that passes daily through the world's major money center banks.

Attacks on US and NATO Computer Systems

During the recent war in Kosovo, computer hackers from Serbia continually overwhelmed and denied computer service access to NATO Internet web servers. US military Internet resources have also been tested and attacked with new viruses, and with computer denial of Internet service attacks. Several sources suggest that Russian and Iraqi hackers may be responsible. Recent attacks erased the US Navy's information appearing on the Internet web site of the Navy's Medical Information Management page. This hacker attack may be only the tip of the iceberg for such information warfare assaults against government, military, academic, and corporation web sites worldwide.[6]

New military technology includes electronic camouflage devices that alter the visual appearance of military vehicles to match the exact colors and materials that the computer systems have detected in the background behind a vehicle. This technique makes a light armored vehicle virtually invisible to the naked eye, at a distance. New metamorphic camouflage suits for soldiers can chemically alter their appearance to match the exact background through which soldiers travel as they approach their target.

Another new technique involves spraying of the door of a target building with a specially designed chemical that transforms the door's metallic structure into an extremely brittle form. Then a strong blow with a battering ram literally disintegrates the door, allowing officers to quickly enter the building. Police now possess new ammunition using liquid rounds filled with pepper spray. These can immediately disable an individual from shock and blurred vision. Newly developed non-lethal gas grenades can now be sent into a target building immediately disabling any potential enemy by causing them to lose muscle control and consciousness without killing them.

The Threat of Nuclear War

A frightening report by *TIME* magazine on September 23, 1998, on the Internet described how close we came to an accidental nuclear war with Russia due to failures in their aging early-warning missile-detection system. *TIME*'s Moscow reporter, Anna Blundy, wrote that the Soviet Union came within twenty minutes of launching a nuclear retaliatory strike against the West on September 26, 1983. A Soviet Oko satellite, a key part of Russia's early-warning space defense system, suffered a major technical failure causing it to falsely signal USSR defense headquarters that America had launched a Minuteman intercontinental ballistic missile against the Soviet Union. A respected Russian magazine, *Kommersant Vlast*, confirmed that the air force duty officer in charge of the missile warning system, Lieutenant-Colonel Stanislav Petrov, received the satellite's launch warning. Petrov had less than ten minutes to decide whether the reported missile attack was real. Fortunately, Petrov decided that it must be a false alarm and a devastating accidental nuclear war was avoided. The fact that this incident could so easily have led to an accidental nuclear war with the United States apparently horrified the Soviet Politburo and led to additional safety features being installed in their missile warning and rocket launch systems.

However, we came perilously close to accidental nuclear war again in 1995 when a research rocket was launched from Norway in a scientific experiment to study the northern lights. Despite the fact that NATO headquarters previously notified Russia's Ministry of Defense about the planned rocket launch more than two weeks earlier (joint notification of rocket launches is required by our treaty), once again the Russian early-missile warning defense headquarters forwarded a missile launch warning to Moscow. Incredibly, Russian President Boris Yeltsin actually used his nuclear-command briefcase preparing to launch a retaliatory nuclear strike against the West before Russia's missile commander realized their mistake and advised Yeltsin that, in fact, it was not a genuine attack.[7] Despite years of unprecedented military negotiations and cooperation between NATO and Russia, the political-military leadership in Moscow had believed that a nuclear missile attack from the West was possible.

Biological Warfare

A PBS *Frontline* broadcast on October 13, 1998, entitled *Plague War*, warned of the growing danger to humanity posed by the development of biological weapons created by Russia, China, and many dictatorships throughout the Third World. A weapons expert warned that the launch of modern biological warfare "would be the closest thing to a living hell as we could know." James Baker, the former US Secretary of State under President George Bush, warned during this special broadcast, that Russian President Boris Yeltsin had repeatedly lied to America about Russia's biological and chemical weapons programs. This occurred despite Russia's many solemn commitments and signed treaties pledging the abandonment of the testing, development, and storage of extremely dangerous chemical and biological weapons. One of the greatest dangers is the attempt by Russian scientists to develop gene-altering weapons that might destroy an enemy's population. Unfortunately, the present economic collapse in Russia has forced many talented chemical and biological weapon researchers to abandon their low-paying (sometimes non-paying) jobs in Russia and accept employment in terrorist states including Libya, Syria, Iran, and other committed enemies of the West.

A Revolution in Military Affairs

Dr. Nick Begich, M.D., presented a fascinating but disturbing report to the World Foundation for Natural Sciences (October 17, 1998) in Interlaken, Switzerland that revealed startling new information regarding new military technologies that were producing a revolution in the conduct of warfare between states.[8]

In his remarkable study, Dr. Begich revealed that it is now possible to utilize new electromagnetic technologies to trigger earthquakes or eruptions from volcanos, or to encourage changes in weather patterns. The astonishing new developments in electromagnetic research have allowed the US military to develop new weapons that will have a dramatic impact in future conflicts. A number of these new systems are almost ready for use in battle. Dr. Begich wrote a fascinating book with his co-author Jeane Manning entitled *Angels Don't Play This HAARP*, which provides compelling documentation of the dangers to our nation as well as the planet from this dangerous technology.

Non-Lethal Weapons

Scientists throughout the world have recently developed a group of sophisticated weapons that are supposedly "non-lethal," yet, such weapons are extremely dangerous to both civilians and soldiers. One of the problems is that they may be utilized more freely by both the police and paramilitary forces against civilian demonstrators, because the police have been taught to view these truly dangerous weapons as "non-lethal." The European Parliament's Foreign Affairs Subcommittee examined the use of "non-lethal" weapons at hearings on February 6, 1998. Witnesses such as the International

Red Cross from Geneva, Switzerland, pointed out that supposedly "non-lethal" weapons could indeed turn out to be lethal. However, the definition of a weapon as "non-lethal" is deceptive since the official definition of "non-lethal" requires that such weapons produce a mortality rate less than 25 percent. Even an obviously dangerous land mine will apparently kill less than 25 percent of its victims. Further, land mines also qualify under the rather arbitrary and misleading definition of any weapon as "non-lethal" as long as less than 25 percent of victims actually die. In other words, many of these new supposedly non-lethal weapons are in fact deadly. Has the technical term "non-lethal" been used to describe these new weapon technologies by weapons designers and military strategists to encourage politicians to vote for and support the development of these new military technologies?

A major concern is that studies confirm that officers are more likely to use such weapons against citizens or opponents than if they only had deadly weapons such as rifles or pistols. Studies from Northern Ireland and Israel reveal the increased frequency of "non-lethal" weapons used even in non-combat policing situations in comparison with the use of normal "lethal" rifles. British soldiers in Northern Ireland were issued "non-lethal" weapons (such as rubber bullets) as well as their more usual deadly ammunition. Intriguingly, the UK troops in Northern Ireland inflicted more injuries and deadly wounds to those opposing them when they used so-called non-lethal weapons.

In other words, soldiers were much more likely to use "non-lethal" weapons against civilians in a riot because they believed the weapons would not kill their victims. In comparison, when soldiers used rifles they usually exercised greater restraint. It is fascinating to observe that the United Nations peace-keeping force in Bosnia that used normal military rifles did not fire a single shot during the course of their peace-keeping operations. Meanwhile, British troops in Northern Ireland who used non-lethal weapons were responsible for countless injuries as well as civilian deaths.

The American Air Force Scientific Advisory Board issued a report on the development of new electromagnetic weapons that can be shaped, pulsed, or focused to interact with the human body to inhibit normal muscular movements, cause sleepiness, or affect emotions. In 1994, Dr. Christopher Lamb, the Pentagon's Director of Policy Planning, issued a directive on the use of non-lethal weapons by the military and the police. Beginning January 1, 1995, the government formally acknowledged the Pentagon's research on new technologies regarding non-lethal weapons for dual use by both the military as well as the police.

The government's plans to use pulsed, electromagnetic, and radio-frequency systems as non-lethal technology for domestic Justice Department law-enforcement use, raises serious concern about the dangers to average citizens. The US Department of Justice, however, has encouraged local jurisdictions to utilize new dual-use technologies. The report by the American Air Force Scientific Advisory Board reveals that these new non-lethal weapons are designed for use against both domestic and foreign enemies of the US government. The same Scientific Advisory Board warned that it is important for the public to understand that just as "lethal "weapons do not achieve 100 percent lethality, neither will "non-lethal" weapons be capable of eliminating fatalities or the commonly experienced collateral damage. The Spring 1998 edition of *Parameters, US Army War College Quarterly*, included a provocative article by Timothy L. Thomas entitled "The Mind Has No Firewall." This article discussed the remarkable new developments that would enable governments to significantly impact both the mental and physical health of people.[9]

A warning about our new military technologies is found in a recent Russian military article as well. This Russian article declared that humanity now stands on the brink of a psychotronic war, which will involve attacks by all parties on the actual mind and bodies of the citizens of the enemy nations. Very High Frequency (VHF) weapons generators have been developed, which are targeted at the mental state as well as the physical body of the target.

In the past, Information Warfare Theory was focused exclusively on the computer hardware and software systems of the enemy but did not specifically target the human operator. The new philosophy recognized that the human operator was also an appropriate target for the weapons systems. The US military analysts reported their findings in *USA Joint Publication 3–13.1* that examined "psychological operations" (PSYOP). The study stated:

> the ultimate target of (information warfare) is the information dependent process, whether human or automated. . . . Command and control warfare (C2W) is an application of information warfare in military operations. . . . C2W is the integrated use of PSYOP, military deception, operations security, electronic warfare and physical destruction.

Information warfare obviously depends upon ultimately targeting all information dependent systems or people of the enemy force "whether human or automated."

The research of Dr. Victor Solntsev of the Baumann Technical Institute in Moscow was included in the report of the *Parameters* article. Dr. Solntsev suggested that a computer virus known as "Russian Virus 666" will actually alter a person's mind. The computer virus is designed to repeatedly appear every twenty-fifth frame on the screen of a computer. The intermittent pulse pattern can force a computer operator into a trance-like state. There are several reports that this computer virus program can also induce a subconscious reaction causing changes in a person's perceptions, or even a heart attack.[10]

The US Army War College developed a report entitled *The Revolution in Military Affairs* in July 1994. Their study suggested that the new conflicts that fell short of outright war (terrorism, revolution, or violence) created a necessity for new weapons and required a significant change in public opinion. The report asserts that this change in opinion does not have to evolve naturally, but can be deliberately shaped by the government. The report also suggested that the attitudes of Americans can be modified slowly to permit the US military to introduce new types of advanced weapons that would normally be rejected by most citizens as evil and inappropriate. Further, the report points out that the military technological revolution will likely serve to produce change that is rapid, fundamental, and permanent.

An article in the *US News and World Report* on July 7, 1997, revealed that American scientists were searching for specific energy patterns to modify the behavior of targeted individuals. Military technology has now been so overwhelmingly transformed that the basic strategies of war have been altered forever. The United States Army War College paper suggested that this new technology was so revolutionary that it was equivalent to the introduction of gun powder in Europe or to the discovery of nuclear power in our more recent history. Interestingly, this paper also suggests that these new technologies would be strongly opposed by the US public.

Speed of Light Beam Weapons

A devastating new type of weapon system is being rapidly developed in military laboratories in the United States, United Kingdom, Russia, China, and Israel. This new group of weapons is called Directed Energy Warfare and includes the military applications of powerful lasers and particle beam and microwave weapons that can be used against targets on land, sea, air, and space. An article by Gerald Green in the *Journal of Electronic Defense* in December 1996 reported on the evaluation of the impact of such beam weapons by the Electronic Industries Association (EIA).

> The EIA's most dramatic and perhaps most controversial prediction concerned the impact that speed-of-light weapons would have on the anticipated Revolution in Military Affairs in the period 2010 and beyond. The EIA predicts that 'whichever side owns the speed-of light weapons will dominate the battlespace in almost every respect.'[11]

Retired Major General George J. Keegan, Jr., Chief of Intelligence of the USAF, wrote an article in a military magazine about the new revolution in beam weapons. One of the most fascinating is a military beam weapon called a "collective accelerator." It uses powerful magnets to accelerate the orbits around the nucleus of atoms to the speed of light. It then pulses the resulting stream of protons hundreds of times per second. Incredibly, every pulse of protons carries an electrical charge of tens of billions of electron volts.[12] The target almost disintegrates when hit.

Weather Warfare through HAARP Technology

Throughout history, people have complained about the weather without any real hope or prospect of changing it. In the 1950s, scientists developed technologies that allowed us to exercise significant control over the weather within our own country or to impact the weather over an enemy nation. Twenty-nine states within the United States have now licensed weather modification programs authorizing companies to utilize this technology to alter the weather within the state to produce rain, for example, to replenish reservoirs when drought hits. One company, Weather Modification Inc. of Fargo, North Dakota, has provided weather modification through cloud seeding since 1954 to the Kings River Conservation District (KRCD) reservoir in the agriculturally vital San Joaquin Valley of California.

The weather-modification companies usually use aircraft or ground cloud-seeding generators to release silver iodide particles into the clouds above a dry area when both temperature and moisture conditions are appropriate to produce rain. The silver iodide particles cause water vapor in the atmosphere to condense into ice crystals around the tiny particles, triggering rainfall. However, present cloud-seeding technology requires sufficient atmospheric moisture to permit silver iodide crystals to trigger the near-saturation condition in the cloud into forming rain or snow. Preventing hurricanes and hailstorms from forming, or creating precipitation from a normal clear blue sky are extremely difficult, but hopeful, scientific objectives of weather-modification experiments. The US House of Representatives subcommittee on Science and Technology (October 1977) revealed that more than sixty nations were presently engaged in constant programs of weather modification.

Anyone noting the changing weather patterns including extreme temperatures, and weather calamities over the last several decades realizes that we are experiencing weather conditions that are very unusual. Historical temperature records reveal that average annual global variations of normal seasonal temperatures have seldom varied more than one-tenth of a degree. However, the

World Meteorological Organization recently reported relatively massive variations in annual global temperatures measuring greater than 0.6 degrees Celsius since 1900. For example, recent Pacific hurricanes have included extraordinary high winds reaching velocities of up to 220 miles per hour, forcing meteorologists to create a new "Category 6" to describe these absolutely unprecedented hurricane storms. Since 1992, the US Department of Energy has declared that floods, heat waves, hurricanes, blizzards and hail storms have resulted in damages exceeding $70-billion as well as hundreds of civilian deaths. There are reports on the Internet that Malaysia successfully contracted with a Russian-based weather-modification company to create a large hurricane that will approach close enough to the coast of Malaysia to clear a significant amount of the city state's smoke and smog, while avoiding serious damage to the land. As a result Malaysia had its smog cleared.[13]

The strategic military advantage of being able to control the weather over your own nation or that of your enemy has been obvious to generals for many decades. In the late 1990s, a US Air Force research study entitled *Weather as a Force Multiplier*, described how the military could use powerful "ionospheric heaters" as well as "clouds generated by chemical condensation trails (contrails)" that would be released from huge airborne tankers to control global weather patterns by approximately the year 2025.

US Navy and Air Force researchers at a top-secret base in Gakon, Alaska, have developed an "ionospheric heater" to influence the atmosphere, which is called High-Frequency Active Auroral Research Program (HAARP). As part of this little-known experiment, the HAARP project has sent tightly focused rays of extremely intense radio-frequency energy into our atmosphere for several years at a time. The brilliant inventor of HAARP, Professor Bernard Eastlund, acknowledges that NATO is interested in modifying weather patterns to influence enemy nations. For example, a 1990 NATO research report entitled *Modification of Tropospheric Propagation Conditions*, outlined how the military might use high-altitude tanker planes to spray chemical polymers including magnetic iron-oxide powder to modify the atmosphere, allowing it to absorb more electromagnetic radiation and thereby heating the air. According to the report, it is possible to use HAARP to achieve large-scale modification of global weather patterns through focused ionospheric disturbances of the atmosphere.

The US Air Force stated that their HAARP transmitter in Alaska will ultimately produce approximately 3.6 million watts of radio frequency power. However, an October 1991 report by the US Air Force Phillips Laboratory, entitled *Technical Memorandum 195*, described future HAARP scientific tests that could utilize a staggering power output of up to 100 billion watts. To put the enormous power range of HAARP in context, a typical US public radio station commonly broadcasts in the power range of 50,000 watts. Some sources have suggested that the radical HAARP program may be a massive American military and scientific effort to respond to the dangers from global warming believed to be caused by the release of green-house gases. Other possible uses for HAARP technology include valuable earth-penetrating tomography that would utilize its X-ray-like functions to reveal mineral deposits — or the possible existence of underground enemy military installations in other nations.

Dr. Begich explains this concept of essentially "boiling the ionosphere" of the atmosphere:

> ... this invention provides the ability to put unprecedented amounts of power in the Earth's atmosphere at strategic locations and to maintain the power injection level, particularly if random pulsing is employed, in a manner far more precise and better controlled than heretofore accomplished by the prior art....[14]

Two thousand years ago, the prophet John warned that in the last days there would be unprecedented destruction from the sun and the sky that would afflict the rebellious humanity living during the seven-year Tribulation period leading up to Armageddon and the return of Christ:

> And the fourth angel poured out his vial upon the sun; and power was given unto him to scorch men with fire. And

men were scorched with great heat, and blasphemed the name of God, which hath power over these plagues: and they repented not to give him glory. (Revelation 16:8–9)

It is possible that weather modification technology in the hands of competing military alliances of the Antichrist and the "Kings of the East" during the cataclysmic conflict of the last days may unleash the destruction foretold by the prophet of God. Remarkably, there are reports that HAARP technology can create enormous destructive explosions equivalent to those produced previously with nuclear weapons without producing any nuclear radiation. This is detailed in US Patent 4,873,928.[15]

HAARP transmitters can also send an enormous burst of powerful electromatic radiation toward the ionosphere and reflect this back to earth directly upon an enemy target base in a controlled pattern that could be enormously destructive. If this HAARP report proves to be accurate, it would be virtually impossible to protect against a powerful but invisible blast of electromagnetic frequency radio waves reflected off the atmosphere from an originating earth station on enemy territory. Furthermore, several reports suggest that this revolutionary technology also has the ability to create an impenetrable electromagnetic shield over our nation to prevent any incoming enemy missiles, bombers, or other weapons attempting to penetrate our national airspace. If these reports are true, then for the first time since the creation of nuclear missiles in the 1950s, this technology could allow us to defend our population and our allies from incoming missiles.

Radio-Frequency Weapons

One of the latest terrorist threats to the West comes from radio-frequency (RF) weapons. Radio-frequency weapons include large but portable van-sized or even small briefcase-size Transient Electromagnetic Devices (TED) that utilize spark-gap electronic generation technology. These devices can be readily made for less than $500 using widely available automotive electronic parts. Electronic frequency weapons generate wide-band radio pulses in the nano-second and pico-second range, utilizing megawatt power and GHz (microwave) frequencies. Directional radio-frequency antennas enable them to be utilized to attack very specific targets. These RF terrorist weapons could be easily disguised as a small satellite dish.[16]

Over the past decade a number of research projects have reported the development of weapons utilizing radio frequencies to produce large amounts of static electrical energy capable of destroying electronic targets such as sophisticated computers. During the 1990s these weapon systems were often described as high-powered microwave (HPM) devices but they are now described as radio-frequency weapons.

A new form of these weapons, transient electromagnetic devices (TED), could be used by terrorists to devastate the electronic infrastructure of all modern societies that are based on sensitive electric micro-circuits and computer systems. Obvious targets include government offices, financial institutions, aircraft, medical, and critical electronic equipment used every day throughout western societies. A report by David Schriner to the Joint Economic Committee United States Congress, on February 25 1998, warning of the terrorist dangers of Radio Frequency weapons was entitled *The Design and Fabrication of a Damage Inflicting RF Weapon by Back Yard Methods*. It detailed that if an electrical radio signal was tuned to the frequency of a targeted radio antenna, then the radio's part attached to the antenna would be heated sufficiently to destroy it in a few seconds. The electrostatic discharge (ESD) produced by such systems is similar to, but much greater than, the static electricity produced when we walk across a rug. Such a targeted electrostatic discharge, if powerful enough, could overpower and destroy sensitive electronics such as the computers that control so much of our economy's sophisticated infrastructure.[17]

In the past few years there has been considerable discussion by national security agencies about the possibility of someone building a transient electromagnetic device. This device would use readily available technology from any electronics supply shop to create a devastating terrorist radio-frequency weapon capable of destroying any industrial or corporate computer systems. A reasonably well-educated criminal or terrorist, with a practical electrical background using education materials from a good technical library, could probably build such an RF terrorist device in a few weeks, with widely available tools and materials. The fact that such materials are readily available from electronic shops in all cities would make it very difficult for the FBI or other national security agencies to trace such an individual.

Nanotechnology "Super-small" Weapons

A fascinating report in the *South China Morning Post* on February 28 1998, declared that the United States had already developed sophisticated and advanced new weapons based on incredibly small devices capable of destroying enemy technology. A German television report from *Agence France-Presse* in Hamburg, Germany on the same day, reported that these tiny military surveillance devices, less than an inch in length, can be equipped with microscopic cameras, microphones, or even weapons. These small military devices could be introduced through the clefts of doors or the external vents of air-conditioning systems without being observed; enabling them to attack human targets or strategic electronic devices. *Panorama* magazine reported that the US military requested a Tennessee university to create an insect-sized mini-robotic device for surveillance missions. A California corporation designed miniature aircraft "microbats" for reconnaissance missions including extremely small remote-controlled attack planes that could contain explosive weapons. These microbats can be controlled remotely to enter a hostile terrorist building or hostage-taking environment. The devices can conduct surveillance or deliver weapons such as tear gas or flash stun grenades. Additional research projects were focused on developing micro-rockets that could penetrate the computer command centers of an enemy target and cause damage by triggering short circuits.

Satellite Surveillance

From the very beginning of the space age, in the early 1950s, both Russia and America have been involved in an enormously expensive space race to establish a network of surveillance satellites orbiting the earth to enable their spy agencies to photograph as well as listen in on the activities of their enemies. While every one of the American branches of the military engage in various satellite activities, the National Security Agency, headquartered in Fort Meade, Maryland, is the primary agency that controls these expensive but incredibly effective surveillance devices. A little-known agency, the National Reconnaissance Office actually designs and builds the satellites, monitoring their activities from at least four major bases in the continental United States.

Canada has recently developed a spy satellite capability that will enable the $305 million Radarsat 2 to photograph enemy or friendly vehicles, as small as tanks moving up to sixty miles per hour on a future battlefield. The American Air Force can spot moving vehicles from cameras operated from airplanes, but there is always a risk of photographic interference from mountainous terrain or risks from anti-aircraft missiles. However, the new Canadian Radarsat 2 satellite will provide advanced surveillance capabilities to both nations that are "state of the art," and considered to be at least two years in advance of any other nation.

One of the largest defense contractors, Lockheed, manufactures the KH11 satellites, which are as powerful as the well-known Hubble Space Telescope but are pointed toward the earth's surface. Reports suggest that since the late 1960s the sophisticated cameras in these spy satellites have been able to photograph the manufacturer's name engraved on a golf ball from up to sixty miles off in space. In light of the massive improvements in satellite construction, photographic analysis, and computer enhancements, one can only imagine the awesome photographic abilities of these present KH11 satellites that continually circle the globe.[18]

These remarkable developments in the area of new weapons will certainly assist in the process of establishing the military domination of the western forces of the Antichrist over the rest of the nations of the world during the initial part of the seven-year Tribulation period. However, many of these weapons may also be used by the "kings of the East," including the nations of Asia to throw off the shackles of domination toward the end of the Tribulation period as described in the prophecies of Daniel. In the end, the book of Revelation describes a titanic battle between the enormous armies of the East against the armies of the West under the Antichrist to determine who will rule the planet for the next thousand years. In a later chapter we will examine the prophecies found throughout the Scriptures that describe the astonishing outcome of that final World War when Jesus Christ will return from Heaven to defeat His enemies and set up His eternal kingdom on earth.

Notes

1. *Toronto Star*, 24 January, 2000.

2. Robin Coupland, "Non-lethal Weapons: Precipitating a New Arms Race," *British Medical Journal* 315 (12 July, 1997).

3. Doug Richardson, "Non-lethal Options," *Defence and Security Review* (www.atalink.co.uk/DSR/CLIENT/richweap.htm)

4. David Van Biema, *TIME*, 16 June, 1995.

5. "All in the Russian Mind? *Bulletin of the Atomic Scientists*, July/Aug. 1998.

6. Internet article by Ellen Messmer, "Serb Supporters Sock It to NATO and US Computers, Brussels: *Network World* 5 April 1999. (http://www.nwfusion.com/news/1999/0405nato.html)

7. Internet report, *TIME*, 23 September, 1998.

8. Nick Begich and Jeane Manning, *Angels Don't Play This HAARP* (Anchorage: Earthpulse Press, Inc., 1995).

9. Timothy L. Thomas, "The Mind Has No Firewall," *Parameters, US Army War College Quarterly*, Spring 1998.

10. Timothy L. Thomas, "The Mind Has No Firewall," *Parameters, US Army War College Quarterly*, Spring 1998.

11. Gerald Green, "Speed-of-Light Weapons Will Dominate the Future Battle Space," *Journal of Electronic Defense*, December 1996.

12. George J. Keegan, Jr., "The New Zap Guns, A Look at the New Revolution in Beam Weapons," *Gung Ho*, January 1982: 35–49.

13. "Malaysia to Battle Smog With Cyclones" *Wall Street Journal*, 13 November 1997, p. A19.

14. Nick Begich and Jeane Manning, *Angels Don't Play This HAARP* (Anchorage: Earthpulse Press, Inc., 1995), p. 8.

15. Nick Begich and Jeane Manning, *Angels Don't Play This HAARP* (Anchorage: Earthpulse Press, Inc., 1995), p.38, 62.

16. Winn Schwartau, *Information Warfare — Cyberterrorism* (New York: Thunder's Mouth Press, 1996).

17. David Schriner, Joint Economic Committee Congressional Hearing on Radio Frequency Weapons and Proliferation, 25 February, 1998.

18. Dean Beeby, "High-Power Spy Satellite Being Built," *Toronto Star*, 20 June, 1999.

5

Global Economic Warfare

The new global economy is bringing about a massive transformation to the world's balance of power. The industrial revolution established the economic, political, and military supremacy of the Western nations over every other nation on earth. The ability of European nations and America to harness the energies from water, steam, electricity, and petroleum greatly assisted in their development of advanced building materials and sophisticated machinery. All of these factors combined allowed the West to produce an awesome industrial machine producing massive quantities of goods, high technology equipment, and powerful weapons on a scale that dwarfed that of any other national group. The result has been a massive accumulation of industrial, political, and military power in the hands of the Western nations during the past one hundred and fifty years. This disparity in power permitted the West to establish and retain its power over colonial territories and exercise regional hegemony.

The new post-industrial revolution since World War II has

further solidified the industrial and military domination of the Western nations over other areas of the world. The new superiority is based on the West's massive investments in research and development, rapid adoption of sophisticated computerized machinery, fiber-optic communications networks, and advanced and expensive military equipment with the capability of overwhelming competition from any other nation. During the last three decades Japan, Taiwan, South Korea, and now mainland China have embarked on a highly motivated and effective catch-up campaign with the West, utilizing industrial espionage to steal advanced Western technology and industrial secrets.

We are entering a time when the production, control, and protection of advanced technological information will determine who will control the world's economy and rule the globe. For example, George A. Keyworth, the science advisor to former president Ronald Reagan, wrote, "We're moving increasingly toward a business environment in which information itself is the product, and in which the strategies by which businesses use information become critical elements of their success or failure."[1]

As we consider our overwhelming dependence on private and business computer data for our enhanced productivity and technical innovation in our Western economy, we realize that our national reliance on unprotected computers has exposed us to the greatest potential threat to the economy that western nations have ever faced. The well-respected economist, Professor David Bell, wrote, "Economics is a continuation of war by other means," in his paraphrase of the earlier dictum of the great political and military strategist, Von Clauswitz, regarding the fact that "war is the continuation of politics by other means."

The Globalist Economic Agenda

The three major global economic agreements, the North American Free Trade Agreement (NAFTA), the General Agreement on Trade and Tariffs (GATT), as well as the World Trade Organization (WTO), are leading us step-by-step toward a one-world government. Recent trade agreements have now placed the economic future of the United States and Canada under the effective control of foreign officials and globalist organizations that do not share our political or religious values nor our love of free enterprise. The leaders from many multinational companies have worked behind the scenes for years spending vast sums of money on political donations and employing thousands of lobbyists to ensure that Congress and the White House would assure the passage of these critical trade agreements that further their globalist economic and political agendas.

North American Free Trade Agreement (NAFTA)

Those who have studied the implications of the North American Free Trade Agreement (NAFTA) repeatedly warned that a large number of North American multinational corporations would quickly move factories and jobs to Mexico and South America. In Mexico, for example, the minimum wage is less than a dollar an hour with few pension benefits, negligible health care, and virtually nonexistent worker safety or environmental regulations. Today a multinational company can choose to base its manufacturing operations in Mexico or other countries with low wages, no unions, no pensions, and no health benefits; or it can build a manufacturing plant in North America, with high wages, strong unions, expensive health benefits, and large pension obligations. There is little surprise when the shareholders and board of directors of a multinational company choose to build its next manufacturing plant in Central or South America, especially when the company can also avoid many corporate taxes by locating in a foreign jurisdiction. These multinational companies transfer existing high-paying American jobs to Third World nations in order to gain the tremendous competitive advantage of low wages and minimal benefits. Then they ship the foreign-manufactured products back to the United States or Canada for sale to North American consumers at prices that no North American manufacturing corporation could possibly match. Welcome to the new world order of free trade!

Henry Kissinger, the former US Secretary of State and a long-serving member of the globalist Trilateral Commission, was one of the chief architects of the New World Order. As an expert in diplomacy, Kissinger is a world-renowned authority on the true intent of international treaties. This is his candid evaluation of the real goal and intention of North American Free Trade Agreement (NAFTA):

> What the Congress will soon have before it is not a conventional trade agreement, but the hopeful architecture of a new international system. A regional Western Hemisphere Organization dedicated to democracy and free trade would be a first step towards the New World Order that is so frequently cited but so rarely implemented.

The General Agreement on Trade and Tariffs (GATT)

When President Clinton signed the General Agreement on Trade and Tariffs (GATT), he transferred significant control of the American economy away from the US Congress and into the hands of the new 117-nation World Trade Organization (WTO). The WTO was created at the conclusion of the Uruguay round of negotiations to replace GATT with a new global economic order. First, Clinton surrendered effective military control of American troops to the United Nations during the peace-keeping missions in Somalia and Bosnia. President Clinton has signed "enabling" legislation that will force the US economy and its laws to be "coordinated" with the foreign bureaucrats who administer the WTO. Without any significant political debate or media discussion, the US economy was placed under the effective control of international global interests as part of Clinton and Gore's planned reduction of American economic sovereignty.

Peter Sutherland, the former director general of GATT and the new head of the WTO, admitted in an interview that "the old GATT procedure effectively had no ability to impose sanctions on the guilty." In other words, under the old GATT treaty, the United States could impose trade sanctions and economic restriction as part of a diplomatic campaign against North Korea, Iraq, or China for their violations of human rights. While this was technically against the rules of international trade, GATT had no legal capability to stop America from using these tools of foreign trade diplomacy.

However, under the new rules of the WTO, America must follow the trade rules imposed by the World Trade Organization. If the United States violates these rules in the future by unilaterally using trade sanctions, then the WTO will automatically impose trade sanctions on American exports. These restrictions on US economic policy will severely limit the options of a future American president to influence another country's actions through trade sanctions.

As Peter Sutherland points out, "The new system will have an appeals body to rule. . . . The judgment on appeal will have to be accepted . . . sanctions can be imposed upon the recalcitrant country." To understand what a massive political change this new WTO regime will bring about, consider this situation: In 1989 when Chinese authorities massacred over one thousand protesting students who demonstrated in favor of democracy in Beijing, America expressed its anger by imposing trade sanctions on China. However, in any future situation, America will find its hands will be effectively tied from using trade and economic sanctions as a tool of foreign policy. Is this another example of the continuing process of surrender of national sovereignty in preparation for the coming one world government?

Sir James Goldsmith, a recently deceased British billionaire, warned in his best-selling book *Le Piege* (*The Trap*), that GATT represented a terrible threat to the workers of industrial nations because their well-paying jobs would be transformed to low-paid workers in Third World nations. Sir James noted, "EC countries will only be 4.5 percent of the world population 30 years hence." He pointed to the growing and persistent rates of systemic unemployment in Western Europe that averaged over 12 percent. Goldsmith declared, "Siemens, the German electronic giant — just to cite one example among scores — announced it will soon employ more workers outside Europe than in Europe. This trend is accelerating. . . ." Sir James also warned that global free trade, furthered by GATT and the WTO, will be responsible for "the wholesale destruction of agrarian communities in the Third World, with millions of peasants displaced by intensive modern farming methods and then jammed into megaslums." The interview with Arnaud de Borchgrave on the *Washington Times* ended with Goldsmith quoting from a World Bank report published in September 1993:

> If by wise policy, or blind luck, a country has managed to control its population growth, provide social insurance, high wages, reasonable working hours and other benefits to its working class (i.e., most of its citizens), should it allow these benefits to be competed down to the world average of unregulated trade? . . . This leveling of wages will be overwhelmingly downward due to the vast number and rapid growth rates of under employed populations in the Third World.[2]

The World Trade Organization (WTO)

Incredibly, the World Trade Organization legislation now allows foreign bureaucrats to exercise oversight control over the economy and laws of trade that impact business throughout the United States and Canada. History shows us that whoever controls the currency and economy of a nation effectively controls that nation. The power-hungry bureaucrats at the United Nations, their globalist friends at the European Union, and the new World Trade Organization are delighted with the prospect of gaining control over the US economy. Those citizens who realize that GATT and NAFTA represent a threat to American jobs and the sovereignty of their country understand the growing danger from the World Trade Organization. Ostensibly the purpose of the WTO is to liberalize trade relations among nations of the world through the lowering of tariff barriers and opening of local markets to all competing nations. However, in January 1995 the WTO in Geneva, Switzerland, issued a WTO mandate to enforce international trade rules. In the past, nations disagreeing with a GATT ruling could ignore it and impose tariffs or sanctions as it saw fit in their own national interest.

An article in the September 15, 1994, issue of *The New American* pointed out the real dangers to our democratic sovereignty:

> The truth is that the WTO bureaucracy would have sufficient power to pressure nations to change their domestic laws. WTO was designed to eliminate a nation's option to ignore GATT dispute panel rulings, as the United States had done in an August 1991 case. . . . The United States promptly ignored the GATT panel ruling, continuing its ban of tuna from Mexico. . . . Senator Jesse Helms observed that under the WTO, dozens or perhaps hundreds of state laws could be attacked by foreign countries. As a matter of fact, the European Union issued a book entitled *Report on United States Barriers to Trade and Investment*. This report contains 111 pages of federal and state laws that the EU claims are barriers and that the Europeans may challenge in the WTO.

In the future, each nation, including the United States, the United Kingdom, and Canada, will be forced to obey the rulings of the resolution panels of the WTO even if these require massive changes in the existing federal, state, or provincial laws. The WTO represents an unprecedented globalist attack on our government's sovereign control over our own economy and business. The GATT treaty that created the WTO is so complicated that the document covers literally thousands of pages of text! Incredibly, only one single US senator even bothered to read through this complicated GATT document that is the greatest single attack on the economic sovereignty of America as well as all other nations in history. It is worth noting that he voted against GATT. If the true intent of the WTO was simply to reduce existing trade tariffs, this could have been expressed in only a few pages of text. Hidden within the tens of thousands of pages of legal language are thousands of special exceptions and lucrative deals for the multinational companies whose well-paid lobbyists have worked for years behind the closed doors in Congress to bring this new WTO trade agreement to fruition.

Any nation found guilty of violating the decisions of the WTO dispute panel will be brought before the world body and forced to either change its laws, pay massive fines, or face mandatory worldwide trade sanctions with all other nations forbidden to trade with it. In the history of mankind there has never been such an attack against the sovereignty and independence of the nation state comparable to the impact of the World Trade Organization treaty. Despite the huge implications of this agreement, the lame duck US Congress that was voted out of office in the November 1994 election, met in special session *after the election* to vote for this treaty *without any debate*. The US Congress voted for this unpopular treaty despite that fact that ninety-nine senators had failed to even read the text of this critical treaty that eliminates US economic and trade independence. Ask yourself, Who were these senators representing when they chose to ramrod this treaty through without debate after many of these Democratic senators had lost the mid-term 1994 elections?

The present White House administration is totally committed to US membership in the World Trade Organization where the majority of its members are Third World nations usually opposed to Western policies. Other international organizations, such as the United Nations Security Council, allow America and the other major super powers to protect their national interest through limited membership rules and an effective veto for the super powers over actions they perceive as being against their national interest. However, in the WTO, each country in the world, including small nations, such as Mongolia or Monaco, has the same voting power as America. In any future trade dispute, America will have only one vote among 117 nations. The United States will have no veto over the actions of this trade body. To gain an appreciation of the likely attitude of the vast majority of the WTO member nations, consider the fact that 76 percent of these nations consistently voted in the United Nations against the United States' interests during 1993. There is no reason to believe that their attitude will be any more favorable to America or Canada in the World Trade Organization. Only now, under the rules of the WTO, America will not have a veto to protect it against the actions of other nations.

Phyllis Schlafly commented on the real reason the globalists wanted America and Canada to join the World Trade Organization:

> The WTO is designed to function as the global trade pillar of a triumvirate that will plan and control the world's economy. The other two pillars are the World Bank, which loans capital to developing nations, and the International Monetary Fund (IMF), which supervises the flow of money around the world. The three-legged plan to plan and control the world's economy was devised at the Bretton Woods Conference at the end of World War II. The World Bank and the IMF got off the ground rapidly (largely financed, of course, by the United States), but the planned global trade arm, then called the International Trade Organization (ITO), was blocked by US senators who concluded that it would diminish US sovereignty and interfere with US domestic laws.[3]

The basic philosophy behind GATT and the WTO is to reduce the tariffs imposed by nations to protect their local industries against the threat from inexpensive foreign imports. In the case of textiles, the reduction of tariffs will basically destroy the American textile industry. The WTO will allow foreign manufacturers in countries that pay workers only five percent of the average wages of American workers to sell their cheap textiles in American stores, thereby destroying the jobs of one million textile workers in the United States. During the negotiations for the WTO treaty the US administration admitted that up to one million American jobs in the textile industry would be lost and that compensation policies would be implemented to minimize the economic loss for these workers.

The World Bank and the International Monetary Fund

The World Bank Group, which is controlled by the UN, is composed of several key sectors including the International Bank for Reconstruction and Development (IBRD), which is the main lending department of the World Bank, and the International

Development Association (IDA), which is the World Bank affiliate agency that lends to the world's poorest nations.

The planned move toward world government involves planned coercion by the globalist's UN World Bank and the International Monetary Fund to force recalcitrant countries to follow the new rules of the New World Order. The World Bank and International Monetary Fund use the "carrot" of promised new loans and the "stick" of delayed approval of debt-restructuring for past loans to force the leaders of these Third World countries to obey the dictates of the elite leaders of the New World Order. In *A Report to the Trilateral Commission—39*, published in 1990, the writers declared their intentions. "With due deference to local circumstances and sensibilities, the Trilateral countries should be frank in advocating the need for reform and modernization of Latin American economies. Such efforts are necessary both to achieve recovery and secure international support — particularly from the Trilateral private sector." In an amazing admission of the true underlying agenda of the Trilateral planners and international bankers, the report continued, "The purpose of this effort is to help Trilateral policy makers find a place for the societies of Latin America and the Caribbean in the future international order."

Throughout South America, "debt-for-equity" conversions are being contracted between local governments and the international bankers. Massively discounted government bonds are traded for equity in the newly privatized companies that were formerly the nationalized companies of South America. Another creative high finance tool, "debt-for-nature" swaps, involves trading millions of acres of land and rain forest in return for eliminating payment of enormous debts entered into during the free-lending 1980s. The huge international banking and industrial groups of the West and Japan are increasing their stake in the Third World with a new wave of neo-colonialism. The fifteen republics of the former Soviet Union have now applied for membership in the World Bank and the International Monetary Fund.

Free Trade Agreements —
A Step Toward the New World Order

As an example of the unheralded economic agenda of the New World Order, consider the new Free Trade Agreement between the United States, Canada, and Mexico. George Bush spoke to a group of Latin American diplomats and American bankers in the White House in 1991. The President promised, "I want to assure all of you here today, as I've assured many democratic leaders in Central and South America and the Caribbean and Mexico, the United States will not lose sight of the tremendous challenges and opportunities right here in our own hemisphere." In order to achieve global domination, it is essential that the leaders of the super powers first achieve regional dominance. The New World Order will begin by first dominating its various regions, one by one, starting with the Western Hemisphere. The world is in the process of being restructured and divided into spheres of influence between the three major economic players, the United States, Germany, and Japan.

The Canada–Mexico–United States Free Trade Agreement is now producing massive economic changes. However, there are already plans for an even larger agreement that will encompass the whole of the Western Hemisphere from the tip of South America to the North Pole. Huge multinational companies will be able to produce their goods in these countries without high taxes, duties or customs. Additionally, they will not have to pay for sophisticated health care systems, pensions or the higher wages required to attract North American skilled workers. This plan will represent disaster for the employee benefits built up over the last three decades by North American workers. Many plants and jobs will move south of the Rio Grand at an ever-accelerating rate. Chile is the first South American nation to sign an initial agreement to participate in the expanded Free Trade Zone.

Who is pushing for these Free Trade Agreements when it is so obvious that the average worker is being harmed? Naturally, it is the huge financial and multinational industrial corporations and the politicians they financially support, pushing us closer and closer to this New World Order.

If nations refuse to join, they will be left out in the cold. If they join, they will lose total control of their economic and ultimately, political destiny. The international drug companies, the worldwide banks and multinational oil corporations will quickly dominate their local economies. The price that the nations must pay to sit at the table of the new, global government is four-fold: (1) Accept a free market economy (2) Pay off international bank debts as demanded by the UN's International Monetary Fund and World Bank (3) Privatize nationalized industries and (4) Remove all barriers to international western investment and trade. Opposition to these agreements is rising in America and Canada from concerned citizens, union workers, and environmentalists, who fear that our politicians are selling out our interests in secret back-room agreements that benefit only those who operate behind the scenes.

As reported in a *Toronto Star* article dated April 25 1992, a seminar with 400 powerful business leaders dealing with this Western Hemisphere Plan was held in Washington, D.C., in April 1992. The chairman of the Americas Society and the Council of the Americas, David Rockefeller, declared that they would "map out a vast free trade zone encompassing the entire Western Hemisphere by the year 2000." Recognizing that their aims are not supported by the public, Rockefeller stated, "It's you, the business community of the Americas, that is going to have to provide the leadership, both the practical and moral leadership, to carry through this process of reform. It's you who will have to stay the course when the politicians, under an increasing barrage of complaints and inducements from various pressure groups, begin to waffle." This indicates that Rockefeller realized that the average citizen and patriotic politician would not be in favor of this scheme when they finally understood its true implications. He encouraged the multinational businessmen, the ultimate beneficiaries of this plan, to "provide leadership, both the practical and moral leadership to carry through this process of reform" against the democratic will of politicians and citizens.

Former President Bush declared, "The Enterprise for the Americas Initiative reflects a revolution in thinking. Through this initiative the United States is not seeking to impose our ideas on our neighbors. Rather, our program is designed to empower them to succeed with free market economic reforms they have chosen on their own." Later in his speech he mentioned that they will demand that these countries eliminate "burdensome regulations" that offend multinational companies.

Strobe Talbott has been a close friend of President Clinton since they were roommates at Oxford University as Rhodes scholars. Since then, Talbott became the number two person in the US State Department and is now Clinton's top advisor on relations with Russia. He wrote an essay for *TIME* magazine in 1992 entitled "The Birth of the Global Nation," outlining his views on the need for global government and the end of national sovereignty. Talbott described GATT and the UN's International Monetary Fund as the "protoministries of trade, finance and development for a united world." He admitted that once a nation appeals to the IMF for massive loans to bail themselves out of a difficult but temporary economic situation, the IMF "can virtually dictate fiscal policies, even including how much tax a government should levy on its citizens. . . . [GATT] regulates how much duty a nation can charge on imports." Talbott admitted that he is an "optimist" about the fact that world government is now inevitable and wrote:

> I'll bet that within the next hundred years, nationhood as we know it will be obsolete; all states will recognize a single global authority. A phrase briefly fashionable in the mid-20th century — 'citizen of the world' — will have assumed real meaning by the end of the 21st. . . . All countries are basically social arrangements. . . . No matter how permanent and even sacred they may seem at any one time, in fact they are all artificial and temporary. . . . Perhaps national sovereignty wasn't such a great idea after all. . . . But it has taken the events in our own wondrous and terrible century to clinch the case.[4]

The United States Monitors Most Nations' Communications

Reliable sources allege that one of the greatest intelligence coups of the last century was accomplished by the United States in its virtually undetected capture of the previously encrypted government communications of over 130 nations as well as tens of thousands of business corporations throughout the world for almost fifty years from those who purchased expensive encryption systems from the supposedly neutral Swiss company known as Crypto AG. This company established its reputation on promises to provide secure communications to governments and corporations throughout the world purchasing their expensive systems, with confidence that their communications would be totally secure.

With a reputation for its neutrality and technologically advanced machinery, Switzerland was uniquely positioned to provide powerful encryption machines to nations throughout the world from Russia to Libya and Iran. Most non-Western nations would naturally be reluctant to purchase encryption equipment from any Western nation such as America or Britain. However, Switzerland's reputation remained intact during the tumultuous events of two World Wars in Europe.

The nations purchasing Crypto's supposedly secure encryption systems relied upon these systems to send top-secret messages to their various government departments, embassies, trade negotiators, intelligence agencies, and spies, et cetera, throughout the world. However, recent disclosures by former employees of Crypto AG and other reliable sources confirm that the American National Security Agency (NSA) and Germany's intelligence agency, Bundesnacrichtendienst (BND), were able to secretly embed a de-encryption key within the cipher text produced by the Crypto AG's system, permitting the NSA and several associated western intelligence agencies to readily decode the cipher and read the secret messages of most of the world's other governments. [5]

The article in the *Baltimore Sun* (1995) reported further, "For years, NSA secretly rigged Crypto AG machines so that US eavesdroppers could easily break their codes, according to former company employees whose story is supported by company documents,"[6] Remarkably, the NSA was able to compromise the Swiss company's secret encryption technology to enable them to read the top-secret messages of many governments and businesses as easily as if they were transmitted in open format for the last fifty years at least.[7]

In effect, the NSA built a secret back-door into the encryption devices manufactured by Crypto AG and various other private security companies to enable them to easily read the communications of thousands of companies and over 130 national governments relying on this supposedly secure technology. Since the National Security Agency was so powerful, it was in a position to strongly influence numerous security companies involved with the creation of encryption codes to compromise these codes in return for strong incentives offered by the American government.[8] The NSA was America's most powerful intelligence agency, with top-secret "Black budgets" involving tens of billions of dollars annually to develop super-secret surveillance projects to protect the nation's secret communications and decode the secrets of every other nation, including America's allies.

The United States occasionally demanded that nations purchase Crypto AG encryption machines as a condition to their receiving financial or military support. Intelligence experts have stated that Pakistan was given substantial American military credits on the condition that it must buy its encryption equipment from Crypto AG. There are reports on the Internet that NSA developed relations with a variety of cryptographic companies including the Swiss companies Crypto AG and Gretag AG as well as the Scandinavian companies Transvertex and Nokia in Finland, and a few private encryption companies in post-Communist Hungary.[9]

President Ronald Reagan inadvertently admitted to the existence of such a capability when he justified his attack on Libya to the public in response to their terrorist attacks. Reagan declared that the United States had intercepted secret communications of the Libyan government, proving their agents planned the bombing of the La Belle discotheque in Berlin's Schoeneberg district in which two American soldiers and a Turkish female were killed, and another 200 people injured.[10] This admission confirmed America's ability to monitor the Libyan's supposedly top-secret encrypted communications between Tripoli and their agents in the Libyan embassy in East Berlin. In addition, according to reports in the Swiss newspaper *Neue Zurcher Zeitung,* America acknowledged its ability to read enemy nations' encrypted communications when it provided French officials with transcripts of secretly encrypted Iranian messages confirming the participation of Ali Vakili Rad and Massoud Hendi in the assassination in France of Shahpour Bakhtiar, the exiled former Iranian prime minister.

The US government security agencies such as the NSA, CIA, FBI, and State Department naturally were the first to utilize the massive amounts of secret intelligence data accumulated through fifty years of spying through the secret encryption back-door trap in Crypto AG's machines and others. However, these agencies constantly cooperate with thousands of American and other Western corporations both in the defense industry as well as general business. Occasionally, these agencies request that a company allow one of their spies to act as one of the business' employees in order to penetrate enemy secrets. Naturally there is always a *quid pro quo* in such relationships and the sharing of acquired industrial espionage secrets with these businesses occasionally occurred as it does on a constant basis with the spy agencies of China, Russia, France, and Japan.[11]

As we approach the final conflict that was prophesied in the ancient Scriptures so long ago, we can see that the growing use of economic warfare between the nations is destroying every bit of privacy that either governments, corporations, or citizens used to enjoy. The increasing use of industrial and economic espionage as well as information warfare technology is destroying even the expectation of privacy. These developments are preparing the way for the creation of a totalitarian world government where virtually no one "small and great, rich and poor, free and bond" will be able to escape the coming Mark of the Beast system as prophesied in the Word of God.

Notes

1. *Hudson Briefing Paper* (Hudson Institute, Herman Kahn Center) February, 1992.

2. Arnaud de Borchgrave, "Goldsmith Sees GATT as Major Disaster," *Washington Times*, 6 December, 1993.

3. Phyllis Schlafly, *The Phyllis Schlafly Report*, June 1994.

4. Strobe Talbott, "The Birth of the Global Nation," *TIME*, 20 July, 1992.

5. "No Such Agency, Part 4: Rigging the Game," *The Baltimore Sun*, 4 December, 1995.

6. "No Such Agency, Part 4: Rigging the Game," *The Baltimore Sun*, 4 December, 1995.

7. J. Orlin Grabbe, "NSA, Crypto AG, and the Iraq-Iran Conflict," Internet site http://www.aci.net/kalliste/speccoll.htm.

8. Wayne Madsen, Internet site http://mediafilter.org/caq/cryptogate/.

9. Internet site: http://mediafilter.org/caq/cryptogate/.

10. "The Tehran Connection," *TIME*, 21 March, 1994.

11. Wayne Madsen at web site: http://mediafilter.org/caq/cryptogate/.

6

The Death of Personal Privacy

An undeclared war on personal privacy and freedom is now being waged throughout the world. This war is very real, although it is often ignored and usually not acknowledged by most citizens. Despite the fact that aggressive attacks on our privacy are occurring every day, the average citizen in the Western world seems unaware of this. One of our most cherished freedoms and human rights — "the freedom to be let alone" — is being eroded by the new technological developments and the desire of government to respond to the growing threat of terrorism, drug trafficking, and crime. A 1998 Harris poll, completed by Louis Harris and Associates for the *Privacy & American Business* publication, found that 88 percent of US consumers were very concerned about threats to their personal privacy. However, 69 percent of those polled stated that they preferred voluntary measures instead of government action to ensure consumer privacy protection.

"You already have no privacy. Get over it."

A panel discussion in New York City entitled "New Media Summit 99: A Deeper View," warned that the rapidly growing use of the Internet, the sophisticated analysis of computer data bank information through "deep mining" of multiple consumer and government-acquired databases, and the lack of meaningful privacy legislation has depleted our personal privacy to an alarming degree. A staggering amount of sensitive information is now available about every one of us — on the Internet, or off line. This information is contained in literally thousands of computer databases established by consumer reporting agencies, government, and business. One panelist, Thomas Evans, president of GeoCities, (Marina Del Rey, CA) summed up the privacy situation in the USA as follows: "You already have no privacy. Get over it."

According to Bob Pringle, the president of InteliHealth, an online Internet health web site, "privacy is basically already dead." (Bob Pringle, www.intelihealth.com) However, David Sobel, the general counsel to the Electronic Privacy Information Center in Washington, D.C., suggests that "Privacy is not dead. It's under assault."

Lawyers are increasingly attacking the information held by Internet web sites with subpoenas, seeking to obtain access to web site access information, emails, and any other files held by the web sites. Sobel stated, "Ninety percent of the people using this medium do not know what's going on behind the scenes." Few users of the Internet realize or pay attention to the fact that everything they do on the Internet, from visiting particular web sites, visiting chat rooms, sending or receiving email, and shopping is all permanently recorded in some computer database somewhere. Who stops to consider the possible implications that could result from researching a topic on the Internet? For example, an innocent search to gain information about a disease could someday be accessed by an investigator during a background check for a future employer. Even the possibility of a link between the prospective employee and the disease could be sufficient to reject the employment application.[1]

The Government Has Your Life on File

The growing surveillance of virtually every aspect of our daily lives is fundamentally altering our way of life. Throughout human history in all societies, nations, and times, people have been able to conduct their daily lives under the natural assumption that their normal activities were no one else's business. Tragically, the incremental development of totalitarian, fascist, and communist governments since 1917, began a process of secret police surveillance of whole societies for the first time in history. Previously, only those individuals who opposed the will and purpose of a ruler by either criminal, military, or political means, were considered worthy of surveillance. Unfortunately, the advances in sophisticated technologies during the last few decades now enable governments to gather copious amounts of information on the assets, activities, financial transactions, health, political, and religious activities of every citizen.

Closed-circuit surveillance cameras now monitor our high-ways, streets, parking lots, and buildings in the interest of public safety and security. These intrusive surveillance cameras are eliminating the fundamental right of privacy that we have previously taken for granted. Our privacy is being progressively eroded by new audio, visual, and identification technologies. The development of miniature security cameras to promote personal safety and provide crime control, has recently been expanded to include surveillance of employees at their desks, in the washrooms, and throughout a building. The growing threat from employee theft and industrial espionage provides a persuasive argument to support the necessity for this intrusion on daily life.

Corporations and governments alike engage in this employee monitoring. Many large corporations also monitor their customers for crime prevention and staff protection. In effect, we are now living in a total surveillance environment resembling the horror described by George Orwell in his frightening novel, *1984*, about the threat of totalitarian government. In fact, the remarkable technology developed during the last decade has produced surveillance possibilities more pervasive and threatening than any faced by the fictional character, Winston, in George Orwell's prophetic novel.

Many government agencies and corporations have introduced security systems requiring all workers to wear an employee badge containing a radio frequency microchip. This enables companies to monitor the location and activity of each worker. When an employee enters the office, the computer records the exact time and quietly monitors his or her every move throughout the day. Security sensors placed at strategic locations throughout the building record the location and duration of all the activities of the badge wearer.

Many office phone systems can secretly monitor private phone calls unwisely made while at work. Computerized office phone systems may contain a record of all possible legitimate business phone numbers. If an employee places a personal call to a friend, the office phone system will record the unauthorized number and produce a report of the employee's private calls and their duration at the next employee evaluation interview.

The International Labor Organization in Geneva reported, "Workers in industrialized countries are losing privacy in the work place as technological advances allow employers to monitor nearly every facet of time on the job." US corporations use secret employee surveillance more than any other nation. The American Civil Liberties Union warned, "Criminals have more privacy rights than employees. Police have to get a court order, whereas in the workplace, surveillance can be conducted without safeguards." Computer network security supervisors in many fully computerized companies secretly monitor the actual keystrokes and productivity of every individual employee using a desktop computer in their daily work. Employees often complain about the stress they experience, knowing that they are being secretly monitored every minute of the day. In many companies, random drug testing, secret cameras, and intrusive psychological questionnaires can create an unhealthy psychological environment.

You would probably be appalled to know that police, security agencies, government officials, and even curious business competitors or neighbors can now acquire virtually any private detail of your life and business. A complete record of your travel destinations, newspapers and books you read, video rentals you make, pay-TV choices you subscribe to, traffic tickets you incur, medical tests, as well as any purchases you make, are all now electronically and permanently "on file" for anyone who can acquire access to the information database. There is a growing public awareness and concern about the issue of privacy for our computer records, especially regarding our health and financial records. Despite these concerns, the US Congress and the Parliament of Canada have failed, so far, to enact serious laws to protect the privacy of their citizens.

Security companies have recently made great technical advances in sophisticated surveillance devices. New pinhole cameras can be placed behind a wall to audibly and visually monitor the next room. The tiny lens (the size of a pinhead) is virtually impossible to detect, unless you examine every wall, floor, and ceiling surface with a magnifying glass. The new infrared cameras can photograph silently and in almost total darkness. Another new surveillance camera can be secretly concealed in a small mobile telephone with the camera lens recording through the tiny hole normally used for the microphone. During a negotiation, the owner can leave the phone in a board room when he leaves the room. As one team discusses their position, the other can secretly record everything said or done.

Surveillance devices that enable you to monitor everything occurring in your home or office while you are away can now be purchased for several hundred dollars. A new remote monitoring device, the XPS-1000, allows you to call your phone number from anywhere in the world by dialing your phone with a special activation code. The device will not cause your phone to ring; but from that moment on, you can monitor every sound in the building. Another tiny device, a micro transmitter surveillance bug powered for three months by a miniature battery, can be secretly left in any room and will broadcast up to one thousand yards to a radio receiver on a FM frequency. The truth is that personal privacy has become an illusion. If someone is truly determined to monitor your activities, they can do it. There is very little you can do to stop them.

The National Identification Center

In 1996, the US government secretly created a National Identification Center (NIC) in Virginia. The NIC permits federal law enforcement as well as the CIA and NSA intelligence agencies to monitor people by using an extremely sophisticated computer system. This advanced computer system consolidates every existing computer record that the US government has accumulated on each citizen. The officially declared purpose of this National Identification Center is to monitor US citizens' compliance with new gun-control regulations passed by Congress. However, the reality is that this national computer center contains complete data files on every citizen. These files provide unprecedented power to those in the government who may in the future wish to establish totalitarian police control. In an October 1993 newsletter to his constituents, Congressman Neal Smith from Iowa revealed the government's real plans.

While discussing the handgun control laws that were the purported reason for the NIC, Representative Smith claimed responsibility for creating a new National Identification Center that will also be used to monitor citizens for "other" purposes. Congressman Smith wrote,

> The Subcommittee on Appropriations which I chair has been actively pursuing an effective solution to this problem. . . . But the program we are implementing will take more time. The solution to screening people . . . is to have a National Center computerized so that local law enforcement offices can instantly access information from all states. In other words, all states that supply that information to the National Center will have a positive identification system which will identify any applicant. . . . We have invested $392 million so far in such a Center, about a four-hour drive from Washington, D.C., and we

hope to have it completed and equipped in about two years. . . . We hope all states will be in the system by 1998 and will supply the information on a continuing basis . . . Meanwhile, we will continue to establish the National Identification Center for this and *other law enforcement purposes.* (italics added)

All governmental intelligence agencies, including the Bureau of Alcohol Tobacco and Firearms (ATF) and the FBI, will be able to access the National Identification Center to identify and monitor every registered gun owner in the United States. However, the real question is this: What "other law enforcement purposes" do the US government agencies intend to pursue? This National Identification Center is only one component of an all-encompassing system of totalitarian police control that is being established, not only nationwide, but throughout the world.

Two of America's most secret government agencies, the National Reconnaissance Office (NRO) and the National Security Agency (NSA), now operate a global surveillance system known as the Echelon Project. This system has the capability of monitoring every single phone call and fax transmission worldwide. The remarkable capability of this surveillance system will be documented in the next chapter. It is impossible to contemplate the growing surveillance capabilities of governments throughout the world without being reminded of the ancient prophecy from the book of Revelation about an unprecedented totalitarian police system in the last days. The prophet John warned, "No one may buy or sell, except one who has the mark or the name of the beast, or the number of his name" (Revelation 13:17).

Your Life in a Computer Database

Government officials, national security agencies, and marketing corporations are constantly seeking personal information about the details of our daily lives, our spending habits, and our assets. Government agencies usually raise the threat of international terrorism, organized crime, the flood of illegal aliens, or those who cheat on welfare or fail to pay child support to justify these inquiries. Computers can now collect and permanently record vast amounts of information in sophisticated databases capable of storing detailed records such as health status, medical treatments, employment status, vehicle ownership, driving records, criminal records, and real estate ownership. In addition, all of our credit records, banking and financial transactions, credit rating, educational transcripts, and travel records are included in these databases and are available to the government and to some corporations and research institutes.

It has been estimated that most Western democratic governments, as well as governments in China and Russia, possess enormous computer databases containing literally thousands of individual details about each citizen. The hurdle facing governments and corporations has been the separation of this information into thousands of different files. Now, however, if the government can assign a unique identification number to each citizen, then all relevant files about that citizen could be gathered instantaneously into one file.

A confirmation of this continuous process of citizen database consolidation was publicized recently in newspapers in Canada including the *National Post* on May 19, 2000. The federal government reluctantly confirmed that up to 2000 different bits of information had been assembled on each Canadian in a secret computer database known as the Longitudinal Labour Force File. As a result of strident public criticism following these revelations, the Canadian government promised to destroy this special computer program that links these files, according to a follow-up article in the *National Post* on May 30, 2000. However, the government will still retain the copious amounts of data on over thirty million Canadians in separate computer database files.

Credit and Debit Cards

Although credit cards were initially rejected by many citizens who favored the use of cash, over the last five decades credit card use has exploded. Now, most people use credit cards for the majority of their everyday purchases. Initially, however, credit cards were seen only as a financial vehicle for business people, travelers, and those who needed to purchase an expensive item. However, today most people would hardly know how to get through a week without their credit cards.

Visa International, which is owned by its member banks, announced that over one billion VISA cards are now used throughout the world, and over 21.3 billion credit-card transactions are processed annually. In 1999, people spent over $1.6 trillion with VISA cards, indicating that an average user placed approximately $1,600 annually on his or her credit card, an amount that was 19 percent higher than the year before. Malcolm Williamson, VISA International's president, stated,

> This is a powerful testimony to how widely accepted payment cards have become as currency. VISA alone has more than doubled its share of worldwide personal consumption expenditure in the last five years. Although one billion cards is hugely significant, we're asking ourselves whether we may never announce the second billion. The reason for this is the huge expansion of options for cardless payments. . . . The card may become redundant. We may move from not only cashless but also a cardless society. Although the number of credit cards may not continue to grow as quickly as in the 1990s, their use to pay for purchases on the Internet will multiply. Visa cards are used for more than 50 percent of all payment transactions on the Internet today. Significantly, Visa is developing new mobile payment devices using cellular phones, et cetera, with companies such as Nokia and Ericsson. (*Financial Post*, May 19, 2000)

SmartCards — A Computer Chip on a Card

We have all used plastic credit/debit and identification cards with a magnetic strip holding electronic data verifying our identity, as well as additional information validating our right to access particular computer databases, such as our bank accounts. While these cards are still used throughout the world, they are increasingly being replaced by higher security SmartCards that contain an increased amount of information. SmartCards contain an embedded computer chip in a credit card-sized plastic containing literally millions of times more digital information than could be carried on a magnetic strip. Perhaps more importantly, SmartCards are capable of providing very high levels of security since they contain detailed identification information of the citizen carrying the card. There is now the potential of replacing dozens of the various cards in your wallet with a single, very secure SmartCard that is virtually immune to attacks by thieves and computer hackers because the data is encrypted and passwords and biometric information are required.

Two decades ago, France experienced a wave of vandalism and petty theft of coins in the public telephones owned by the French Public Telephone and Telegraph System. France's solution was to create a SmartCard embedded with a computer memory chip that would hold a predetermined value. The customer could then insert the card into the public telephone and the amount of the call would be automatically deducted from the remaining value in the card's memory. However, this new system also made it much easier to trace and record all public telephone calls made in France.

With many new advances in the miniaturization of embedded computer chips to maximize memory, the latest generation of SmartCards is now available in almost every nation on earth. More than a billion SmartCards, now in use worldwide, can perform functions including

- Cash transactions, such as rechargeable stored value cards carrying a predetermined value
- Confidential transferring of urgently needed medical data to paramedics and hospitals
- Authorization of a satellite TV receiver to de-encrypt satellite and cable signals
- Minimization of credit and debit card fraud
- The control of access to high security offices and computer systems
- Access to travel on air planes, trains, subways, and buses

But ultimately, the growing utilization of SmartCards will also make it possible for future governments to track the activities, communications, and financial transactions of all citizens, from the cradle to the grave.

Multiple-Application SmartCards

Currently, the industry is strongly advocating its use as a multi-application card. The latest generation of a multi-application SmartCard could hold your driver's license, car registration, medical insurance file, credit and debit information, subway and bus prepaid access, and access to your computer and office. The multi-application SmartCard is designed with individually encrypted digital keys that only permit access to the specific organization (bank, driver's license bureau, et cetera) that legitimately need the data. Any unauthorized attempt to access the data on a stolen SmartCard would be unproductive. One security system causes the SmartCard to shut down permanently all card functions if any unauthorized individual tries to penetrate the system by randomly trying various passwords. After only three unsuccessful password attempts, the SmartCard's security system is activated.

The US government's General Services Administration (GSA) has 400 employees testing a new multi-application SmartCard that utilizes a Java computer software system. This card has a computer chip on one side and a magnetic strip with a written signature for Automatic Teller Machines (ATMs) and stores on the other. So, in addition to providing employees' access to their office in Vienna Virginia, the new card also acts as a credit/debit card, a calling card for telecommunications, and a digital signature card for authenticating secure communications. It can also be used to track the security of General Service Administration property. It can even be used by government employees to board flights on some American Airline planes. The cards can also be imprinted with biometric information including fingerprints, as well as voice or iris recognition, for access to high-security areas.

Even low-technology areas, such as Mexico, are now using SmartCards. In Reynosa, Mexico, low-wage workers who may lack bank accounts are often robbed when they carry home their weekly wages in plastic bags. MetaCo LLC, a payroll company in Rochester, New York, developed a novel solution for the companies employing these workers. They created a SmartCard called MetaCard. Each worker has his or her fingerprints scanned and electronically encoded in the MetaCard, preventing anyone else from using the card. The employee can use the card as one might a time-clock for work attendance, by swiping it in the SmartCard reader as they enter and leave the factory. Each week, the company electronically deposits the correct wages into the card's memory chip, allowing the employee to use the card at the factory cafeteria to access cash, or to automatically deposit unused funds in an interest-bearing bank account, if they choose.[3]

The benefits of SmartCard technology are so apparent that their use is growing at an annual rate of over 40 percent. People and corporations increasingly use them as a safe and legitimate substitute for cash. In fact, the latest studies suggest that less than three percent of the money in North America as well as most other nations exists in the form of actual paper currency and coins. We are already an almost cashless society, with the exception of small economic transactions of under $50. This is where SmartCards are most likely to have their greatest impact. As people become more comfortable with their use, paper currency and coins will lessen considerably, and the advantage of eliminating all the other cards in our wallets and purses is obvious.

All sensitive information will be protected through your personal biometric information encoded in the smart card's computer chip. The biometric information will measure your unique physiological and behavioral characteristics including an iris scan, the unique rings, burrows, freckles, and filaments within the lens of your eyes. Cameras with an infrared scanner can also scan the retina of the eye to read the pattern of microscopic blood vessels on the reflective rear retina wall of your eye. New machines can measure your precise hand geometry, identifying you by measuring the length of your fingers, and the translucency and thickness of your skin. Infrared scanners can also reveal and record the patterns of veins on the back of your hand. New voice recognition software can confirm a person's identity out of millions of phone calls, through precise measurement of your voice tone and timbre. Incredibly, a machine can also puff air over the back of your hand, analyze your unique body odors, and permit the device to detect up to thirty separate trace chemical elements providing positive identification. Optical or sonic fingerprint scanners can now read the thousands of whorls, loops, and arches of your fingertips.[4] However, along with these advantages come serious disadvantages; use of SmartCards can cause a very real and growing danger to personal privacy.

SmartCards — A Violation of Personal Privacy

Recently, South Koreans rejected the government's proposed introduction of a national identification SmartCard that was to be carried by each citizen over the age of seventeen. This proposed SmartCard ID would have contained digital information in an embedded micro chip that could include a photograph, fingerprints, driver license, medical insurance card, Korean national pension card, and proof of residence. The new president of South Korea, Kim Dae Jung, himself a former political prisoner in Korea, was suspicious of the potential abuse of such data by monitoring the activities of each citizen by a future police state, or even by the KIA, the secret intelligence agency. Australia and Taiwan also recently postponed the introduction of a SmartCard national ID system. However, the government of Malaysia is proceeding with a similar card containing identification information, health, and immigration data.

While the growth of the use of SmartCards is virtually inevitable, many citizen groups have expressed concerns that our right of privacy, our "right to be left alone," could be dangerously compromised. Many warn that the multi-application SmartCard could provide access to computer-linked databases holding vast amounts of confidential information. If a sophisticated thief, a private eye, or an intelligence agency acquired access to any multi-application SmartCard, they may be able to break its security system and copy the information.

Another concern is that illegal access to this information could allow an investigator to determine someone's travel arrangements to a particular political or religious event. Knowing that you got off the bus or subway at a certain station, near a meeting location of concerned citizens, could enable police or intelligence agencies to access the database of the transportation system. They could then determine each person who got off at that station within an hour of when you did. It may then be possible to identify the likely participants at that meeting.

An International Standard for Privacy

These privacy concerns have motivated representatives of the fifteen nations of the European Union (EU) to create a new international standard for privacy. The basic rules of this privacy legislation are as follows

- All privacy regulations apply to both government and private organizations
- Data collection should be limited to that which can be obtained legally and with the knowledge and consent of the subject, except where this is impossible or inappropriate (e.g., criminals)
- Data on individuals should be limited to the original purpose and kept up to date. The purpose of data collection should be specified and subsequent use of data should be limited to that original purpose
- No personal data should be disclosed to others without the consent of the subject or without a legal order
- All personal data must be kept secure through all reasonable precautions
- All citizens should be able to access, review, and challenge inaccurate data held in databases
- The controller of the database should be legally and criminally accountable for abiding by these privacy principles
- The policies and practices of organizations holding databases on individuals should openly reveal this information to those who inquire about it
- Private data collected by European Union member corporations and states may not be transmitted to organizations in nations

that do not have privacy regulations equal to the European Union

The introduction of similar privacy legislation in North America and other democratic nations could provide significant protection against abuse. The Organization of Economic Cooperation and Development (OECD) is an international group of 29 developed nations from North America, Europe, and Asia, that has also suggested the establishment of privacy standards for both government and businesses. One small but positive step in the right direction was taken by the US Congress when it recently created a privacy office within the Office of Management and Budget to examine the issue of the growing danger to our private information.[5]

Despite such privacy concerns, Donna Farmer, president and CEO of the SmartCard Forum, an industry spokesperson for the SmartCard industry, raises a valid counterargument. In an article on privacy concerns and SmartCards, in *Card Technology* magazine, Donna Farmer suggested that SmartCards could assist in the prevention of privacy attacks. Farmer stated, "Think of how much information is in the clear in my wallet. On a SmartCard that data would be encrypted. It would be hundreds of times more secure." At the same time, Farmer admitted, "As we move into a digital age, people have to be much more aware of their own personal security."[6]

One potential solution is to design the smart "stored value" card to allow payment, but to be programmed not to inform the merchant or person receiving the electronic fund of the purchaser's identity, or enable them to track any previous purchases. For example, the European-based Mondex International SmartCard allows a customer to transfer funds from their card to their friend, or to a merchant's account in order to make a purchase. However, the merchant's bank accepting the store's Mondex card deposit of their sales receipts is not able to identify the purchaser. VISA International is also providing for customer privacy through the use of their disposable VISA Cash Card. This card also does not permit merchants to identify the customer.

Identity Theft — A New Threat to Your Credit and Privacy

One day I was walking through a parking lot and saw a lost wallet on the ground that had probably fallen out of a pocket or purse when someone entered or exited their car. When I called the person to verify the address in order to send their wallet to them, they were naturally quite elated. While they were delighted to recover the cash, their real appreciation was for the return of their identification documents. Almost any lost or stolen wallet or purse contains critical personal documents such as your driver's license number, your social security card, various credit and debit cards, et cetera. In addition, some people even write down their PIN number for their credit/debit cards, rather than safely memorizing it.

However, the nightmare of identity theft or impersonation crime is a growing threat to everyone. To illustrate the problem, consider the plausible story of Tammy, who, for example, lost her purse to a thief as she boarded a subway car. Despite the fear, the anger, and the annoyance of lost time spent contacting credit card companies, banks, and government offices, she felt her life was finally getting back on track only after about two months. But, the first realization of the threat to her identity came five months later when a social welfare auditor called to check on welfare claims. Tammy had never collected a penny of welfare in her life. She thought, "This must be a simple clerical mistake due to someone having the same name." However, after investigation, it turned out that someone was using her stolen identity papers to defraud the welfare system.

Then the collection notices from credit agencies started coming in from around the country, for various items supposedly purchased by Tammy. An apartment collection agency called and told her that she owed four months' back rent on a one-bedroom apartment that had been rented to a lady who had disappeared. This lady had easily acquired the apartment using Tammy's stolen identity cards with her excellent credit and employment history. It took months to convince the landlord and their lawyers that she was innocent and not liable. Meanwhile, Tammy's credit history was being systematically destroyed by some unknown criminal. Despite letters of explanation to each bank, creditor, the Department of Transportation, and each of the credit bureaus, the nightmare still wasn't over. When her income tax refund did not arrive at the usual time, she began to worry. She finally called the local office of the Internal Revenue Agency. In response to her request about her overdue refund, Tammy was mortified to learn that the thieves were so brazen that they actually filed an income tax return with counterfeit W-4 forms in her name, requesting a sizable refund. The thieves were now in possession of her income tax refund. It took several months to verify and correct the problem so that she could receive her legitimate tax refund.

Tammy's trials and tribulations with identity fraud followed the theft of all her identification documents and credit/debit cards. These criminals can even cause a great deal of harm by simply acquiring a credit card slip with your name and number on it. Once in possession of that information, they can use your good credit to apply for credit cards from other banks and financial institutions. Unfortunately, sophisticated computer desktop publishing programs, inexpensive desktop scanners, and powerful laser printers now permit anyone with good computer skills to create genuine-appearing corporate checks, educational transcripts, et cetera, to defraud companies, government agencies, and individuals.

To avoid the crime of identity theft, it is wise to regularly check your credit records with local credit rating agencies to see if any unfamiliar company has recently requested credit information on you. If so, consider this as a red flag that some thief is attempting to apply for credit using your name. Always check your account statements for anything unusual and never leave your wallet or purse unattended. Finally, watch carefully when a clerk or waiter scans your credit card to make sure they are not making an additional imprint of your card for illegal use. Carefully examine your returned credit card to verify that another card was not given back to you, mistakenly or not.

After years of public indifference to the growing threat to our privacy, there are some hopeful signs of public awakening to the dangers posed by these new surveillance technologies. When the

US Congress passed legislation in 1996 to allow individual states to utilize social security numbers for driver's licenses, there was so much public opposition that Congress voted to hold a moratorium on implementing this practice. It was recently revealed that Intel Corporation had included a secret serial number within each Pentium III chip that would allow the identification of the individual computer user. Naturally, computer users and privacy groups protested this potential infringement of their privacy. Additionally, Microsoft embedded a hidden identification number in all documents produced by a computer using their software. The huge protests against Microsoft's abuse of privacy forced the company to offer a free software program on the Internet that would eliminate the identifying number. However, the vast majority of existing Microsoft software customers are unaware of the problem, or lack the necessary computer expertise to fix it.

If we are to protect what little privacy we have left, we need to encourage citizens in all nations to become aware of the growing surveillance they are subjected to. We should encourage a healthy debate about the relative advantages and disadvantages of each technological discovery. However, the greatest argument in favor of increasing surveillance is that each new device or technology does provide a significant benefit to either citizens or organizations. While I believe that citizen involvement and thoughtful protest against government and corporate abuse of our right to privacy can and should slow the relentless attack on our private information, the direction of our society and its continuing technological development is obviously moving us relentlessly toward the total surveillance society described in the ancient prophecies found in the book of Revelation. When we look at the whole picture it seems obvious that, despite misgivings, we will continue step-by-step toward a total surveillance society in which our right to privacy is only a distant memory.

Notes

1. "Panel: Privacy Doesn't Exist Anymore," *Direct Marketing News*, 5 July, 1999.

2. *Financial Post,* 19 May, 2000.

3. "SmartCards Simplify Payroll for Mexican Factory Workers," *IDSystems*, March 1999.

4. Betsy Pisik, "Smart Card Security," *The Washington Times*, 16 April, 1995.

5. Robert Gellman, "How Much Clout Will US Privacy Office Have?" *Government Computer News*, 24 May, 1999.

6. H. Farmer, "Big Brother Casts a Shadow Over Smart Cards," *Card Technology*, March 1999.

7

Big Brother Is Watching

How would you feel if you knew that anyone could immediately and secretly access virtually every private detail of your life? Such access could include government security officials, the police, your employer, your employees, or other inquisitive individuals such as your neighbors. The details of your travel habits and hotel destinations, your purchase of books, newspapers, magazines, movie rentals, pay-TV choices, traffic tickets, medical tests, and almost every purchase you make are now recorded on computer databases that are accessible to a surprising number of people, businesses, and government agencies. Enormous amounts of revealing information about your life remain "on file" for anyone who can access the thousands of computer databases storing this sensitive information. There are many information marketers, such as credit agencies, that automatically purchase or barter to obtain the information about your lifestyle, voting record, purchases, tax records, and real estate ownership.

From the moment we wake until we go to sleep, closed-circuit surveillance cameras constantly monitor our highways, streets, parking lots, and buildings. In the United Kingdom it is estimated that an average citizen will be photographed over one hundred times every day by closed-circuit cameras. This continual surveillance is fundamentally altering our way of life. These intrusive surveillance cameras are eroding the basic sense of privacy that most of us have previously taken for granted throughout our lives. Our privacy is being diminished by the development and implementation of these new surveillance technologies. The introduction of security cameras to provide traffic safety and crime control has expanded to include surveillance of employees at their desks, in washrooms, elevators, and throughout the factory or store.

The strong corporate arguments in favor of such continuous employee and customer monitoring include crime prevention, protection of staff, and employee drug-prevention programs. However, the result is that many employees now live a secretly monitored life that scarcely differs from that described by the author George Orwell in his frightening novel, 1984. Technological developments have produced surveillance possibilities that are far more thorough and effective than the spy capabilities of the Big Brother totalitarian government of George Orwell's prophetic novel.

A National ID Card for Everyone

There is a growing public perception in the media and in Congress that the United States needs a better method for identifying and monitoring the movements of all legal and illegal immigrants. The Commission on Immigration declared, "All US citizens and legal immigrants would get the equivalent of a national ID card under an expected proposal to Congress by the Commission on Immigration Reform." (*US Today*, July 13, 1994) The fear that the United States is being swamped by illegal immigrants from Central and South America is growing and is leading to proposals for a national ID card for everyone in the country. For example, a White House spokesperson speaking on the administration's plans to stem the tide of illegal foreign workers stated, "We're moving in the direction of a national registry as proposed in September by a bipartisan congressional commission." In the same article, the Commissioner for the Immigration and Naturalization Service, Doris Meissner, declared, "You cannot have meaningful employer sanctions [regarding illegal foreign workers] without either a tamper proof document of some kind, or a system that approximates that." (*Los Angeles Times*, January 10, 1995)

In 1993, President Clinton proposed the mandatory use of a high-technology national identity card as part of the transformation of health care legislation. The White House argument was that the identity card would protect all health care records, from visits to your family doctor to medical prescriptions or hospital treatments. However, regardless of the political justification, a national identity card is essentially a sophisticated device for tracking the details of your personal life. The overwhelming changes to the entire healthcare economy, proposed by Hillary Clinton, raised such a profound political backlash that the whole proposal died. Yet the Clinton administration proceeded to offer other apparently credible justifications to make the mandatory introduction of a national identification card seem necessary.

Officials argued that such an ID card could be utilized to catch welfare cheaters who "double-dip" by collecting benefits in two different jurisdictions or by using fake ID. Another justification for this card is to track down deadbeat parents seeking to evade payment of court-ordered child or spousal support. Other persuasive arguments in favor of a single national ID card are that it could replace a variety of existing identification papers, such as draft cards, passports, driver's licenses, voter registration cards, or even a birth certificate. The key requirement for an effective national system would be a SmartCard manufactured at low cost (less than $3.00) so that each citizen could be given an identification number permitting government databases to link all relevant data from the thousands of separate and presently uncoordinated databases.

The 1996 Health Insurance Portability and Accountability Act (the Kennedy-Kassebaum law) provides the US Department of Health and Human Services (HHS) with the power to assign "unique health care identifiers," enabling every part of the government's health care system to electronically tag, track, and monitor every American's medical records. Each citizen would have to submit an identification document with a unique number if they wish to receive health care, or the health provider will not be paid. This unique identification number will allow medical data to be collated into a comprehensive file without your knowledge or approval. Such information could be accessed by potential employers, insurers, or others who wish to conduct research on your life. The 1998 Patient Protection Act (H.R. 4250), which was passed by the House of Representatives on July 24, 1998, allows any company that develops personal medical records on US citizens to gather, exchange, and then distribute the records, as long as the information will only be used for "health care operations" (a phrase that is not defined in the Act). In 1991, the Canadian province of Ontario proposed that every citizen should be issued with a personal healthcare SmartCard that would hold their personal identification and medical records.[1]

A "Directory of New Hires" was established by law in 1996 under the Welfare Reform Act, officially called the Personal Responsibility and Work Opportunity Reform Act. Each employer in the United States must now send the name, home address, and Social Security Number of every new or promoted employee to the federal government. This information will eventually be incorporated into the all-encompassing computer database.

As of October 1, 2000, every state in the USA must use a state driver's license that contains the Social Security Number of the driver that "can be read visually or by electronic means" (1996 Illegal Immigration Reform and Immigrant Responsibility Act — Section 656.b). The plan is to convert existing driver's licenses into national ID cards, making it possible for the federal government to track virtually everyone wherever they go. It is important to remember that the federal government promised the American people that the Social Security number would never be used for purposes of national citizen identification when it was first introduced in 1932.

Many states are now modifying their driver's licenses to use it as a SmartCard. This card will contain both a computer chip and a magnetic strip, with biometric information including a digitized fingerprint, voice print, retina scan, or DNA print. These new SmartCards will track all your activities. For example, the smart card about to be introduced by New Jersey will have the ability to track bridge and highway tolls, credit card records, medical visits, and even state library systems' late book fines.

A national ID card will soon become necessary for daily functions. It will be extremely inconvenient, if not impossible, to go about one's business without possessing this national ID document. The risk that you might lose your national ID card, or have it stolen, raises some very serious concerns. There are already proposals for a more secure identification system if the ID SmartCard was replaced by a computer chip surgically implanted beneath the skin so that it could never be lost or stolen. Several companies have created a miniature computer-chip radio transponder that can be safely implanted. Such a chip could be injected at the same time as a vaccine, or implanted independently. The tiny chip — the size of a grain of rice — contains a multiple-character alphanumeric identification code that provides foolproof permanent ID, impossible to counterfeit. Whenever the implantable chip is near an electronic radio scanner, a beep sounds and the unique alphanumeric ID number appears on the scanner receiver. The average citizen may find this concept disturbing, but there is already a growing tendency for both government and business to use such computer chips to provide foolproof identification for domestic animals, pets, and for special medical situations.

Implanted ID Computer Chips for Pets

The widespread use of implanted ID chips for pets, containing medical records of the animal and the owner's address, has made people familiar with the potential of this technology. All zoos now surgically implant their animals with ID and radio-locator chips. This technology is also being suggested for use with young children. Any parent can understand the desperate panic felt when a young child disappears from sight. Some companies have suggested that implanted radio ID chips in children would allow a parent to track them at all times. Radio frequency (RF) scanners in theme parks, malls, hospitals, and other public places, would allow a child to be located instantly. Such chips would assist in the prevention of child abduction. There have been reports of executives traveling to high-risk kidnapping nations, such as Colombia, having had a surgically implanted RF chip so that the police could locate and rescue them if they were kidnapped.[2]

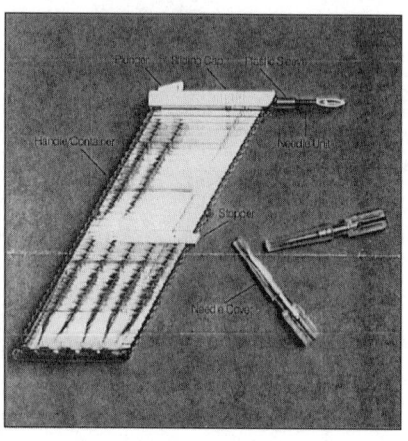

ID Chip Dispenser that is used in millions of pets.

The concept of placing a computer chip with all our personal information beneath the skin has great advantages. Such a surgically implanted chip could assist in the radio monitoring of released prisoners under house arrest. It could also provide precise location by Global Positioning Satellite (GPS) systems. GPS devices could then ensure the safe identification and tracking of medical patients, such as those with Alzheimer's. If someone suffered a heart attack or other medical emergency, an implanted GPS device would allow the 911 paramedics to instantly locate the victim.

Despite the many advantages, the implementation of such ID devices would also eliminate our privacy forever. And yet the widespread use of implanted radio locator ID chips may be inevitable, according to a spokesperson for the World Future Society, Andrew Cornish, who suggests that, at least initially, the use of such implanted ID chips would be voluntary. However, he acknowledges that things that are introduced as "voluntary" often become compulsory as time passes.[3]

Fear of Crime and Terrorism Sets the Stage for a Total Surveillance Society

In the last few decades, even in the historically non-violent United Kingdom, the fear of both terrorism and random criminal violence has grown to alarming proportions. As a result, United Kingdom citizens have demanded, or at least agreed to, an unprecedented introduction of surveillance technologies. These technologies have put the entire civilian population under almost constant observation during their public activities. Despite the popular notion in America and around the world, that US citizens are at the greatest risk for random violence, the truth is that there are more serious offenses in the United Kingdom than in America. A report in *USA Today* revealed that the "chances of being mugged in England are greater than in America. Crime rates for serious offenses such as assault, burglary, robbery and motor vehicle theft were all higher in England and Wales than in the USA, according to a study by a Cambridge University professor and a US Justice Department statistician." (*USA Today*, October 12, 1998) In 1995, the last year for which complete statistics were available in these two countries, there were 20 assaults per 1,000 citizens in Britain, as compared to only 8.8 per 1,000 in the United States. According to a 1998 study reported in London's *Sunday Times*, the robbery rate in Britain is 140 percent higher than in America, and their burglary rate almost doubles that of the United States. It is the fear of violent crime that has led to an unprecedented demand for police surveillance for protection.

Electronic Cash Transactions — Credit and Debit Cards

Automatic Teller Machines (ATMs) are an integral part of the financial life of many in the civilized world. We have become accustomed to memorizing our Personal Identification Number

(PIN) and preventing anyone else from looking over our shoulder as we use it. To enhance the security of ATM transactions and to track fraudulent use of stolen or counterfeit credit and debit cards, most ATMs now secretly photograph every customer's face as they complete their transaction. While this technology assists the police in finding and convicting a fraudulent thief after the crime, the photo will not prevent the criminal use of stolen or counterfeit cards.

Digital I Ring — Dallas Semiconductor.
Used to control manufacturing processing, access to ATMs, to access
your computer, utilize vending machines.

ID Computer Chips on a Ring

As an example of the remarkable advances in security technology and the growing acceptance of such innovations, consider the IButton Ring which was introduced by Dallas Semiconductor Corp. of Dallas, Texas. The IButton is a computer chip that is contained within a tiny stainless steel MicroCan that can be worn as a ring, key ring, watch, or attached to clothing. Over twenty million IButton computer chips are used throughout the world to communicate to desktop, laptop, and hand-held personal computers. When you touch the IButton ring to the receptor device, information is instantaneously transferred at the rate of 142 thousand bits per second. This device can contain identification and biometric information as well as store funds or medical information. In Mexico customers simply touch the IButton ring to the Bluedot Receptor on the gas pump and the money is automatically deducted from their bank account. In Argentina and Brazil IButtons are used by millions to pay parking meters. Over a million and a half riders in Turkey use the IButton for tickets to ride the new mass-transit system. This type of technology is likely to be used globally to increase security and avoid the need for cash. However, there will be a permanent computer record of every single transaction including the time and place.

Passwords

Corporate security specialists have found that the misuse of computer passwords has seriously compromised the security of many company computers. Employees often choose passwords that are very easy to remember; selecting codes based on variations of family birthdays, the name of their dog, or even their home address. Any competent computer hacker can make educated guesses for passwords that people may choose, based on the hacker's access to the employee's personal information. Additionally, there are password search programs that hackers share with each other on the Internet, which quickly try tens of thousands of password variations. Even more worrisome is the fact that many people foolishly write their password down and leave it in their office where an unauthorized person could discover it. Using the same password for years without change, or giving a password to another employee in an emergency situation and then forgetting to change it afterwards, can cause problems leading to the violation of computer and bank security. Billions of dollars in losses have already resulted.

Consequently, new advanced security systems are now being introduced worldwide. While some may question the need for sophisticated, expensive, and secure technology, a study by the Computer Security Institute in San Francisco (*Financial Post*, January 24, 2000) discovered that 62 percent of companies surveyed admitted that their computer systems had recently suffered breaches of security. Interestingly, the study revealed that 55 percent of unauthorized breaches of computer systems were committed by the company's own employees.

Biometric Identification Systems

Although identification and debit/credit cards with either magnetic strips or embedded microchips have been successfully used for decades to provide correct identification (ID) and access to secure computer systems, companies are increasingly turning to new biologically based biometric identification systems to enhance their security. These new biometric systems incorporate some element of your unique physical makeup to provide personal ID that cannot be counterfeited by any other person. Biometric systems utilize biological information such as iris eye scans, fingerprints, hand geometry, and even computer facial recognition systems.

Iris Scan Identification

The newest generation of bank ATMs contains sophisticated closed-circuit television cameras capable of unobtrusively photographing each customer's iris as they stand in front of the ATM. This detailed picture of the iris is instantaneously compared with the computer databank's file of iris patterns for each legitimate bank customer. This validates their identity without the need to memorize a PIN. Since the detailed pattern of each person's iris is as unique as your fingerprint, this technological advance helps banks to vastly improve their ATM security. There are more than four hundred specific "degrees of freedom," or measurable features and characteristics of the iris, that can be instantly measured and compared to an original iris image to identify a particular person. Fingerprint comparison only uses approximately sixty measurable features to make an absolute identification in a court of law.[4]

Recently, the sophistication of this security technology was demonstrated by Bank United in Houston, Texas. The bank's executives asked identical twins, Michael and Richard Schwartz, to switch their bank ATM cards and attempt to confuse the iris scan camera system. In only three seconds, this system, called EyeTM, was able to detect that the twin offering his brother's bank card was not the individual whose iris pattern was recorded earlier in the bank's security computers. This iris-scanning technology will be spreading rapidly among the world's banks. However, many other institutions have quickly adopted this effective ID system for other security needs. For example, the Charlotte/Douglas International Airport in South Carolina will soon use iris scanners to control employee access to sensitive, secure, and restricted areas of the airport.

Fingerprint and Hand Geometry Scanners

Many military bases, as well as high security organizations such as banks, are now introducing fingerprint scanners to control access to sensitive high-security areas. Some hospitals, such as LaPorte Hospital in Indiana, have introduced the NEC Technologies Inc. new HealthID fingerprint recognition system to their hospital staff, as well as to their patients. These fingerprint scanners ensure only authorized access to confidential patient medical files. The absolutely reliable identification of every patient will avoid the risk of inadvertently giving a patient the wrong medical procedure or medication.

NEC Technologies Inc. is the world leader in developing advanced fingerprint recognition systems, with the majority of these being used by governments and large corporations. They recently developed a fingerprint-recognition system called TouchPass. This system permits organizations using Microsoft Windows software and IBM-compatible personal computers to control access to their confidential data by requiring employees to verify their fingerprint ID before using their computer. Compaq Computer Corporation is now marketing a miniaturized fingerprint scanner for under $100, permitting companies to allow only authorized personnel to access their sensitive financial and technical files.

Unfortunately, many of the current fingerprint scanners cannot acquire a readable fingerprint from each person's hand. Existing technology measures the difference in the electrical capacity between the dead skin layer that forms tiny ridges and swirls on your fingertip, and the air space between the ridges. For example, if a person's skin is very dry due to old age or disease, or the skin's surface is contaminated due to excessive oil, et cetera, the system will not be able to read the fingerprint correctly. An engineer, working for Harris Corporation in Melbourne, Florida, invented an integrated circuit fingerprint, using existing personal computer technology called FingerLoc. When a fingertip is placed on the computer chip, the tiny sensors detect the electrical potential from underlying ridges and valleys in the sub-surface layer of live skin just below the surface of the dry dead skin. This innovative technology provides a much higher level of security; it can read any fingerprint regardless of the individual's actual skin condition.

Another innovation to control secure access to computerized ID or banking systems was recently introduced by some financial corporations offering electronic banking services from your personal computer. Realizing that personal passwords are relatively insecure, one financial corporation, ING Direct Canada, is offering their customers a new computer mouse that is specially manufactured by SecuGen Corporation in California. Amazingly, the surface of the computer mouse can recognize the legitimate customer's fingerprints, immediately comparing them to those on file in the corporation's computer database, and granting the customer secure access. If any unauthorized person attempts to impersonate this customer, the corporation's sophisticated security system will instantly detect the attempt and terminate their communication.

Facial Recognition Computer Systems

A significant challenge facing identification systems was the inability of computer software programs to accurately differentiate between the details that compose the photograph of a human face. However, a brilliant computer software program has been developed that uses a new process called "fuzzy logic" that mimics the ability of the human brain to identify one individual face from hundreds of thousands of others. Another promising new facial recognition system digitalizes a photograph of a human face using 65,536 pixels to create a ten-dimension "feature vector."

These systems allow the computer to instantaneously compare two different photos of individuals and accurately identify each. The national security agencies, immigration, and police agencies are very interested in the possibilities of using this face-recognition camera system to monitor and identify individuals from hidden surveillance cameras at immigration ports and international airport entry points. These systems would greatly enhance the ability of government authorities to identify and arrest terrorists, drug dealers, spies, or international criminals. However, the development of facial-recognition computer security systems in tandem with long distance closed-circuit television cameras in public places, is a significant link in the chain that could produce the global totalitarian police state of the coming Antichrist as described in the book of Revelation.

A British Broadcasting System (BBC) radio article on October 21, 1998, reported that a sophisticated facial-recognition camera system called Mandrake is now being tested in London, UK. The system uses advanced facial geometry calculations to instantly make its comparisons. The Mandrake close-circuit television system photographs all individuals in a given area and compares the "target faces" of known criminals with the thousands of innocent individuals in a crowd. Polls in England revealed that 60 percent of the population claimed that crime prevention was their number one social priority. During the test, one hundred and forty fixed-position street cameras and eleven mobile camera units were deployed throughout one borough of London. The photographic images of thousands of citizens walking on the streets were instantly transmitted to the computer database at the security center. They were compared in seconds with a group of target faces of known criminals. When the computer found a match, the Mandrake system highlighted the target face and gave an alarm. The security operator double-checked the target image against the photos of the criminals and contacted the police.

A small town named Newham, just outside of London, has installed over two hundred closed-circuit television cameras in an attempt to reduce crime in the community. At the present time there are no laws protecting the privacy of UK citizens from the growing use of closed-circuit surveillance cameras. Using a new advanced facial-recognition software program developed by Visionics Corporation of Jersey City, New Jersey, the system can automatically scan the faces of anyone passing in front of the camera and instantaneously compare the image with the dozens of faces of known criminals.[5]

A Mass Population Identification and Tracking System

When the United Nations or the United States intervenes in a humanitarian refugee situation, the ability to identify and track homeless refugees is of utmost importance in order to effectively administer medicine, food, and water, and maintain security. Many of the refugees cannot speak English and have difficulty communicating with the medical staff or aid workers. The refugees often have similar sounding names, and unfortunately they often try to mislead the refugee and immigration officers regarding their identity and their status. For example, in the early 1990s, the US military administered a group of approximately 50,000 Haitian and Cuban asylum seekers in the US base in Guantanamo, Cuba. Many of the thousands of refugees shared the popular name "Immanuel," or "Jesus." This produced serious problems in identification. A large number of these individuals were infected with AIDS and many had serious criminal records requiring special controls.

To assist in identifying the individuals of special interest to the US Army, the technicians modified an existing remote radio frequency and identification transponder technology known as the Deployable Mass Population Identification and Tracking System. These special identification computer devices were designed to fit into a black plastic wristband, quite similar in appearance to a wristwatch. The radio transponder contains a unique identification code that is permanently transmitted to the individual's wristband unit. This unique ID number identifies the refugee and instantly calls up his name, address, history, medical, criminal, and immigration status on the computer screen of the security scanner, confirming identification. This mass population ID tracking system allows the US Army to monitor and verify the location of every one of the 50,000 refugees within the 45 square miles of the huge Guantanamo military base.

Obviously, this technology could be adapted to allow the government to monitor any population group over any geographical area. One of the most significant problems associated with any of these computerized identification systems is the possibility of some group counterfeiting the transponder codes, and the risk that individuals will either exchange, modify, or lose their wristband transponder ID. A proposed solution to these problems is the surgical implanting beneath the skin of these ID radio frequency computer chips.

Population Control Device, used by US Military for Haitian Refugees.

Surveillance Controls at Our Borders

When you casually drive your car up to any international border between Canada and the United States or between Mexico and the United States, a sophisticated long-distance camera automatically scans your license plate. Instantly the computer system compares your license plate against the national motor vehicle registry computer files, the customs search-and-seize list, and national police and security files of the United States, Canada, and Mexico. When the customs agent leans out of the booth toward your car window and asks you where you live, where you were born, and who is the registered owner of your vehicle, he or she already knows the answer! In the five seconds you wait to drive across the red line to approach the customs agent, the optical scanning system that read your license plate instantly accessed Immigration, Customs, and State Department computer records, including your vehicle registration, driver's license, and police records. It will indicate if you have outstanding parking tickets, or if you took two trips to Canada during the last four years. The custom and immigration computers of the United States and Canada record each time you enter and leave the country. Unless your answers to the customs agent's questions agree with the information displayed on his screen, he or she will send you to the station for further interrogation.

The introduction of laser scanning technology, such as we use in grocery stores, gives some idea of the ease with which a totalitarian control system could be implemented. Scanning devices, including high speed and long distance optical readers, are now used in many buildings, highways, and high security areas. The license plate of each car crossing a bridge or driving through a tunnel can now be scanned by a similar camera system, in order to determine if any traffic warrants are outstanding. An instantaneous computer check compares the files of the state's motor vehicle records, parking citations, and outstanding warrants against your car's license plate. If you forgot to pay your speeding or parking tickets, a police officer with a radio-modem-computer link is waiting for you.

DNA and Genetic Testing

One of the greatest scientific developments of the past century is the discovery that each cell in the human body contains Deoxyribonucleic Acid (DNA), embodying the complete genetic blueprint to build, maintain, and repair every organ and process within your body. The DNA genetic information is absolutely unique and differs from every other human being on earth, except for identical twins. Therefore, your DNA is as unique as your fingerprint to provide scientifically valid identification. DNA testing has proven to be a phenomenally useful discovery in the criminal justice system. Police are now able to apprehend, convict, and occasionally acquit individuals by confirming the identity of an individual at a crime scene. In the last few decades, scientists have developed sophisticated laboratory techniques to examine the smallest of biological samples in order to determine the exact identity of the person. It is practically impossible for a human to spend time in a room without leaving a number of DNA samples, including microscopic saliva traces, blood specks, flakes of skin, sweat, or single strands of hair.

Justice authorities confirm that more than 50 percent of all violent crimes, including rape and murder, are committed by individuals who have been previously arrested for precisely the same crime. Since 1994, the US Congress has mandated that each state collect DNA samples from all violent offenders, as well as any prisoners currently incarcerated. The new system requiring that all DNA data must be instantly linked to the national computer database was introduced by the FBI in October 1998. This new database, the National DNA Index System (NDIS), presently has 140,000 DNA criminal profiles. The NDIS helps the police, and courts, in every state to instantly compare the crime-scene DNA samples to the national database of previously convicted criminals. Since 1995, a similar DNA database in the United Kingdom has been used to identify over 30,000 criminals.

The incredible value of DNA evidence is beyond question. A motorcycle police officer in St. Petersburg, Florida, was following a potential suspect who they thought might be involved in a string of robberies and rapes. When the police officer noticed that the suspect spit onto the highway while stopped at a traffic light, the officer stopped his car, took a paper towel, and wiped up the evidence. When the sample was analyzed, the DNA from the saliva matched the DNA sample found on the rape victim. Within a few days the criminal was arrested.

Unfortunately, there is presently a huge backlog of biological samples that must be tested, and the present DNA tests can take weeks or longer to produce an acceptable result. At the present time there are more than 400,000 DNA samples awaiting analysis, and more than 200,000 additional samples that need to be re-analyzed using the new, more sophisticated Short Tandem Repeats (STR) DNA analysis technique. This time-delay problem results in countless criminals being able to continue their crimes even though positive evidence proving their guilt is probably already in the justice system.

The National Institute of Justice, the research department of the US Department of Justice, has funded scientific research in laboratories around the nation to design computer chips the size of credit cards capable of analyzing the DNA of biological samples found at crime scenes. The main goal of this research program is to create portable technology for police investigators at a crime scene, to immediately identify the DNA of the perpetrator, and to instantly compare that DNA sample with those of previous crime suspects.

One company, called Nanogen, based in San Diego, CA, is developing a portable DNA microchip-analyzing device in a plastic cartridge that can be fitted into a briefcase and used with a networked laptop computer. Nanogen's device will be able to interface with the FBI's DNA database, and instantly compare the DNA found in biological samples at a crime scene with the DNA of an existing criminal. The current DNA technology involves dissolving the biological evidence (hair, saliva, or skin) in a chemical solution that is then extracted through chemical reactions. The extracted DNA is placed in the plastic cartridge in the briefcase reader where the short tandem repeats of the DNA sample are analyzed. These repeats produce a unique DNA "fingerprint" that can be instantly compared with the DNA samples of millions of criminals on computer file with the Department of Justice. If thirteen different repeat sections of DNA are identified and successfully matched with an existing criminal profile, the courts will usually agree that an absolute identification is confirmed.[6]

However, the continuing development of genetic testing suggests that in the very near future we will be able to test the genetic profile of a newborn child only minutes after it is born. This vital genetic information may be used in the future to determine where that citizen will someday be allowed to work or who they will ultimately marry. In addition, the child's DNA could determine whether they will be able to qualify for medical or life insurance, government healthcare, or major social services. The Privacy

Commissioner of Canada, Bruce Phillips, has warned of the danger that the vital genetic information of each citizen may be shared as casually with private corporations and other governments as our supposedly private individual credit information files are shared today.[7]

One of the greatest challenges to DNA evidence is the problem caused by DNA cross-contamination at the crime scene. Unless a detective is very careful it is quite easy to contaminate the criminal DNA sample with samples from investigating police officers at the scene. Each individual sample of hair, skin, or blood must be individually picked up by the gloved hand of a qualified detective, and placed in a sterile container. Since the officer must use a clean set of gloves for each particular piece of biological evidence, it is not uncommon for a detective to use dozens of pairs of disposable rubber gloves at one crime scene to collect multiple biological specimens.

It is obvious that the continued accumulation of DNA evidence from criminal suspects and prisoners, and from members of the military and police force members, will ultimately make it possible to immediately identify most suspects in criminal investigations. However, the down side to these developments is, again, an infringement of our privacy. Eventually, it may be impossible for anyone to escape the police and intelligence agencies of any future government.

New Auto Surveillance Technology

New technology has been developed that allows any vehicle to be tracked accurately by a Global Positioning Satellite (GPS) system. Experts estimate that $8 billion will be spent in the year 2000 on GPS equipment.[8] When a new Chrysler Intrepid was recently stolen by three car thieves in Toronto, Canada, they were astonished to find that they were under the surveillance of the police force and quickly arrested. The three thieves had stolen the car from a Thrifty Car Rental Agency but they had the misfortune to choose a car equipped with the high technology GPS anti-car theft system developed by NavLynx Technologies of Toronto, Canada.

After stealing the car, the thieves were astonished to hear

the phone ring and the voice of an operator from NavLynx Technologies headquarters telling them "You are driving an unauthorized car." They were asked to identify themselves and warned that if they refused, they would be arrested. The frustrated thieves immediately threw the phone out of the car window as they sped along the highway at almost 100 miles an hour. Using the new built-in technology, the NavLynx company operator informed police of the speed and exact location of the stolen car. When the police informed the company supervisor that they were in close pursuit of the car, the company then sent a radio signal by satellite to the device and disabled the car's ignition system, bringing it to a stop in front of the pursuing police cars. The NavLynx Technologies can track the car anywhere with its Global Positioning System, identifying its location and speed, as well as locking doors and opening or closing car windows.[9]

A number of security companies, such as LoJack and Teletrac, offer vehicle recovery systems that can detect radio signals from a hidden beacon in stolen cars or trucks. An article in *Forbes Magazine* on September 22, 1997, reported one consumer's use of the Teletrac system in his wife's car; he was worried about her having to drive to work through a dangerous part of the city. The customer used the tracking system called Ozz, and dialed in the special number. The Ozz computer immediately announced, "The vehicle is traveling west on the Santa Monica Freeway near Fairfax at 30 miles per hour."[10] Teletrac is also developing a personal radio beacon detector that can be worn by a patient with Alzheimer's, or a young child, enabling their location and recovery if they wandered away. While this type of system can provide enhanced personal security, it is obvious that such information can also be misused. Numerous new cars are being equipped with such technology. While the advantages of GPS systems are obvious for safety concerns or for recovering a stolen vehicle, the potential disadvantage is equally clear.

Telephone and Laptop Computers

At an airport in Brussels, as a businessman ran toward the gate, he paused to phone his secretary, entering his credit card number into his cell phone. Unfortunately, he was unaware that cyber thieves were waiting to intercept his call and gather his special phone numbers through the use of very sophisticated portable scanners. In the following days, his credit card number and phone number were used by these thieves to make numerous illegal phone calls to colleagues around the world. Most users of analog cellular phones are unaware of the ease with which electric scanners can intercept relevant radio frequencies to listen in on private calls. The late Princess Diana, Prince Charles, and former US Speaker of the House of Representatives, Newt Gingrich, were embarrassed to discover that their most private phone calls were intercepted by enemies who publicly revealed their secrets to the world's media.

However, newer digital cellular phones use advanced encryption techniques, making the interception of calls by scanners almost impossible for the average hacker. Yet, there are new computer and cellular phone digital-scanning devices, which can be acquired from high-tech surveillance shops, allowing their possessor to crack most digital encryption. While more secure encryption systems may be developed, at the present time it may be prudent to refrain from discussing confidential information over cellular phones.

In addition to the threat of telephone message interception, the very existence of a cellular phone provides a complete and permanent phone company record of your phone's precise location. Even when you are not using your phone, as long as your battery has power, it is continuously sending out a radio signal that is picked up by the thousands of antenna that each mobile phone system places throughout the city as well as in rural areas. This locator signal permits the mobile phone system to locate and transmit an incoming phone message to your cellular phone. However, what few mobile phone users may realize is that the phone company computers keep a permanent record for years, of the locator signals sent by your phone. Therefore, if the police or an intelligence agency ever needed to, they could determine the precise location of your phone at a certain time on a certain date.

By October 2001, the US Congress will require that all manufacturers of cellular phones design their products so that wireless phone-service providers will be able to pinpoint any 911 caller's location to within four hundred feet. Ted Rappaport, the director of the Mobile & Portable Radio Research Group at Virginia Tech, Blacksburg, Virginia warned, "Big Brother could really be a problem if position location technology is used improperly. . . . There are a lot of people who would want their privacy protected when making a cellular call, and the technology used to locate 911 could be used to locate any wireless call."[11] A private source told me that this was how the Los Angeles Police located O. J. Simpson when he fled from his home in his white Bronco vehicle.

Millions of business people travel the world with their laptop computers. These computers often contain corporate secrets. There are many reports of illegal theft of these portable computers, as well as the secret attacks on the confidential data carried on the computer hard drives of these corporate business people. A report by Safeware Insurance Company, based in Columbus, Ohio, reveals that 265,000 laptop computers were stolen from business people in the United States in 1996. The numbers are rapidly growing every year. While many of these thefts are random attacks by opportunistic thieves, an increasing number are committed by industrial espionage thieves specifically targeting corporate information hidden in the hard-drive files of the laptop computer carried by a corporate rival. The Gartner Group, one of the world's most respected computer consultants, warns, "Theft of goods is probably the number one security threat."[12]

Many companies are responding to this threat by equipping employee's laptops with sophisticated tracking devices. NEC's CompuTrace software helps a company to trace any future use of a stolen computer, and to track down thieves. The first time a thief uses the stolen laptop, the software sends out a secret signal to NEC identifying the location and phone number of the line used.

Email

Increasingly, electronic mail (email) is replacing handwritten or typewritten mail. Email messages are an efficient form of communication. Email can also be easily intercepted and scanned for key words or numbers. The interception of personal or corporate emails can be done routinely by sophisticated computer software programs. Unfortunately, most email interception is virtually undetectable to the party whose privacy has been violated.

A spokesperson from the United States Department of Justice defended the government's intrusive monitoring of email and other Internet communications by claiming that democratic societies must balance the individual right to freedom and privacy with the nation's need for public security from organized crime, terrorism, and foreign enemies. Acknowledging that eliminating general surveillance of our communications would be desirable in an ideal world, spokesperson Scott Charney stated that it would only work, "if everyone were law abiding, but they are not."[13]

The Internet

The Internet is transforming the world's private, corporate, and governmental communications. The astonishing growth of the Internet is unprecedented in the history of technology. The number of global subscribers more than doubles every year. The Internet began as a small communications network designed by the Defense Advanced Research Project Agency, the research branch of the Pentagon, to connect various military bases and university science laboratories working on defense projects. However, it quickly grew to connect hundreds of thousands of academics, scientists, and researchers. The original intent for the Internet was non-commercial, but by the early 1990s the Internet was transformed into the largest communications system in history. Today hundreds of millions of individuals, and millions of corporations as well as organizations, depend on the Internet for both internal and external communications. This makes it extremely easy for intelligence agencies to monitor daily the billions of communications in search for any chosen target.

A single, private corporation has been able to establish itself as the sole controller, gatekeeper, and virtual toll collector for every individual, business, or organization that wishes to participate on the web. The US government initially granted this exclusive monopolistic right to a tax-supported organization called Internet Network Information Center (INIC) operating under the direction of the National Science Foundation, in order to issue domain names for all web-sites. It provided this vital service to web users without charge. In order for anyone to search the Internet to locate another web site, it is essential that each web site possess a unique electronic address. This address is known as an Internet Protocol (IP) address, and allows the substitution of an easily remembered name. For example, my web site: GrantJeffrey.com, is simpler to recall than what might otherwise be a number like: "123.273.486.8."

The US government required that anyone in the world who wanted to set up their own web site with a unique Internet address, ending in any of the well-known suffixes: .com, .edu, .org, .net, or .gov, must register their domain name with Internet Network Information Center. However, in 1993, the government transferred the domain registry to a private corporation called Network Solutions, Inc. (NSI) in Herndon, Virginia. Many Internet users were outraged when, in September 1995, NSI demanded that anyone wanting to register a new domain address must pay NSI $100, and those wanting to renew an address must pay $50 per year. This monopoly yields a very profitable revenue each year. NSI was acquired by Science Applications International Corporation (SAIC), a privately held company with over 20,000 employees working in 450 locations throughout the world.

The most disturbing aspect of this exclusive arrangement is the implied control. SAIC is operated by numerous individuals who have worked for decades within the Pentagon and national security intelligence organizations. The board of directors of SAIC includes individuals such as Bobby Inman, the former head of the National Security Agency (America's most important intelligence agency), Robert Gates and John Deutch, both former directors of the Central Intelligence Agency, William Perry, the Secretary of Defense, Melvin Laird, the former Secretary of Defense, and Donald Hicks, the former chief of research and development at the Pentagon.[14] Why is the national security community so intent on controlling the key entry points into the major communication system that links the governments, corporations, and billions of citizens?

Organizations and national security agencies that are able to control and monitor the Internet are in a position to exercise total access to billions of daily communications. We now live in a surveillance society. Virtually every email, chat-room conversation, web search, or Internet communication is now available for analysis by security and intelligence authorities. Presently — fortunately — we live in a democracy where the existence of political checks and balances, together with the judicial system, provide some measure of confidence that major privacy violations may be stopped. However, it is obvious that in the hands of any future dictatorial government, this powerful surveillance technology could make it almost impossible to escape the control of totalitarian police and security forces. The next chapter will explore the capabilities of the global surveillance system that can monitor almost all electronic communications on earth. This system is known as the Echelon Project.

Your Life Is Available on the Internet Forever

Many of us have grown up in a world where most of our family information was kept very private. The salary and financial details of one's neighbors and fellow employees were not discussed. Only one's banker knew the details of one's financial history, and he was obliged to confidentiality as a part of his job description. That world is long gone, and it is unlikely to return.

Today we live in a world where any inquisitive neighbor, fellow employee, boss, friend, or enemy can relatively easily access the most intimate details of your financial life, credit history, real estate holdings, criminal records, divorce settlement, educational background, or interests on the Internet. Surveillance technology is now available to civilians that would formerly have been available only to intelligence agencies. Even our government agencies are beginning to release to the public personal and financial data that they have collected from their trusting citizens.

For example, the Federal Bureau of Investigation has responded to the demands of citizens to access the once-secret FBI files. As a result of the Freedom of Information Act, anyone with a computer can access the FBI's new web site (foia.fbi.gov) and read thousands of unclassified or formerly classified government documents, including files on Elvis Presley, Frank Sinatra, and John F. Kennedy. FBI files are available on such diverse topics as aviator Amelia Earhart, who was lost at sea, or the infamous Project Blue Book on UFO sightings.[15]

The Internet is profoundly transforming our society, communications, and private lives in revolutionary ways. Without realizing it, millions of people are inadvertently creating permanent computer records of their life, activities, purchases, and interests that will someday come back to haunt them. Your electronic data shadow will follow you throughout your life, whether or not you are aware of it. Most people think of email and the Internet as simply a vehicle for instantaneous communication — like a phone call. However, the Internet is a computer database that records virtually everything you write and every site you visit. It never forgets. These records may be stored for decades. There are a number of computer databases that archive vast amounts of Internet information. One site, called the Internet Archive (www.archive.org), a nonprofit archiving organization, conducts searches of millions of Internet web sites every sixty days and collects copies including text and images.

At the present time there are approximately 45,000 news groups on the Internet that contain individual messages, comments, and jokes. Most participants believe their personal messages disappear forever when the "thread" of the news group no longer displays their comment. However, a number of computer databases, including Deja News and Internet Archive, search these news groups and record those messages. Imagine applying for a promotion or a new job in the future and finding that a series of promising interviews abruptly ceases with no explanation. While you may never find the real reason, the prospective employer may have searched one of these Internet archives and discovered some inappropriate comments or web site visits that reflected poorly on you.

The founder of Internet Archive, Brewster Kahle, has hired

over thirty employees to monitor sophisticated computer software search engines, called "spiders," that continuously search more than 300 million Internet web sites and Usenet sites and store the vast amounts of information every two months. They have already accumulated ten trillion bytes of computer information off the Internet. To place that enormous collection of information including personal data in context, it would take ten million standard one-megabyte floppy disks to hold that amount of information.

Bruce Schneier, co-editor of *The Electronic Privacy Papers* and a well respected consultant on computer encryption, wrote:

> The odd thing is, we perceive the Net as a conversation and not as public record, and it turns out to be public record to a larger extent than people are aware of. . . . You can easily imagine in 20 years a candidate being asked about a conversation he had in a chat room while he was in college. We're becoming a world where everything is recorded.[16]

David Sobel, the general counsel for the Electronic Privacy Information Center based in Washington, D.C., warns, "We're now entering an era where tens of millions of people are speaking on the record without any understanding of what it means to speak on the record, and that's certainly unprecedented. . . . It is suddenly becoming impossible to escape your past."[17]

For the first time in history, foolish and unwise comments that you made thirty years ago during an Internet political or religious discussion news group may come back to haunt you. Sobel warns, "If you define privacy as the right of individuals to control information about themselves — as we do — then mega-archiving systems clearly raise significant privacy issues. These systems convert every passing thought and contemporaneous musing into a permanent, retrievable record — without, in many cases, the knowledge or consent of the creator."[18]

Despite the obvious dangers to your personal privacy posed by use of the Internet, it is implausible for any business or professional person to avoid it. The Internet is virtually indispensable for research and communications. While there is a growing concern among academics and intellectuals about the risks to our privacy, the process is now irreversible.

John made a remarkable prophecy almost two thousand years ago in the book of Revelation. He indicated that a future world dictator would develop a comprehensive police control system that would make it absolutely impossible for anyone, "small and great, rich and poor, free and bond," to escape his police control system in the last days, before the return of the Messiah. The development in our generation of these unprecedented systems of communication surveillance and police control is a significant indication that we are living in the last days, as prophesied in the Scriptures.

Notes

1. "Experimental Health Cards Will Carry Patients' History," *Toronto Star*, 25 July 1991.

2. Mark David, "If Chips a Are for Pets, Why Not for Kids?" *Automatic ID News*, August 1994.

3. Jon Van, "In Future, Tiny Chip May Get Under Skin" *The Chicago Tribune*, 7 May 1996.

4. John Burneil, "ATM Makes Eye Iris Identification," *Automatic ID News*, September 1995.

5. Nancy Senger, "We're Watching (Out For) You," *Business Solutions*, September 1999.

6. Vince Beiser, "Cops Covet DNA Chip," 1 June 1999, http://www.wired.com/news/print/0,1294,19878,00.html.

7. John Douglas, "Genetic Privacy Threatened: 'Human Bar Codes' Envisioned," *National Post*. http://www/hackcanada.com/canadian/freedom/human_bar_codes.text.

8. Ann Marsh, *Forbes Magazine*, 22 September 1997.

9. Bob Mitchell, "Car Phone Orders Thieves to Pull Over," *Toronto Star*, 20 January 2000.

10. Ann Marsh, *Forbes Magazine*, 22 September 1997.

11. Tim Friend, "Using Cell Phones to Reach Out and Find Someone," *USA Today*, 16 December 1997.

12. *Mobile Computing and Communications*, October, 1997.

13. Javier Bernal, *Public and Private Security in the Internet*, 6 August 1999, http://www.socio.demon.co.uk/magazine/6/enfopol_echelon.html).

14. John Dillon, "Networking With Spooks," Internet: http://mediafilter.org/caq/internic.

15. *Federal Computer Week*, 30 August 1999.

16. Joseph Lasica, "Your Past Is Your Future, Web-Wise," *The Washington Post*, 11 October 1998.

17. Joseph Lasica, "Your Past Is Your Future, Web-Wise," *The Washington Post*, 11 October 1998.

18. Joseph Lasica, "Your Past Is Your Future, Web-Wise," *The Washington Post,* 11 October 1998.

8

Project Echelon

A Global Surveillance System

Echelon is the most ambitious intelligence effort in history and was launched by the US National Security Agency (NSA) following World War II. Their goal was to create a truly global spy system, code-named Echelon, a top-secret Anglo-American project, which would be able to capture and analyze almost every phone call, fax, e-mail, Internet, radio, and telex message throughout the world.

It was originally established and now maintained by five western nations: the United States, United Kingdom, Canada, Australia, and New Zealand. In 1948, these five countries created a secret intelligence agreement called UK–USA to spy on Russia and its Warsaw Pact allies during the Cold War. Echelon involves the United Kingdom's General Communications Head Quarters (GCHQ), the Canadian Communications Security Establishment (CSE), the Australian Defense Security Directorate (DSD), and New Zealand's General Communications Security Bureau (GCSB).

Now they use their technology cooperatively, spying on the communications of citizens of other member countries in order to escape the legal prohibition against spying on the private communications of their own citizens. This arrangement enables them to "technically" deny that "they" are illegally intercepting the electronic communications of their own citizens. They then forward the relevant intelligence intercepts. They each intercept and gather electronic signals from almost every telephone call, fax transmission, and email message throughout the world every day. The intercepted communications are compiled and analyzed by the powerful banks of advanced super computers at the National Security Agency in Fort Meade, Maryland, and searched for messages containing certain key words identified by the member intelligence agencies in Echelon "dictionaries." While most of the West's other intelligence surveillance systems are focused on enemy nations' military targets, weapons, and capabilities, Echelon is unique in that its primary espionage focus involves non-military civilian targets including the messages of governments, corporations, and individuals in almost every nation on earth.

Can you imagine the attitude of the Europeans, Russians, Chinese, and Japanese if they knew that their most private communications were being acquired instantaneously by a worldwide intelligence "vacuum cleaner" that is constantly sifting millions of simultaneous calls and messages in search of those using any of the thousands of key words, key telephone numbers, passwords, or voice prints of targeted individuals?

Echelon — The Greatest Threat to Privacy

Three-quarters of a century ago, Louis Brandeis, a well-respected judge on the Supreme Court, warned against the danger to our freedom from the constantly increasing capabilities of the government to monitor the communications and private lives of the average citizen. In 1928, during a case involving police wire-tapping, Supreme Court Justice Louis Brandeis wrote a profound dissenting opinion about the fundamental right of each citizen to privacy in both our thoughts and private papers within a democracy. In this written dissenting opinion Brandeis wrote against the government's abuse of the citizen's Fifth Amendment right — that of not having to incriminate oneself by being forced to give evidence against oneself, as well as the Fourth Amendment prohibiting illegal search-and-seizure:

> When the Fourth and Fifth Amendments were adopted, 'the form that evil had theretofore taken' had been necessarily simple. Force and violence were then the only means known to man by which a government could directly effect self-incrimination. It could compel the individual to testify — a compulsion effected, if need be, by torture. It could secure possession of his papers and other articles incident to his private life — a seizure effected, if need be, by breaking and entry. Protection against such invasion of the sanctities of a man's home and the privacies of life was provided in the Fourth and Fifth Amendments by specific language. *Boyd v. United States*, 116 U. S. 616, 630, 6 S. Ct. 524, 29 L. Ed. 746. But time works changes, brings into existence new conditions and purposes. Subtler and more far-reaching means of invading privacy have become available to the government. Discovery and invention have made it possible for the government, by means far more effective than stretching upon the rack, to obtain disclosure in court of what is whispered in the closet.

> Moreover, "in the application of a Constitution, our contemplation cannot be only of what has been, but of what may be." The progress of science in furnishing the government with means of espionage is not likely to stop with wire tapping. Ways may some day be developed by which the government, without removing papers from secret drawers, can reproduce them in court, and by which it will be enabled to expose to a jury the most intimate occurrences of the home. Advances in the psychic and related sciences may bring means of exploring unexpressed beliefs, thoughts and emotions. "That places the liberty of every man in the hands of every petty officer" was said by James Otis of much lesser intrusions than these. To Lord

Camden a far slighter intrusion seemed "subversive of all the comforts of society." Can it be that the Constitution affords no protection against such invasions of individual security? [Supreme Court decision — *Olmstead et al. v. United States*, June 4, 1928][1]

Justice Brandeis expressed valid and well-founded concerns about the potential dangers to our democratic and constitutional rights, posed by the invasion of our privacy and freedom. Justice Brandeis would be astonished today, if he knew that all democratic governments in the new millennium routinely perform constant surveillance on almost every one of the phone calls, emails, Internet searches, faxes, and telex communications of every citizen on the chance that they may now, or at some point in the future, become a legitimate target of the police or the national intelligence agencies. There has been little discussion or political concern expressed regarding this invasion of privacy because the vast majority of citizens have no idea that our communications are routinely intercepted by spy agencies. Brandeis also warned us to be most on guard against the growing threats to our freedom and privacy when government authorities attempt to justify their intrusive surveillance activities for seemingly beneficial reasons:

It is also immaterial that the intrusion was in aid of law enforcement. Experience should teach us to be most on our guard to protect liberty when the government's purposes are beneficent. Men born to freedom are naturally alert to repel invasion of their liberty by evil-minded rulers. The greatest dangers to liberty lurk in insidious encroachment by men of zeal, well-meaning but without understanding. [Supreme Court decision — *Olmstead et al. v. United States*, June 4, 1928][2]

The National Security Need for Intelligence

The importance of electronic espionage is acknowledged by all students of history. This fact was demonstrated by the famous Zimmermann Telegram that motivated the United States to join the other western allies in the defeat of Germany and Austria during the final years of World War I. The western allies such as England, Canada, France, Australia, and Germany were all exhausted physically, financially, and psychologically by almost four years of war. The United States strongly refused to become involved in yet another "European war." However, if the western allies were to prevail, it was essential that America join them to defeat Germany. A top-secret team of British naval code breakers was able to unlock the secret German cipher that kept all of their government and military communications secret.[3]

The German foreign minister sent a top-secret message to Herr Zimmermann, the German ambassador to the United States, which instructed him to negotiate with the Mexican government to invade the southern United States with German assistance and arms. In return for allying itself with Germany, Mexico would receive California, Texas, and New Mexico at the successful conclusion of the war. In addition, Germany promised it would unleash its dreaded U-boats against all American shipping in the Atlantic Ocean. The British naval code breakers had illegally wire-tapped the encrypted message from an American telegraph cable that ran from Germany through the United Kingdom and then on the Atlantic seabed to the United States. Rather than admit they had illegally tapped into an American telegraph cable, the British staged a fake burglary of a Mexican telegraph office and falsely claimed they obtained the secret German message there. Simultaneously leaking this information to the US newspapers, and sending it diplomatically to President Wilson, the British motivated the American government to declare war on Germany.

Unfortunately, by the 1930s, the lesson about the need to learn our enemy's secrets was almost forgotten. The US Secretary of State, Harry Stimson, who served under President Roosevelt, was offended by the idea of espionage and shut down the State Department's "Black Chamber" intelligence operations and pioneering military surveillance and code-breaking capabilities. Secretary Stimson naively declared, "Gentlemen do not read each other's mail." While such a quaint attitude might have been appropriate centuries earlier, the United States and all western democracies were now faced with ruthless dictators and totalitarian governments in many parts of the world. The growing threats to national security demonstrated the imperative need for the best national intelligence capabilities to survive against opposition from Hitler, Stalin, Mao, and other dictators attacking the foundations of free governments.

Following the end of World War II, the five English-speaking allies met in 1948, to establish UK–USA. Each of the five member nations would be responsible for acquiring all of the electronic communications coming from every nation within their appropriate sphere. England's GCHQ station at Menwith Hill is the largest overseas intelligence interception of the NSA and was originally established in 1956 by the US Army Security Agency to perform surveillance on targets throughout Europe, Africa, and Russia west of the Ural Mountains.

America's NSA covers Russia east of the Ural Mountains and most of North and South America. Australia's facility covers southeast Asia including India and Indonesia as well as the South Pacific islands. Another key western ally is Israel. Israel provides detailed intelligence of secret activities within the Middle East as well as Russia to its supportive western allies. Israel's secret surveillance facility is called Unit 8200 and is located in the northern suburbs of Tel Aviv, known as Herzliya. Unit 8200 accumulates and analyzes the intelligence collected from a large number of interception satellite receiver stations throughout Israel, including Mt. Hermon in the northern Golan Heights, Nahariyah on the border with Lebanon, Mitzpah Ramon in the southern Negev Desert, and a remote southern site called Dahlak Island in the Red Sea off the Horn of Africa.[4]

How Does Echelon Work?

The *Britannica World Language Funk and Wagnalls Standard Dictionary* defines "Echelon" as "one of the different fractions of a military command arranged from front to rear, to which a particular combat mission is assigned." Echelon utilizes the most advanced spy satellites, illegal wire-taps, and the fastest super computers in the world. Together they monitor all global electronic traffic. Targets include all local, cellular, and long distance phone calls, fax and telex transmissions, Internet communications including web surfing, news groups, chat rooms, emails, and all global radio traffic. The Echelon system design involves the careful positioning of communications stations throughout the world to collect all down-linked satellite, microwave, cellular and ground-based fiber-optic communications traffic. One of the primary targets is the interception of data from the series of twenty international telecommunications satellites (Intelsat) satellites that circle the globe above the equator, relaying most of the planet's daily email, fax, and telex communications.

The global Echelon system has three separate but essential functions: interception, analysis, and reporting. The interception function of Echelon includes a global communications monitoring system. The analysis function of Echelon is completed in "real time," at NSA headquarters, by a huge number of advanced super computers and thousands of human analysts. The reporting function involves a detailed system informing various intelligence agencies in the respective nations, and their political masters.

The Echelon intelligence system intercepts and then processes the acquired information utilizing NSA's computer analysis, including sophisticated voice recognition, artificial intelligence neural networks, and Optical Character Recognition (OCR) programs. The computer programs search for key words or special phrases listed in the Echelon Dictionary and alert the computers to flag the target message. It is then recorded and transcribed for future analysis. Any useful information collected by Echelon is forwarded to the intelligence agency that originally requested the intelligence intercept. Obviously, the vast majority of intercepts are messages that contain no requested key words or phone numbers. Therefore, these millions of useless messages are erased by the Echelon computers and are never listened to or analyzed by a human operator.

The NSA is the senior partner of Echelon. The United Kingdom plays the second most important role in monitoring worldwide communications based on the GCHQ, the largest British intelligence and espionage agency with 4,000 intelligence specialists at its headquarters in Cheltenham. In addition to controlling Menwith Hill's operations, utilizing more than a dozen powerful VAX computers, GCHQ runs additional interception stations including the RAF base at Morwenstow on the coast of Cornwall. Britain's GCHQ, with a budget of more than $1 billion and 15,000 staff, coordinates all electronic intelligence monitoring of Africa, Europe, and western Russia, while the American NSA monitors the rest of Russia and the nations of the former USSR.

The governments' justification for Echelon's universal surveillance program is that our society must be protected against the so-called "Four Horsemen of the Infocalypse": terrorists, drug dealers, sexual predators, and organized crime. However, this historically unprecedented monitoring of even our everyday private and business conversations is an attack on our fundamental human right to freedom and privacy — "the right to be left alone" as articulated by Supreme Court Justice Brandeis several decades ago. While initially used for valid purposes of espionage against enemy states, criminals, and terrorists, surveillance technologies could easily be used by authorities in the future as a tool of control against ordinary citizens. Simon Davies wrote, "History demonstrates that information in the hands of authority will inevitably be used for unintended and often malevolent purposes."[5]

A number of additional secret interception stations were built throughout the world during the last decade in order to monitor almost all messages transmitted on the international telecommunications network and the growing Internet. Echelon stations monitor microwave land-based communications networks, satellite communications, as well as radio communications. The Echelon system coordinates over fifty global interception stations capable of spying on virtually all global government, corporate, and personal electronic communications.

Unlike most other intelligence activities that seek to acquire specific communications or calls from a targeted individual or agency, the Echelon interception system does not target any particular individual's telephone, fax, Internet or email in its communications acquisition phase. Echelon uses a "giant vacuum cleaner" approach to intelligence acquisition activities in that the system attempts to acquire virtually all electronic communications. Then it uses sophisticated super computers with artificial intelligence neural networks to analyze the captured data. After acquiring billions of messages every hour, the system's powerful computers sift through the mass of communications using sophisticated artificial intelligence programs in search of important data connected with particular intelligence targets, projects, organizations, phone numbers, and codes.

Echelon processes the information utilizing the capabilities of the NSA, including optical-character-recognition software to automatically read documents, as well as highly accurate voice-recognition programs that can translate conversations from over seventy languages. At Echelon's Menwith Hill site in Britain, an extremely sophisticated voice recognition program called Voicecast, can actually target any voice pattern, so that every subsequent telephone call that person makes will be captured and then transcribed by the agency for future analysis. Voicecast utilizes advanced voice recognition and high-speed super computers programed to detect individual voice prints of targeted individuals. Menwith Hill's facility taps into every one of Britain's national and international electronic communications networks. The Echelon system works twenty-four hours a day, seven days a week.

An Abbreviated List of Sample Echelon Dictionary Key Words

An abbreviated list of key words used by the Dictionary Oratory program to search for possibly relevant material is given below as an example of the topics an intelligence agency may consider potentially interesting. This list of key words was provided as an example by several individuals in the intelligence community and reported on the Internet at: (Echelon code word list — Michael Owens Ed. Internet Office News: http://www.internetofficenews.com). The real list of key words would involve thousands of possibilities constantly updated by Dictionary Managers:

Explosives, guns, assassination, conspiracy, primers,

detonators, nuclear, ambush, motorcade, IRS, BATF, hostages, munitions, weapons, TNT, presidential motorcade, grenades, rockets, fuses, mortars, incendiary device, security forces, intelligence, infiltration, assault team, evasion, detection, mission, body armor, charges, timing devices, booby traps, silencers, Uzi, AK-47, napalm, Air Force One, special forces, Terrorism, National Information Infrastructure, Hackers, Encryption, Espionage, FBI, Secret Service, White House, Military Intelligence, Infowar, FINCEN, RCMP, GRU, SAS, Echelon, Dictionary, Spetznaz, Psyops, TELINT, enigma, Bletchley Park, Clandestine, NSO, argus, Security, sniper, Electronic Surveillance, Counter terrorism, interception, Gamma, Keyhole, SEAL Team 3, Merlin, white noise, top secret, Coderpunks, TRW, counterintelligence, industrial espionage, Minox, Keyhole, Rand Corporation, Wackenhutt, Scud, SecDef, SWAT, Fort Meade, NORAD, Delta Force, SEAL, virtual, Black-Ops, Area 51, TEMPEST, Pine Gap, Menwith, Sayeret Mat'Kal, Sayeret Golani, Delta, GRU, GSS, Crypto AG.

Recent reports indicate that Echelon's "Oratory" voice-recognition program for spoken communication now uses thousands of new key words, phone numbers, and individual voice prints of targeted individuals. Each of our voices is as unique as our fingerprint or iris scan. High-volume analysis by voice-recognition computers may be very difficult to perfect. However, when they do develop the necessary voice-recognition programs, it will be possible to apply the same universal analysis techniques that are now applied to written communications.

At the present time, within seconds of making a phone call anywhere in the world, a wanted terrorist or spy can be quickly identified and his exact location instantly targeted by his unique voice print. The terrorist's call can be quickly terminated, monitored, or re-directed to one of his enemies to create chaos in the subversive group. Within seconds the locations of the phone call can be precisely identified. Don't believe what you see in action movies, where the actor hangs up the phone in less than thirty seconds and thereby foils the ability of the FBI or NSA to accurately trace his call. In reality, only a few seconds are needed to allow the authorities to determine your phone number and location.[6]

The Need for Encryption Data Protection

One of the most useful and effective techniques to protect valuable corporate data from corporate espionage is to encode the information using encryption technology. Encryption refers to the transformation of electronic data or voice messages into a new form that cannot be read or interpreted by any intercepting party who lacks the proper de-encryption key. The basic technique of encryption is to change the information contained in a given message by applying a secret algorithm or mathematical formula to the letters of the message. This will produce a new encrypted message that appears to be pure gibberish to anyone who lacks the secret algorithm.

To simplify the concept, imagine that we wish to encrypt the word "nuclear." First, assume we convert the word "nuclear" to numbers, based on their position in the alphabet. In a simple alphabet-numerical conversion, the word "nuclear" would appear numerically as "14-21-3-12-5-1-18." In the simplest form of encryption, the word "nuclear" is encrypted by multiplying the numbers that represent the seven letters that compose the word. To simplify it even further, multiply the numbers representing "nuclear" by the number "3." In this case: each number representing the letters of the original word will be multiplied by "3." For example, "14" will be multiplied by "3" to yield "42" and "21" will yield "63." Finally, the numbers "14-21-3-12-5-1-18" that originally equaled "nuclear" are now encrypted to read "42-63-9-36-15-3-54." While this incredibly simplified example could easily be figured out by trial and error, it would be almost impossible to figure out the original word "nuclear" if the numerical equivalents were multiplied by a number with 256 digits.

The only way to detect the underlying message of such an encrypted word would be to calculate a staggering number of possible variations. Only the most advanced computers in the world have the high speed to calculate every one of the trillions of possibilities.

Encryption is now essential for businesses, governments, and individuals. Effective encryption of data would make it extremely difficult for private or government spies to intercept most communications. In 1998 the European Parliament analyzed the issue of electronic espionage and the growing risk of interception of global telecommunications in light of the need to protect the fundamental right to privacy. The EU report outlined the absolute need for the widespread use of encryption. Philip Zimmermann, a brilliant computer programmer, has developed an extremely effective data-encryption program known as Pretty Good Privacy (PGP) and has made it freely available on the Internet. He said,

> If privacy is outlawed, only outlaws will have privacy. Intelligence agencies have access to good cryptographic technology. So do the big arms and drug traffickers. So do defence contractors, oil companies, and other corporate giants. But ordinary people and local and alternative political organizations mostly have not had access to affordable ways of protect their privacy.... Privacy is a right like any other. You have to exercise it or risk losing it.[7]

Official Confirmation of the
Global Surveillance System — Echelon

In my 1995 book, *Final Warning*, in a chapter about the government's surveillance of our phone calls, faxes, and computers, I was forced to depend solely upon confidential information developed from interviews with my military and intelligence sources in North America, Europe, and Israel. At that time it was impossible to obtain official documentation confirming the existence of the global Echelon surveillance system. However, during the last few years official sources have confirmed that Echelon is real.[8]

However, Echelon is still so top-secret that both US and British government officials continue to publicly deny that it exists. Yet the British Broadcasting Corporation (BBC) news reported on December 19, 1999 that Australian officials have admitted that the powerful Echelon system does exist. Bill Blick, Australia's Inspector General of Intelligence and Security, confirmed to the BBC that their Defence Signals Directorate (DSD) is part of the Echelon network. "As you would expect there are a large amount of radio communications floating around in the atmosphere, and agencies such as DSD collect those communications in the interests of their national security." Furthermore, he admitted that these intercepted communications are shared with other allies such as Britain, Canada, and the United States.

In 1991, a retired British intelligence officer who had worked for GCHQ spoke anonymously in a documentary to the UK producers of Granada Television's *World in Action*. The officer revealed the existence of the worldwide Echelon surveillance program. He admitted that all of the data were passed through an analysis program called *Dictionary* that examined millions of messages for anything of interest to the spies. He also stated that a select group of British Telecom staff worked closely with the GCHQ intelligence staff to make sure that every message was carefully examined. This intelligence official declared, "At any time GCHQ is able to home in on their communications for a routine target request." He revealed that the phone-tap procedure in the United Kingdom is controlled by a computer program named *Mantis*, while the telex interception program is called *Mayfly*.[9]

A report was prepared in 1998 for the European Parliament of the European Union by its Director General of Research documenting in considerable detail the global threat to our privacy by the Echelon system. This report, entitled "Development of Surveillance Technology and Risk of Abuse of Economic Information," warns that Project Echelon "presents a truly global threat over which there are no legal or democratic controls." The EU report noted that Project Echelon is "part of the Cold War developments based on an agreement signed by the United Kingdom, United States, Canada, Australia, and New Zealand. . . . Echelon is designed for primarily non-military targets: governments, organizations and businesses in virtually every country."[10]

Nicky Hager, a journalist, conducted many interviews with

agents and technicians working with New Zealand's Signal Intelligence Agency. They described a vast network of Echelon communication interception stations throughout the world.[11] His sources revealed that "thousands of simultaneous messages are read in real time as they pour into each station, hour after hour, day after day, as the computers find intelligence needles in telecommunications hay stacks."[12]

An October 1998 report from the German intelligence agency, known as *Verfassungsschutz*, also confirmed the existence of the Echelon global intelligence system. This German agency warned other German government agencies and businessmen of the need to utilize powerful encryption in their private communications because of the ever-present danger that the British, American, Canadian, Australian, and New Zealand intelligence agencies are listening in on all of their communications. *Verfassungsschutz* warned German business that "without filtering, Echelon monitors all email, telephone, facsimile, and telex communication sent via satellite around the world."

Bo Elkjaer, a German reporter, published a report on the Internet on April 3, 2000, entitled "German Spies: Echelon Exists." This report includes his interview with a spokesman for German intelligence, Mr. Dietrich, in which Elkjaer asked if this official warning from *Verfassungsschutz* did or did not confirm that Echelon truly existed. He specifed, "This is the confirmation of Echelon's existence, isn't it?" The official spokesman, Mr. Dietrich, responded, "Yes."[13]

It is against the law for the US intelligence agencies, specifically the NSA and CIA, to spy on the communications and activities of American citizens on US soil. It is also illegal for the Canadian Secret Intelligence Service (CSIS) to spy on the communications of Canadian citizens, or for British intelligence to spy on UK citizens. In fact, when recently questioned about this, Kevin Mills, the official spokesman for the Communication Security Establishment (CSE) in Ottawa, Canada, denied that his agency spies on or gathers information on the activities of Canadians. Mills declared, "Any capability that CSE might have, is not targeted against

Canadians." However, this denial is simply not credible in light of the revelations about Echelon.

A former member of Canada's Communication Security Establishment, Mike Frost, who resigned in 1990, publicly told the *Canadian Press* that the five UK–USA countries simply agree to spy on each other's citizens and then send the captured material to the interested intelligence agency through highly encrypted computer transmission. Frost wrote *Spyworld* to detail his spying activities and stated, "They circumvent their own legislation by asking the other countries to do it for them. We do it for them, they do it for us and then they can stand up in the House [of Commons] and say we do not target the communications of Canadian citizens." Frost also explained how the intelligence agencies' "embassy collection" operations used their nation's embassy buildings in various foreign capitals to act as interception stations for the Echelon system.

Embassy buildings are ideal intelligence collection sites because they are usually located near the target government's major ministries in their capital, normally at the center of the nation's microwave communication networks. After secretly transporting the sophisticated satellite computer receivers and processors inside their staff's diplomatic bags into their own embassy, Frost claimed that the NSA spies would set up their radio and microwave reception dishes on the roofs of the embassy, often disguised as air conditioning and heating pipes.[14]

When the director of the Australian intelligence agency, the DSD, was asked about Echelon during an interview on Australian television, he admitted to the mutual swapping of communications intelligence against their own citizens. He declared, "DSD does cooperate with counterpart-signals intelligence organizations overseas under what is known as the UK–USA relationship."[15]

Duncan Campbell reported in the British newspaper, the *New Statesman*, that a US newspaper, the *Cleveland Plain Dealer*, had reported that an intelligence employee confirmed that Echelon at Menwith Hill was used to target the phone calls of US Senator, Strom Thurmond. Although Senator Thurmond reportedly looked into it and professed that he was convinced it wasn't true, the published evidence is overwhelming that this powerful global espionage capability does exist.[16] Recently, evidence was released that NSA developed a new global computer network, called *Platform*, that uses the most sophisticated computers in the world to instantaneously coordinate over fifty Echelon interception systems throughout the world.

Warnings About Echelon

A number of "highly placed intelligence operatives" working with the British GCHQ spoke with reporters from the London *Observer*. "We can no longer remain silent regarding that which we regard to be gross malpractice and negligence within the establishment in which we operate." They confirmed that British intelligence used Echelon illegally to monitor the activities of several charities, including Amnesty International and Christian Aid.

When asked to comment about Project Echelon, Representative George Barr, the Republican Congressman from Georgia who serves on the House Judiciary and Government Reform committee, expressed deep concern that the intelligence system is now recording the communications of all Americans. Representative Barr stated, "I am concerned there are not sufficient legal mechanisms in place to protect private information from unauthorized government eavesdropping through mechanisms such as Project Echelon." (*Toronto Star*, June 19, 1999)

When Barr spoke last year in Congress, and publicly called for Congressional hearings, it was the first time in history that the threat Echelon posed to the freedom and privacy of Americans was raised in the US Congress. Congressman Barr stated,

> As a former intelligence officer, I support legitimate intelligence activities. However, I also believe Congress has a duty to make absolutely certain the massive capabilities our intelligence agencies have developed, are allowed to be used only with adequate safeguards against abuse. The massive technological changes that have occurred since the last significant update of our foreign intelligence surveillance laws, mean our existing legal structure is not

adequately protecting the privacy rights of Americans. My concerns in this area are heightened by the reluctance of intelligence agencies to fully cooperate with congressional oversight. This acknowledgment underscores the need for open public hearings on the legal standards intelligence agencies use when they intercept the communications of American citizens. If these reports are accurate, the sheer power and potential for abuse created by Project Echelon demands congressional attention.[17]

In a telephone interview, the well-informed Representative Barr, who served previously as an official with the Central Intelligence Agency, stated,

> By all appearances, what we have is a massive government program that scoops up unbelievably huge numbers of private communications, indiscriminately, without any oversight or court involvement. . . . There's a very important, but fine, line between legitimate foreign intelligence gathering and unconstitutional eavesdropping on American citizens, and it appears that line has been crossed.

During recent hearings about the dangers of electronic surveillance, Congressman Barr warned about the growing dangers:

> Under current law, electronic communications receive less legal protection than traditional mail, or even telephone conversations. Furthermore, the rules for electronic surveillance and foreign intelligence gathering that do exist are so vague and inconsistent that they simultaneously threaten privacy and impede law enforcement. . . . Federal agencies, from the Securities and Exchange Commission to the Department of Justice, have recently shown a disturbing tendency to apply a vacuum cleaner surveillance approach to the Internet, sucking in all kinds of irrelevant data, then isolating, storing and manipulating items of interest. . . . This approach rejects time-honored principles that have

done a remarkably good job of balancing privacy and law enforcement. These principles include the Fourth Amendment's particularity requirement and statutory provisions, such as the Privacy Act.[18]

Barry Steinhardt, the associate director of the American Civil Liberties Union, wrote about the official admission of the Echelon Project by Representative Barr:

> It wasn't until this year that a member of Congress (Representative Barr) had ever actually uttered the word 'Echelon' on the floor of the House. . . . There is this science-fiction quality to this that is hard for people to accept. But it appears to be quite real. People are just beginning to get over the hump of disbelief. . . . The troubling aspect is that Echelon is this huge system that operates without any oversight or scrutiny from anybody.[19]

In April 1999, the American Civil Liberties Union wrote to the members of Congress about the dangers of Echelon. When the official spokeswoman of the NSA was asked about the existence of Echelon, she replied, "We don't confirm or deny the existence of Echelon."[20] A careful study of history reveals a depressing record of intelligence, defense, and law enforcement agencies expanding and evading the legal constraints enacted by Congress or Parliament to protect our civil liberties. Following the end of the Cold War, military defense groups and powerful intelligence agencies throughout the world have sought new missions and projects to justify the need for expanding budgets to transfer military technologies to civilian applications.

Professor Christopher Simpson of the American University has studied Project Echelon for many years. Dr. Simpson, who has written four books on national security issues, stated,

> We're talking about tens of millions of volumes if it was printed out on pages. . . . Certainly every time an international telephone call is made. . . . As we move into this interconnected electronic world, you've got Big Brothers, and you've got Little Brothers. Little Brothers

are companies like supermarkets and Internet companies that keep an eye on you. And you've got Big Brother that keeps an eye on you. The Biggest Brother of all is the Echelon system.[21]

Professor Simpson confirmed that Echelon could recognize individual voices during phone calls and could easily track who is calling whom. The Free Congress Foundation is a conservative think-tank in Washington, D.C. In 1998, the Free Congress Foundation researched and published a detailed report that openly denounced Project Echelon's "shameless and illegal targeting of political opponents, business competitors, dissidents and even Christian ministries."

The Federation of American Scientists provides public policy surveillance on the defense and intelligence activities of the American government. Their senior research analyst on government surveillance, Steven Aftergood, has stated, "The intelligence agencies have been given extraordinary powers to conduct surveillance, and we need to make sure that those powers are being exercised responsibly and in conformity with the law."[22]

The US National Security Council proposed in July 1998 that American intelligence should constantly monitor the computer networks of banks, telecommunications corporations, transportation companies, and non-military government operations in an attempt to protect America's important communication data networks. Only one month later, Attorney General Janet Reno's Justice Department proposed legislation to allow her department and the FBI the legal authority to place hidden encryption-breaking devices and secret surveillance software programs in American citizens' computers, in their homes, and in their offices during criminal investigations. At the same time the FBI is publicly supporting a proposal for new technical standards in the design of the Internet infrastructure to enable their agents to set up court-authorized wire-taps on personal computers without anyone becoming aware of it.[23]

Some of the media are in outright denial that our communications are constantly being intercepted by the intelligence agencies of the West. However, major, respected news sources are finally investigating the Echelon surveillance system, confirming both its existence and its pervasive intrusion. Recently respected news outlets including *The Times* of London, the *New York Times, La Monde* and the BBC have focused on the mounting European public and governmental outrage at the abuses of Echelon. The *Sunday Times* (London) ran an article on May 31, 1999, by reporter Nicholas Rufford, that quoted a number of high intelligence staff within the French, German, and Italian intelligence agencies, expressing outrage at the wholesale intelligence gathering of all communications within allied Western nations.

In 1985, the United Kingdom passed the Interception of Communications Act permitting Echelon and Project P415 to legally intercept all international communications to and from Britain. Section 3(2) of the Act allows government ministers to issue warrants to intercept international messages "in the interests of national security" or for the broader purpose of "safeguarding the economic well-being of the United Kingdom."

The major concern of continental Europeans is the ongoing development of an enormous intelligence-gathering communications station that the NSA is now expanding at the existing 560 acres English base known as Menwith Hill, Field Station F83. It has its own independent electrical power station to ensure uninterrupted operations. Menwith Hill is probably the largest espionage station on the planet. Approximately two-thirds of its staff are American intelligence agents. Located near Harrogate, on the North Yorkshire moors, thirty huge satellite reception radomes, code-named *Moonpenny*, looking like giant golfballs, sit somewhat conspicuously among the flocks of English sheep within the security fences of the well-guarded base. Security is very tight. A high perimeter fence and armed guards in watchtowers surround the facility, and the grounds are patrolled by vicious guard dogs. Anyone who approaches the base perimeter is immediately confronted with military security.[24]

The English newspaper, the *New Statesman*, reported in August 7, 1980 that the Menwith Hill facility was now tapping into all of

England's national and international communications networks. European papers have now revealed that Menwith Hill is the most extensive communications intelligence collection station on the planet. It has dozens of highly sophisticated VAX computers. The base has almost five acres of buildings and more than twenty-two satellite terminals for downloading millions of simultaneous messages. Menwith Hill's station utilizes a multitude of secret interception systems to collect intelligence data from the communications of many nations and corporations, including the Vortex, Magnum, and Orion spy satellite systems. It monitors all of the communications of the European states, Russia, and the rest of Asia. Echelon collects virtually all European electronic communications from governments, corporations, and private individuals, and intercepts all trans-Atlantic communications to and from North America. Menwith Hill is under the actual control of the American NSA, in cooperation with British intelligence who share the intelligence spoils.

This remarkable spy station was purposely built on property that carries the three main digital fiber-optic cables from Europe through England to America — each of which is simultaneously transmitting up to 100,000 calls. These highly important communications cables conveniently go directly through the Menwith Hill facility building to enable their computers to download every single communication without delaying any of the calls. Echelon uses a vast array of intelligence collection platforms to accomplish its complex task. In addition to satellites circling the globe, high altitude aircraft, navel vessels, a fleet of mobile surveillance vans, and tapping of undersea fiber-optic cables, Echelon utilizes secret interception technologies that penetrate mobile or desktop computers as well as all phone and radio communications.

During a September 1998 trial, British Telecom, the phone company responsible for the trans-Atlantic cables, inadvertently admitted to spying on messages of European and United Kingdom businesses and citizens. British Telecom mistakenly released previously top-secret documents to the opposing attorneys who confirmed that reports in the media regarding the wholesale spying were accurate. Although defenders of the system declare that the sole purpose of the Menwith Hill facility is to monitor international calls, a former employee has told reporters that there is gross corruption in the agency, and the monitoring of private calls, corporate calls, and domestic calls is occurring.[25]

France and Russia have established huge systems of spy satellites encircling the globe to gather electronic communications from North America and other nations. France has set up listening posts in France, Corsica, French Guyana, New Caledonia, and the United Arab Emirates. France has been very aggressive in using its espionage capabilities to gather industrial information. Recently Canadian intelligence advised Canadian businessmen flying on Air France planes to refrain from discussing business secrets because French intelligence had implanted sophisticated microphones in the head rests of the seats in business class.[26]

In many super-competitive nations the government's intelligence and secret police agencies work hand-in-glove with the country's businesses to acquire and then share the resulting intelligence information. When high-level business people are identified on a flight list, the intelligence agencies may initiate action. Such a target can be assigned a room in a luxury hotel that the intelligence agencies have equipped with photographic, audio, and electronic surveillance capabilities. Telephone cables are tampered with to allow the capture of any electronic computer communications by Internet or email. When a businessman leaves his room, staff quickly download information from the hard-drive of his laptop computer. Even if it is encrypted, the chances are extremely high that such encryption systems can be broken by a national intelligence service. Even when a careful business person takes the trouble to shred valuable corporate documents, they may unknowingly be handing them over to the competition. It has been suggested that some innovative and clever spies have altered industrial-type shredders to include a microscopic camera lens that photographs the document seconds before it is cut into thousands of tiny pieces.

A working paper of the Scientific and Technological Options Assessment Programme (STOA) of the European Parliament examined the intrusive espionage technology utilized by various governments. According to this report, the Echelon system involves advanced artificial intelligence computer programs including the Memex program. The accumulated electronic data collected from intelligence targets in Europe are then transferred from the United Kingdom by satellite to the American National Security Agency headquarters at Fort Meade, Maryland. Much of the intelligence concerns potential terrorist threats but economic intelligence, including the intense monitoring of the participants in the GATT trade negotiations, forms a significant part of the surveillance efforts.

The European Union's Scientific and Technological Options Assessment Programme (STOA) report states that,

> . . . espionage is espionage. No proper Authority in the USA would allow a similar EU spy network to operate from American soil without strict limitations, if at all. Following full discussion on the implications of the operations of these networks, the European Parliament is advised to set up appropriate independent audit and oversight procedures and that any effort to outlaw encryption by EU citizens should be denied until and unless such democratic and accountable systems are in place, if at all.

The researchers of the European Union concluded in their report that: "Within Europe, all email, telephone and fax communications are routinely intercepted by the NSA, transferring all target information to Fort Meade in Maryland, via the crucial hub of Menwith Hill in the North Yorkshire moors of the United Kingdom." ("Spy Station F83," London's *Sunday Times*, May 31, 1998).

Despite their obvious concerns about Echelon, the European Union has recently entered into an intelligence agreement with the US Federal Bureau of Investigations to cooperate in establishing a global surveillance system to intercept all electronic communications in order to respond to the threat of "serious crime" and concerns about "national security." The Council of the European Union and the FBI have now agreed on a plan for a global telecommunications wire-tapping system: "The legally authorized interception of telecommunications is an important tool for the protection of national interest, in particular national security and the investigation of serious crime."[27]

The FBI, representing the United States, as well as Canada, Australia, New Zealand, and fifteen additional European nations, have now agreed to set up a global surveillance system targeting all communications, especially on the Internet. The expert committees of the International Law Enforcement Telecommunications Seminar (ILETS), which represent these nations, drew up the necessary technical requirements to allow them to intercept all traffic on the Internet. This was documented in the *Enfopol 98* document that was reported on the Internet by *Telepolis*, the European *Online Magazine* in 1999. The plans include establishing secret Internet interception systems that would create a "virtual interface" through the installation of special software collection programs at Internet access points. These secret espionage posts would be operated remotely by the member government's intelligence and police agencies.

Echelon — Project P415
Upgrading Echelon's Global Surveillance
for the New Millennium

The massive Echelon intelligence system is about to undergo a huge upgrade of its already astonishing intelligence capabilities using the latest high technology inventions. These improvements will enable the upgraded system to monitor the entire human population 24 hours a day. The enormously powerful global intelligence gathering system is called Project P415. Menwith Hill, UK, and the National Security Agency headquarters in Fort Meade, Maryland, are the key centers of the newly enlarged global surveillance program. Billions of dollars of new funding are upgrading Echelon's computer analysis systems, personnel, and satellites. Intelligence oversight committees of the US Congress have received confirmation that Echelon's newly enhanced surveillance system will enable western intelligence agencies to monitor virtually all radio, phone, and military communications throughout the globe.

If a Russian tank radio operator in Chechneya makes a radio call to his commander at headquarters, his voice will be instantly recorded on US computers. America has advanced battlefield radio transmission capability that also enables our military intelligence agencies to create a radio message in a future conflict containing the voice of the tank radio operator modified by computer technology to send an erroneous and confusing message to other tanks during an attack.

Since the Cold War, the UK–USA intelligence agreement has now been expanded to include Communist China, Germany, and other nations. New listening posts were set up in the city of Bad Aibling in Germany. Two very secretive joint US–China communications monitoring sites were built at Qitai and Korla, quite close to the Russian Siberian border in the western Xinjiang Uighur Autonomous Region of the People's Republic of China. These top-secret stations are supposedly focused solely on missile and satellite intercepts from Russia and are staffed by a joint team of Chinese People's Liberation Army signals intelligence officers, as well as NSA, and CIA staff.

According to a statement by Bob Tizard, the Defence Minister of New Zealand, additional spy satellite interception facilities have also been established in northern Australia at Geraldton, as well as Shoal Bay, and in New Zealand at Blenheim. Meanwhile, at the Canadian intercept station at a former Canadian armed forces base at Leitrim, just south of Ottawa, Canada purportedly listens in to South American electronic communications. Japan contributes to the effort to monitor Asian and Russian intelligence through their intercept station at Misawa in northern Japan.[28]

Twenty-five years ago, during the famous Church Senate hearings on the misuse of the intelligence resources of America by the Nixon Watergate team, Senator Frank Church wisely warned about the possible danger to American freedom and privacy if our intelligence resources and surveillance capabilities were ever unleashed against our own citizens. Church warned about the growing technology of surveillance by the National Security Agency. Senator Church stated,

> That capability at any time could be turned around on the American people and no American would have any privacy left. There would be no place to hide. If this government ever became a tyranny, the technological capacity that the intelligence community has given the government could enable it to impose total tyranny. There would be no way to fight back, because the most careful effort to combine together in resistance to the government, no matter how privately it was done, is within the reach of the government to know. Such is the capacity of this technology.[29]

The truth is that the danger to representative democracy and individual freedom is far greater today than it was when Senator Church first raised his warning in 1975. Unless the intelligence agencies that operate Echelon and related surveillance systems are placed under the direct control of the US Congress and Senate, our fundamental freedoms might easily be eliminated forever in the interests of the campaign to defeat terrorism, organized crime, drug lords, and foreign enemies.

Echelon was designed and built during the dangerous Cold War period. We are now entering a time when the number of potential enemies who could attack our Western nations grows each year. As the cost to produce biological, chemical, and even, nuclear weapons is dropping radically, the number of terrorist and ethnic groups willing to use these weapons against America and the West is growing dramatically. While I hate the thought of government intelligence agencies monitoring our private and corporate communications, I am forced to admit that our governments would be remiss in their responsibilities to defend our nations if they failed to utilize the sophisticated communications intelligence capabilities they have developed. We all now live in a very dangerous neighborhood. Therefore, it is essential that our intelligence agencies use the best equipment available to detect enemy attacks.

History reveals that almost every technological advance was

initially abused by the political and police authorities that rule nation states. The first use of technology by authority tends to be in the area of communications control, security, policing, and the military. However, history also reveals that almost every new technology is eventually used by citizens to assist in accomplishing their desires for free communication, privacy, and political freedom.

The introduction of the printing press in Europe was immediately monopolized under exclusive license by the authorities of that day. However, free men then used the printing press to print democratic pamphlets and Bibles. This facilitated the Protestant Reformation, the Enlightenment, and the greatest advance in political and religious freedom in history. The computer and the Internet are the latest new technologies that present danger to our political and religious freedoms. However, this new computer technology is a double-edged sword. It will allow determined men to develop sophisticated encryption techniques that will make it very difficult for authoritative governments to keep all communications under total surveillance.

The lesson of history, as illustrated by England's Lord Acton nearly a century ago, was that "power corrupts; absolute power corrupts absolutely." A balanced appraisal of the growth of political, military, and social control throughout history reveals that no one has ever held such potential political and police power as the Echelon system provides to the intelligence and security agencies of the West. In light of the overwhelming evidence that the western powers, as well as Russia and China, utilize these powerful surveillance technologies to examine every communication of private citizens, corporations, and governments, we can conclude that our liberty now stands in the greatest jeopardy of all time.

Echelon has known all about you for many years. Now you know something about Echelon. The only hope to make certain that this technology remains a servant of democratic government, and not its master, is to ensure that there is a system of democratic oversight to "watch the watchers." It is my hope that the growing revelations from media around the world about the capabilities and dangers associated with Echelon will encourage our governments to demand democratic accountability of these necessary but inherently dangerous technologies.

In the past, students of the Bible's prophecies wondered about how the prophet John's prediction about the Antichrist's global monitoring of citizens could ever be fulfilled literally. Until the last decade it was simply impossible for any government, even Nazi Germany, or Communist Russia and China, to provide continuous monitoring of every single citizen no matter how many informers or secret police were employed. However, the development of the Echelon surveillance system and the parallel systems utilized by Russia, China, and the European Union suggest how it will be possible for a future world dictator to exercise total surveillance control over the world's population. The only hope for freedom will be found in the certain promise of the Word of God that Christ will return and liberate humanity from this satanic oppression.

Notes

1. Bruce Schneier and David Banisar, *The Electronic Privacy Papers* (New York: Wiley Computer Publishing, 1997).

2. Bruce Schneier and David Banisar, *The Electronic Privacy Papers* (New York: Wiley Computer Publishing, 1997).

3. Barbara W. Tuchman, *Zimmermann Telegram* (New York: Ballantine Books, March 1985).

4. Wayne Madsen, "State Department Misses Boat on Telecom Snooping," *Network Security*, March 1998.

5. Javier Bernal, *Public and Private Security in the Internet.* 6 August 1999, http://www.socio.demon.co.uk/magazine/6/enfopol_echelon.html

6. *New Statesman*, 7 Aug. 1980.

7. Javier Bernal, *Public and Private Security in the Internet,* 6 August 1999, http://www.socio.demon.co.uk/magazine/6/enfopol_echelon.html)

8. Grant R. Jeffrey, *Final Warning* (Toronto: Frontier Research Publications, Inc., 1995).

9. Nicky Hager, "Exposing the Global Surveillance System," *Covert Action Quarterly*, No. 59.

10. *An Appraisal of the Technologies of Political Control*, STOA Inteim Study, Updated Executive Summary, Updated — September 1998, Luxembourg, 6 Jan. 1998, PE 166 499, Directorate General for Research — European Union.

11. Nicky Hager, "Exposing the Global Surveillance System," Covert Action Quarterly, No. 59.

12. Javier Bernal, *Public and Private Security in the Internet,* 6 August 1999, http://www.socio.demon.co.uk/magazine/6/enfopol_echelon.html

13. Internet web site: http://www1.ekstrabladet.dk/VisArtikel.iasp?PageID=44662 (DK)

14. Mike Frost, *Spyworld*, DIANE Publishing Co., October 1994.

15. Joseph Farah, "Echelon: See, I Told You So," WorldNetDaily, November 4 1999.

16. Duncan Campbell, *New Statesman*, 28 April 1988.

17. Joseph Farah, "Echelon: See, I Told You So," *World Net Daily*, 4 Nov. 1999.

18. Charles Smith, *The Information Vacuum Cleaner*, 2000 WorldNetDaily.com, 9 April 2000.

19. Joseph Farah, "Echelon: See, I Told You So," *World Net Daily*, 4 Nov. 1999.

13. Charles Smith, "The Information Vacuum Cleaner," internet site 2000 WorldNetDaily.com 9 Apr. 2000.

14. Kathryn Balint, "Spy in the Sky," Union-Tribune Publishing Co., 17 Oct. 1999.

15. Kathryn Balint, "Spy in the Sky," Union-Tribune Publishing Co., 17 Oct. 1999.

16. Kathryn Balint, "Spy in the Sky," Union-Tribune Publishing Co., 17 Oct. 1999.

17. *New Statesman*, 7 Aug. 1980.

18. Scientific and Technological Options Assessment Programme of the European Parliament.

19. Kathryn Balint, "Spy in the Sky," Union-Tribune Publishing Co., 17 Oct. 1999.

20. Kathryn Balint, "Spy in the Sky," Union-Tribune Publishing Co., 17 Oct. 1999.

21. Kathryn Balint, "Spy in the Sky," Union-Tribune Publishing Co., 17 Oct. 1999.

22. Kathryn Balint, "Spy in the Sky," Union-Tribune Publishing Co., 17 Oct. 1999.

23. Kathryn Balint, "Spy in the Sky," Union-Tribune Publishing Co., 17 Oct. 1999.

24. Patrick S. Poole, "Echelon: America's Secret Global Surveillance Network," Internet site: www.FreeRepublic.com.

25. Patrick S. Poole, "Echelon: America's Secret Global Surveillance Network," Internet site: www.FreeRepublic.com.

26. John J. Fialka, *War By Other Means* (New York: W. W. Norton & Company, 1997), p. 93.

27. Interception of Communications, report to COREPER, ENFOPOL 40, 10090/93, Confidential, Brussels, 16.11.93.; Council General Secretariat to COREPER/COUNCIL, ENFOPOL 166, 12798/95, Limit, 14.12.95.

28. Duncan Campbell, *New Statesman*, 12 August 1988.
29. Frank Church, US Senate hearings, 1975.

9

The World's First Super State — the Revived Roman Empire

Two thousand years ago the Roman Empire was the dominant empire on earth. Rome stood in total military and political control of the destiny of over one hundred million subjects in an empire that stretched from the western coasts of Britain and Spain to the eastern borders of the empire in the deserts of Arabia. When the Roman Empire finally disintegrated due to failures of leadership, political will, and military power against the relentless waves of barbarian invasion, an enormous and military vacuum was created in Europe. The destruction of Rome set the stage for the Dark Ages that lasted for almost one thousand years of intellectual, religious, economic, and military chaos.

Prophecies about the Ancient Roman Empire

The ancient prophecies of the Old Testament clearly predicted over five hundred years before it came to pass that the Roman Empire, the fourth world empire described in the prophecy of Daniel, would ultimately become the greatest empire the world had ever seen. "And the fourth kingdom shall be strong as iron: forasmuch as iron breaketh in pieces and subdueth all things: and as iron that breaketh all these, shall it break in pieces and bruise" (Daniel 2:40). According to Daniel's prediction, Rome was destined to conquer all of the ancient nations that stood in its path. However, at the time when Daniel wrote his divinely inspired prophecy (approximately 580 BC) Rome was a small city state of little consequence, even in the Italian peninsula. Without divine inspiration, it would have been impossible to predict that the small city state of Rome would rise from obscurity to rule the world.

The Roman Empire began as an insignificant city state but quickly rose to master all of Italy during the third century before the birth of Jesus Christ. Centuries of continuing military and economic warfare followed between Rome and the city state of Carthage in North Africa. The Roman legions finally conquered the armies of Carthage and the powerful Greek city states during the second century before Christ's birth. The disciplined military legions of Rome under the leadership of the Caesars ultimately conquered almost the entire known world by the 1st century of the Christian era.

In 66–63 BC the powerful legions of the Roman general Pompey conquered both Syria and Judea, including the Holy City Jerusalem. During General Pompey's siege of Jerusalem, the Roman legions slaughtered 12,000 Israeli soldiers in the final assault on the city and the fortified Temple Mount. The Jewish historical records indicate that the blood of the Jewish defenders of the Temple ran as high as their ankles in the Court of the Israelites as the Jews desperately fought to the last man against Pompey's Roman troops as they entered the sacred Holy Place. In 63 BC, Rome became the ruler of Israel.

Caesar Augustus ruled as emperor of Rome during the life

of Jesus Christ. During that period the Roman legions expanded the empire to include the territories of the present nations: Egypt, Romania, Bulgaria, Hungary, Bosnia, Herzogovina, Croatia, and Serbia. The eagles of the Roman ensigns soon dominated the nations of northern Europe, including the newly acquired territories of England, Switzerland, Germany, northern France, and Belgium. No other empire in history ever ruled so vast a geographical territory for such a long period of time as the fourth "iron" kingdom of Rome, which extended from 63 BC to AD 1453 when the Byzantine Easter Roman Empire was finally conquered by Islamic armies.

Most other conquering empires absorbed the culture, tradition, and technologies of the peoples they had just conquered. However, the Roman Empire was distinct from all other empires in that its unremitting policy required that its governors crush the laws, religion, language, and society of every conquered nation. Rome's policy required that they destroy the existing culture and replace it with Roman laws and culture. More than fifteen centuries have passed since the last days of Rome's undivided power, yet the impact of Rome on subsequent societies and their history is unprecedented. Remarkably, after thousands of years, Europe, the Middle East, and even North America have retained forms of government, language, culture, and laws that are clearly derived from those of ancient Rome.

Jewish Expectations about the Roman Antichrist

Philo was a famous 1st century Jewish writer who wrote about the future Antichrist who will arise to oppress Israel in the final generation before the return of the Messiah. In his book *De Praemiis et Poenis*, Philo declared, "For a man will come forth, says the prophecy (Septuagint Translation of Numbers 24:7), who will go out and conduct a great war, and will overcome a great and powerful nation, as God Himself will assist His saints."[1] In the *Book of Zerubbabel*, an apocalyptical (non-biblical) book written by an unknown Jewish author, there is a reference to the Antichrist by the name "Armillus." This name was related to the name "Romulus" suggesting his connection with Rome. A number of early *Targums*,

Jewish paraphrases, and commentaries on the various books of the Old Testament, also identified Daniel's "Prince that shall come" (Daniel 9:26) as a future leader of the Roman Empire. Daniel had prophesied, "the people of *the prince that shall come* shall destroy the city and the sanctuary; and the end thereof shall be with a flood, and unto the end of the war desolations are determined" (Daniel 9:26). Since the "people" who destroyed Jerusalem and their temple sanctuary were the Romans, many of the ancient Jewish sages taught that Israel's last great enemy will arise in the last days from the Roman Empire.

One of the greatest tragedies in Israel's history occurred when Emperor Hadrian killed over a million and a half Jewish soldiers and civilians when he defeated the armies of the Jewish general Simeon Bar Kochba. On this ninth day of the Hebrew month of Av (August), 135 AD, General Simeon Bar Kochba lost his three-year war of independence against Rome. Several Israeli rabbis have spoken to me of the "spirit of Hadrian" returning in the last days to battle Israel until he will be defeated by the coming Messiah.

Jewish sages have debated for many centuries about the time when the Messiah will finally appear. Some sages wrote that every Jew in Israel needed to repent at one moment to motivate God to send their long-prophesied Redeemer.

> All the predestined dates have passed and the matter (of Messiah's coming) depends only on repentance and good deeds. . . . Rabbi Joshua said: If they do not repent, will they not be redeemed? But the Holy One blessed be He, will set up a king over them, whose decrees shall be as cruel as Haman's whereby Israel shall engage in repentance, and he will then bring them back to the right path."[2]

This remarkable Jewish prophetic interpretation of a coming evil king suggests that God will use him to finally bring Israel to repentance when "He will set up a king over them." This rabbinic interpretation parallels the Christian one regarding Daniel's prophecy that God will allow the Antichrist to rule over Israel to bring them to repentance. The rabbis thought this "king" would be "as cruel as Haman," their ancient Persian enemy who tried to destroy all of the Jews throughout the Persian Empire (approximately 460 BC).

The Revival of Rome in the Last Days

The prophet Daniel recorded his fascinating vision about the revival of this fourth world empire, Rome, in the final days preceding the coming the Messiah. Daniel wrote:

> After this I saw in the night visions, and behold a fourth beast, dreadful and terrible, and strong exceedingly; and it had great iron teeth: it devoured and brake in pieces, and stamped the residue with the feet of it: and it was diverse from all the beasts that were before it; and it had ten horns. I considered the horns, and, behold, there came up among them another little horn, before whom there were three of the first horns plucked up by the roots: and, behold, in this horn were eyes like the eyes of man, and a mouth speaking great things. (Daniel 7:7–8)

Daniel's ancient prophecy remarkably predicted that the ancient Roman Empire would arise again in the last generation of this age. Once more Rome will take its place on the stage of world history as the dominant world power during the closing events leading to the return of Jesus Christ as the promised Messiah. Daniel also predicted that the final restoration of the fourth empire, Rome, would be in an unprecedented form of a super state confederacy composed of ten nations that would be led by a powerful dictator. The leader, the "little horn," will defeat three nations in a crisis and seize power over the ten nations.

From the time of the disintegration of the western Roman Empire in approximately AD 410, until the closing days of World War II, the peoples of Europe, the Middle East, and northern Africa have experienced ceaseless struggles. Warfare continued between the growing nation states of Europe that grew out of the ancient provinces of the Roman Empire. Throughout the centuries the dream of recreating the Roman Empire has motivated many political, religious, and military leaders. The first attempt began with the failed plan of Charles the Great, known as Charlemagne, in AD 800, to recreate the empire as the Holy Roman Empire. This debacle was followed by numerous attempts over a period of many centuries by various Roman pontiffs to fill the political and military vacuum by creating a new empire under the tutelege of the Roman church to unite the warring factions of Europe.

Despite powerful efforts by England's King Henry II to create a true European empire uniting the territories of England and France in the late 1100s, that effort was abandoned after his death. Almost six centuries later, during the revolutionary chaos throughout Europe that followed the French Revolution, Emperor Napoleon seized power in AD 1800 to pursue his brilliant military plan to recreate an empire. Despite his numerous military victories, the opposing continental European powers joined with the growing military forces of England to create a powerful alliance that finally defeated Napoleon's dreams of conquest. Following his disastrous attempt to defeat Russia in the midst of a bitter winter, the French Grand Army of 450,000 soldiers was destroyed and finally reduced to only a few thousand surviving troops. Over a century later, the Italian dictator Mussolini tried and failed to recreate the Roman Empire in the 1930s through the development of his own fascist forces and his disastrous alliance with the German Fuerher, Adolph Hitler.

At the same time, Adolph Hitler created a powerful political, economic, and military colossus that threatened the whole world between 1939 and 1945 in his mad attempt to create his "Thousand Years" Third Reich as a revival of the ancient glories of the Roman Empire. The prophecy about the revival of the fourth world empire symbolized by the mysterious metallic image was recorded in Daniel 2. The metal image of a man had "feet and toes, part of potter's clay, and part of iron, the kingdom shall be divided; but there shall be in it of the strength of the iron, forasmuch as thou sawest the iron mixed with miry clay" (Daniel 2:41).

In Daniel 7:7 the prophet described a parallel vision of a fourth terrible beast that "had ten horns" representing the ten confederate nations that would arise in the last days within the geographic territory of the ancient Roman Empire. These two prophetic visions suggest that the fourth gentile world empire of Rome will finally revive in the last days in the form of ten allied nations within its ancient historic boundaries. This description of the "ten toes" and the "ten horns" of the revived Roman Empire may describe the future course of the European Union that may be the embryonic power base of the coming Antichrist's world-government that is prophesied to arise at the close of "the times of the Gentiles," and just prior to the Second Coming of Christ.

> Thou sawest till that a stone was cut out without hands, which smote the image upon his feet that were of iron and clay, and brake them to pieces. Then was the iron, the clay, the brass, the silver, and the gold, broken to pieces together, and became like the chaff of the summer threshing floors; and the wind carried them away, that no place was found for them: and the stone that smote the image became a great mountain, and filled the whole earth. . . . And in the days of these kings shall the God of heaven set up a kingdom, which shall never be destroyed: and the kingdom shall not be left to other people, but it shall break in pieces and consume all these kingdoms, and it shall stand for ever. Forasmuch as thou sawest that the stone was cut out of the mountain without hands, and that it brake in pieces the iron, the brass, the clay, the silver, and the gold; the great God hath made known to the king what shall come to pass hereafter: and the dream is certain, and the interpretation thereof sure. (Daniel 2:34–35, 44–45)

Antichrist and the Revival of Rome

The prophet Daniel rose from the lowly position as a conquered Jewish slave in exile to become the respected prime minister of Babylon, the greatest empire of the ancient world. His remarkable ability to interpret dreams and prophetic visions brought him to the attention of King Nebuchadnezzar. The king of Babylon had a strange dream on a great metallic human-like image composed of four different metals: gold, silver, bronze, and iron. Daniel interpreted the king's strange dream and explained that this image symbolized the future prophetic course of four world empires from the time of Daniel in the 6th century BC until the end of this age. This remarkable prophecy envisioned that there would be only four major empires that would rule the world from the Babylon Empire in 606 BC until the time of the Second Coming of Christ as Messiah-King.

> Thou, O king, sawest, and behold a great image. This great image, whose brightness was excellent, stood before thee; and the form thereof was terrible. This image's head was of fine gold, his breast and his arms of silver, his belly and his thighs of brass, his legs of iron, his feet part of iron and part of clay. Thou sawest till that a stone was cut out without hands, which smote the image upon his feet that were of iron and clay, and brake them to pieces. (Daniel 2: 31–34)

The first empire represented by the head of gold was Babylon (Daniel 2:37–38). The second empire represented by the chest of silver was Media-Persia, which was followed by the third empire of Greece depicted by bronze thighs. Finally, the fourth empire was the Roman Empire represented by the two iron legs correctly predicting the division of the fourth empire into Eastern and Western Rome. The final portion of the metallic image was the two feet composed of iron and clay, which represent the final stage of the revived Roman Empire in the years leading up to the Battle of Armageddon. The prophetic meaning of the great metallic image reveals that the decrease in value of the metal from the head of gold, chest of silver, thighs of bronze, legs of iron, and feet of both iron and clay) indicates a regression from the monarchy of Babylon as symbolized by gold to the iron and clay representing a combination of dictatorial rule and democracy in the final stage. However, the increasing strength of the metals symbolized the fact that each successive empire would have greater military power. History demonstrates the fulfillment of this remarkable prophecy.

This astonishing prophecy of Daniel predicted that, despite all the plans and ambitions of kings, emperors, and generals to conquer the world during the past two thousand years, no fifth world empire ever succeeded in replacing the fourth world empire, Rome. Many conquerors tried and failed including: Mohammed, Charlemagne, Genghis Khan, Frederick Barbarossa, Napoleon, the British Empire, Adolf Hitler, Mussolini, and Russia. Each of these in their turn tried to construct a fifth world empire to replace ancient Rome, but each failed utterly. God alone knows the future and He will bring it to pass despite the well-laid plans of men.

> Forasmuch as thou sawest that the stone was cut out of the mountain without hands, and that it brake in pieces the iron, the brass, the clay, the silver, and the gold; the great God hath made known to the king what shall come to pass hereafter: and the dream is certain, and the interpretation thereof sure. (Daniel 2:45)

The Lord motivated Daniel to prophesy that the last world empire would be a unique revival of the ancient Roman Empire in the form of a confederacy of ten nations presumably within the geographic territory of the old Roman Empire at its greatest extent.

Later in his career, God gave Daniel another prophetic vision that depicted the final destiny of the revived Roman Empire:

> After this I saw in the night visions, and behold a fourth beast, dreadful and terrible, and strong exceedingly; and it had great iron teeth: it devoured and brake in pieces, and stamped the residue with the feet of it: and it was diverse from all the beasts that were before it; and it had ten horns. I considered the horns, and, behold, there came up among them another little horn, before whom there were three of the first horns plucked up by the roots. (Daniel 7:7–8)

This additional prophetic vision of Daniel suggests that the ten nations will initially join together into the world's first super state in the form of a ten-nation "Roman confederacy." Later, a dynamic new leader of Western Europe (the "little horn") will take advantage of a future crisis in Europe and violently seize control of three of the ten nations by military force. The remaining seven nations will submit to the Antichrist and accept his dictatorial rule over their population. The Antichrist's conquest of these three European nations will be the first military success on his road to supreme world power. The Antichrist will rule for an unknown number of years, but the Scriptures declare that in his position as the head of the revived Roman Empire he will guarantee or "confirm" a treaty or "covenant" with Israel for a period of seven years (Daniel 9:27). Daniel foretold the Antichrist's future covenant with the revived nation of Israel in his prophecy:

> And he shall confirm the covenant with many for one week: and in the midst of the week he shall cause the sacrifice and the oblation to cease, and for the overspreading of abominations he shall make it desolate, even until the consummation, and that determined shall be poured upon the desolate. (Daniel 9:27)

He will possess absolute power over every nation on earth as well as exercising his satanic power over the tribulation saints who find faith in Christ during this time of brutal persecution. After the resurrection of the departed as well as all living Christian saints, millions of Jews and Gentiles will certainly examine the Scriptures in a search for answers about why so many Christians have disappeared. Millions from every race will eventually reject the propaganda of the world dictator and will place their faith in God as a result of their Bible study, as well as the message of the Two Witnesses and the 144,000 Jewish witnesses (Revelation 7:14–17 and 11:3–12). These converts from every nation on earth will be the "tribulation saints" who are described in the book of Revelation:

> After this I beheld, and, lo, a great multitude, which no man could number, of all nations, and kindreds, and people, and tongues, stood before the throne, and before the Lamb, clothed with white robes, and palms in their hands. . . . These are they which came out of great tribulation, and have washed their robes, and made them white in the blood of the Lamb. (Revelation 7:9,14)

The prophecies indicate Antichrist's power over the saints will be limited to only 1260 days from the time of his sacrilegious defiling of the rebuilt Temple in Jerusalem until the moment of his destruction three and a half years later at Jesus Christ's return to earth at the Battle of Armageddon.

> And he shall speak great words against the most High, and shall wear out the saints of the most High, and think to change times and laws: and they shall be given into his hand until a time and times and the dividing of time. (3½ years) (Daniel 7:25)

The prophet John also prophesied about the Antichrist's persecution of these saints:

> And he opened his mouth in blasphemy against God, to blaspheme his name, and his tabernacle, and them that dwell in heaven. And it was given unto him to make war with the saints, and to overcome them: and power was given him over all kindreds, and tongues, and nations. (Revelation 13:6–7)

The North Atlantic Treaty Organization (NATO) was established in 1948 by the victorious allies of World War II to ensure the common defense of the nations of western Europe against the growing threat of Russia and the Warsaw Pact nations of Eastern Europe. Europe held its first election for the European Parliament in June 1979, creating the first directly elected, multinational super state assembly in history that was set up to deal with European community problems. The process of creating a super state began in 1957 with the Treaty of Rome and the negotiations of the European Common Market (officially known then as the European Economic Community).

Without realizing it, the nations of Western Europe have begun their first tentative steps toward fulfilling Daniel's ancient prophecy of the ten-nation super state based on the territory of the Roman Empire. The Treaty of Rome, which was signed in Rome, set the stage for the European Union to become an economic, political, and military colossus. The French intellectual Jean Monet, the spiritual father of the "United States of Europe," revealed the ultimate political objective of this new super state when he said, "Once a common market interest has been created, then political union will come naturally."

The World's First Super State

A poll reported from European Union headquarters in Brussels in January 1985 revealed that 52 percent of Europeans supported the idea of transforming the ten-nation European Common Market into a true confederacy to be known as the United States of Europe. The new confederation would include a powerful economic and customs union, as well as a defense and political union somewhat similar to the ten provinces of Canada or the United States of America. These embryonic stages of the coming European super state are the beginning of the fulfillment of Daniel's prophecy of the final revival of the Roman Empire. The European Union is gradually but inexorably adopting additional new member states as it expands into an economic, military, and political colossus. Norway and Switzerland both declined to become member states several years ago but are now earnestly reconsidering their choice. A significant portion of the citizens of these nations now see the prospect of joining the European Union as a necessary evil and virtually inevitable. However, a strong minority still vehemently reject membership and openly declare that joining the EU would destroy their historical national sovereignty and ancient culture.

The astonishing speed and success of this integration of the European economies together with growing forces of globalization have presented Norway and Switzerland with the terrible prospect that their treasured historical independence may be a political luxury they can no longer afford. Support for EU membership is growing rapidly with polls showing that 47 percent are now in favor with only 40 percent opposed. The poverty-stricken nations of formerly communist Eastern Europe, including Bulgaria and Romania, desperately hope that they might qualify as new members. They see EU membership as a promise of future economic prosperity and the only real hope to defend their weak democratic governments from communists hoping to be restored to power.[3]

The Euro — The First Super State Currency

The president of Germany's powerful Bundesbank (central bank) declared in 1998 that "a European currency will lead to member nations transferring their sovereignty over financial and wage policy as well as in monetary affairs." Europeans are finally realizing that the European Union could mean the practical abolishing of their own historic nations, their laws, their money, customs, and even control over their political future. The European Union's introduction of the Euro currency in January 1, 1999, for use by business and government was a significant step toward creating the world's first super state economy, an effective common market, and the elimination of all trade barriers between the Union's member states.

Step by step the members of the EU are replacing their national currencies with a new standardized European currency called the Euro. Euro banknotes and coins will not come into public circulation until January 1, 2002. However, all paper and electronic transactions can now be made in euros. This great experiment will alter the world's economy for every international business both within and outside Europe. The eleven member states of the EU voted in the 1992 Maastricht Treaty to introduce the Euro including Austria, Belgium, Denmark, Finland, France, Germany, Greece, Ireland, Italy, Luxembourg, Netherlands, Portugal, Spain, Sweden, and the United Kingdom. However, in the late 1990s, the UK refused to surrender their beloved British pounds and voted in Parliament to wait a few years to see how well the Euro experiment worked. However, the clear advantage is that the Euro obviously simplifies foreign exchange problems for corporations in EU member states and thereby reduces exchange costs.

The EU is also moving rapidly toward the elimination of travel restrictions and customs barriers between member states. The creation of the Euro currency as the single currency of the new Europe paves the way for fully integrated tax systems as well as a common fiscal and monetary policy. Fifteen centuries after the fall of the Roman Empire, the powerful nation states of Europe are being systematically transformed into virtual provinces of the world's first true super state.

Recently, the Euro dropped in value from its initial valuation in January 1, 1999, of $1.09, to less than $.90 US. This initial unplanned-for devaluation of the new European super currency has caused many Germans and Frenchmen to express deep concerns about the economic danger if the Euro does not strengthen in comparison to other world currencies, especially the US dollar. However, this weakness is likely to be temporary in light of Europe's growing economic power.

The introduction of the Euro currency may prove to be a key step in creating a socialist Europe. The finance minister of Austria, Rudolf Edlinger, presented a political manifesto entitled *The New European Way — Economic Reform in the Framework of Monetary Union*. According to an article by Herbert London in *The Journal of Commerce*, Edlinger argues that the EU needs tax harmonization with a common tax on capital and wages as well as a set of common rules for the economic and social well-being of all European citizens. Complementing this, the German Finance Minister Oskar Lafontaine has argued for a common wage policy.[4]

New European and Global Standards

Over 800,000 companies throughout the world already use the Uniform Code Council (UCC) identification and communication standards to verify quality standards in manufactured products. A new international organization, the Global Manufacturing and Retail Initiative was formed in May 1999 to develop standards to simplify service for the global supply chain for the world economy's retail sector. A set of supply-chain standards for the global retail sector is being developed internationally to simplify service. If all 800,000 companies eventually join, this will represent another significant step toward achieving a global economic policy.[5]

The CE Mark

The European Union has also mandated the use of the CE mark for any product to be sold within their European common market according to the New Approach Directives (an EU regulation) according to an article by David Taylor in *Business Standards*. The CE marking guarantees a corporation's compliance to the essential requirements of the New Approach Directives and is absolutely essential if a product is to be sold freely within the individual member states of the EU. Strangely, although the CE mark is found everywhere, there is some confusion over what the letters actually represent. Most European authorities suggest CE is an abbreviation of the French phrase *Conformite Europeenne* (European Conformity). The Maastricht Treaty authorized the bureaucrats of the European Union to negotiate with other inter-governmental organizations to create rules and standards for harmonizing international trade within the European Union.[6]

Any company in the rest of the world proposing to sell products within the European Union must now submit to the CE certification procedures of the EU. The presence of the CE marking will certify that the product has met all safety requirements as required by the Official Journal of the European Communities. The CE marking was designed to facilitate continent-wide trade in the European Union by removing existing trade barriers between member countries. However, it also effectively acts as a barrier to any corporation that has not yet received permission to apply the CE mark to its product. Any American or other foreign company that wishes to affix the CE marking to products designated for sale in Europe must have the written approval of the designated EU authority, which is appointed by the EU to audit all products and quality systems under the directives. After a given corporation is approved, a notified EU authority will conduct a risk assessment of the proposed product, determining which directives apply to it and outlining the potential safety risks posed.[7]

The evidence is now overwhelming that the nations of Europe are joining their forces economically, politically, and militarily to create a super state that will soon rival the United States as the world's greatest super power. The prophecies of the Bible foretold the revival of the Roman Empire after thousands of years to become the leading power in the world. These remarkable developments in Europe should awaken the interest of Christians everywhere that we are entering the last days leading to the return of the Messiah as prophesied by the Scriptures.

Notes

1. Philo, *De Praemiis et Poenis*, section 15-20. Loeb Classical Library (London: Harvard University Press, 1961).
2. *Sanhedrin* 97a., *Talmud* (London: The Soncino Press, 1987).
3. *The Journal of Commerce*, 29 Dec. 1998.
4. *The Journal of Commerce*, 22 Dec. 1998.
5. *Automatic ID News*, June 1999.
6. *Business Standards*, May/June 1999.
7. *Quality*, Jan. 1999.

10

The Rise of Antichrist

> Remember the former things of old: for I am God, and there is none else; I am God, and there is none like me, Declaring the end from the beginning, and from ancient times the things that are not yet done, saying, My counsel shall stand, and I will do all my pleasure. (Isaiah 48:3).

The Scriptures contain thousands of specific prophecies that God will send His Messiah to redeem mankind and establish His kingdom of righteousness. The Bible's prophecies also warn that a False Messiah, the Antichrist, would arise in the last days to deceive the Jews and Gentiles. Hundreds of these prophecies have been fulfilled throughout history, especially in this century, that has witnessed the return of the Jews to Israel, the revival of the ancient Hebrew language, and the beginning of the revival of the Roman Empire. God declared that these fulfilled prophecies are the unquestionable proof that He is in control of the future. The focus of most of the prophecies is the period of time known as the "last days" leading to the return of the Messiah.

Through centuries of bitter exile the Jews longed for the coming Messiah who will redeem the earth from the curse of sin and suffering. Their rabbis wrote about their hopes and fears for this awesome period known as the "birthpangs of the Messiah." Just as a woman endures pain and danger to give birth to her child, the years preceding the Messiah's appearance will be similar to those "birthpangs." Today, after the miraculous return of the exiles to the Promised Land to recreate Israel in 1948, we are entering the most exciting and dangerous time in history. The fulfillment of the messianic dreams of forty generations of Jewish exiles is at hand. The Jewish people comforted themselves during the centuries of exile by remembering the prophecies of the Messiah who would return the exiles to their land and re-establish the throne of David forever. In 1200 AD, the great Jewish scholar, Moses Maimonides, listed messianic expectation as a necessary Jewish religious belief in his *Thirteen Principles of Faith.* "I believe with perfect faith in the coming of the Messiah. Even if he delays I will wait every day for him to come." Tragically, their messianic expectation could lead many Jews to accept the Antichrist's false claims to be their Messiah.

The Christians in the early Church were fascinated by the Bible's prophecies about the Antichrist, his career and his ultimate destruction. Jesus Christ warned His disciples about the coming Antichrist's "abomination of desolation." The words of Jesus were:

> Therefore when you see the 'abomination of desolation,' spoken of by Daniel the prophet, standing in the holy place (whoever reads, let him understand), then let those who are in Judea flee to the mountains. (Matthew 24:15–16)

He reminded us that Daniel declared that the Antichrist, the "prince that shall come," will defile the "holy place" in the rebuilt Temple. These prophecies were discussed widely in the first-century Church and gave believers a clear understanding of the future prophetic crisis at the end of this age involving the Antichrist and his reign of terror. The major prophets all spoke of the coming Antichrist, the Battle of Armageddon and the ultimate victory of the Messiah.

The apostle Paul, in his second letter to the church at Thessalonica, described the confusion created by false teachers about the sequence of future events concerning the coming Antichrist. In attempting to allay their fears, Paul tells them that the "Day of the Lord" will not appear until the "falling away" and that "man of sin be revealed." Paul tells the Thessalonians,

> That ye be not soon shaken in mind, or be troubled, neither by spirit, nor by word, nor by letter as from us, as that the day of Christ is at hand. Let no man deceive you by any means: for that day shall not come, except there come a falling away first, and that man of sin be revealed, the son of perdition; Who opposeth and exalteth himself above all that is called God, or that is worshipped; so that he as God sitteth in the temple of God, showing himself that he is God. (2 Thessalonians 2:2–4)

Paul reminded the church at Thessalonica about his earlier teachings to them regarding end-time events, including the appearance of the Antichrist, the Man of Sin. He also discussed details of the end-time scenario including the resurrection of the saints in I Thessalonians Chapter 4 and 5. The book of Revelation described the career of the Antichrist in great detail in Chapters 4 to 19. The widespread reading of the epistles of Paul and the book of Revelation made these topics a major matter for discussion in the early Church. Many books and letters that have survived from the first three centuries of the Christian era contain long quotations from Revelation and Daniel concerning the final battle between Christ and Antichrist.

The Apocalypse of Peter is a non-biblical Christian commentary from the second century (approximately AD 140) that discusses the conversation of Jesus with his disciples on the Mount of Olives are recorded in Matthew 24 and Luke 21. This work is a type of literature called "apocalyptic" that includes revelatory writings that disclose the hidden secrets about the end of time. Whoever the writer was, this book was not accepted into the canon of the New

Testament because it was not believed to be an inspired biblical writing. But it does illuminate the thinking of some Christians in the New Testament Church about the Antichrist. It gives us an insight into the way Christians understood prophecy in the first centuries after Christ.

> And when they shall see the wickedness of their deeds (even of the false christs), they shall turn away after them and deny him to whom our fathers gave praise, the first Christ whom they crucified and thereby sinned exceedingly. But this deceiver is not the Christ. And when they reject him, he will kill with the sword and there shall be many martyrs. Then shall the boughs of the fig-tree, the house of Israel, sprout, and there shall be many martyrs by his hand: they shall be killed and become martyrs. Enoch and Elias will be sent to instruct them that this is the deceiver who must come into the world and do signs and wonder in order to deceive. (*Apocalypse of Peter* — Second Century)[1]

The writer of the *Apocalypse of Peter* expected that a series of false christs would ultimately be followed by the final Antichrist, "this deceiver is not the Christ." His words "he will kill with the sword" together with the reference to the teaching of the Two Witnesses reveals the writer's familiarity with the book of Revelation. The unknown writer believes that the Two Witnesses will be Enoch and Elijah (Elias). This interpretation was common in the early Church, during the first several centuries of the Christian era. However, it is likely that the second of the Two Witnesses will be Moses. The supernatural miracles performed by the Two Witnesses are similar to those of Moses and Elijah in their earlier ministries. They both appeared together on the Mount of Transfiguration. Another clue to his identity is that the passage in the book of Malachi that refers to Elijah returning in the last days just before the Great Day of the Lord, also refers to Moses.

> Remember ye the law of Moses my servant, which I commanded unto him in Horeb for all Israel, with the

statutes and judgments. Behold, I will send you Elijah the prophet before the coming of the great and dreadful day of the Lord. (Malachi 4:4–5)

The *Didache* is one of the earliest of the church writings that has survived. Most scholars date it during the first decade of the second century (AD 100 to 110). The writer of this document clearly believed in an imminent resurrection of the Christians. The *Didache* declares:

Be ye watchful for your life! Let not your lamps be extinguished nor your loins ungirded, but be ye ready! For ye know not the hour in which your Lord cometh. . . . For as lawlessness increases, they shall hate one another and shall persecute and betray, and then the world-deceiver shall appear as a son of God, and shall work signs and wonders, and the earth shall be delivered into his hands, and he shall commit crimes such as have never been seen since the world began. . . . Then shall created mankind come to the fire of testing, and many shall be offended and perish, but those who have endured in the faith shall be saved by the (Christ). . . . And then shall the signs of the truth appear, first, the sign of a rift in heaven, then the sign of the sound of a trumpet, and thirdly, a resurrection of the dead. . . . But not of all, but as it was said, "The Lord will come and all his saints with him. . . . Then shall the world see the Lord coming on the clouds of heaven."[2]

The author of the *Didache* believes in the coming of a personal Antichrist (the world-deceiver) as the persecutor, betrayer of truth, and a man of lawlessness. He declared that "the world-deceiver shall appear as a son of God, and shall work signs and wonders." This Antichrist will possess miraculous powers, derived from Satan and will use "signs and wonders" to deceive the world about his true nature. He will "appear as the son of God" attempting to deceive the world, especially Israel, about his identity. The *Didache* described his initial success: "the earth shall be delivered into his hands." The Apostle Paul described him as the "son of perdition" and the *Didache* said, "he shall commit crimes such as have never been seen since the world began."

Another early Church non-biblical manuscript, *The Apocalypse of Baruch* (Chap. 4), wrote about the ultimate destruction of the Antichrist, Israel's last great enemy, by the Messiah on the top of Mount Zion. Its description parallels the Old Testament prophecy of Zechariah 13 and 14, where the prophet describes Christ's final victory over the Antichrist's armies' attack on Jerusalem. The Seventh Book of the *Apostolic Constitutions*, from the second century, refers to the second coming of Jesus and His destruction of Antichrist, ". . . with the angels of His power, at the throne of His dominion to judge the world-deceiver, the Devil, and to requite each according to his deeds."[3]

The apocryphal Christian book *Ascension of Isaiah*, also from the second century, provides additional insight into the early Church's understanding of the Antichrist and the Second Coming. The author refers to the name of the future Antichrist as *Beliar*. "Many in Jerusalem and in Judah will he cause to depart from the true faith. Beliar will dwell in Manasseh." This speculation about the Antichrist living in Manasseh (Samaria — the West Bank in Israel) is quite interesting in light of other verses that claim he will be connected to the Romans "of the race of Augustus," referring to Roman emperor Caesar Augustus.

> These are the days of the completion of the world. And after it has come to its consummation, Beliar, the great prince, the king of this world who has ruled it since it come into being, shall descend; he will come down from his firmament in the form of a man, a lawless king, a slayer of his mother. . . . This ruler will thus come in the likeness of that king and there will come with him all the powers of this world and they will hearken to him in all that he desires. . . . All that he desires he will do in the world; he will act and speak in the name of the Beloved and say 'I am God and before me there has been none else.' And all the people in the world will believe in him, and will sacrifice to him and serve him saying, 'This is God and beside him there is none other.'

And the majority of those who have united to receive the Beloved will turn aside to him and the power of his miracles will be manifest in every city and region and he will set up his image before him in every city and he shall rule three years, seven months and twenty-seven days. . . . And after (one thousand) three hundred and thirty-two days the Lord will come with his angels and with the hosts of the saints from the seventh heaven with the glory of the seventh heaven, and will drag Beliar with his hosts into Gehenna and He will bring rest to the pious who shall be found alive in the body in this world and to all who through faith in him have cursed Beliar and his kings. But the saints will come with the Lord in their garments which are stored on high in the seventh heaven. . . .[4]

This writing identified the future Antichrist as a man possessed by Satan who will be "the king of this world" and who assumes the position of a "great prince" and "lawless king." The writer declared that he "will come with all the powers of this world" in confirmation of Revelation 13:13–14,

. . . he doeth great wonders, so that he maketh fire come down from heaven on the earth in the sight of men, And deceiveth them that dwell on the earth by the means of those miracles which he had power to do in the sight of the beast; saying to them that dwell on the earth, that they should make an image to the beast, which had the wound by a sword, and did live.[5]

The phrase "he will act and speak in the name of the Beloved and say 'I am God'" exactly parallels the warnings of Jesus, "I am come in my Father's name, and ye receive me not: if another shall come in his own name, him ye will receive"(John 5:43). His statement that "he will set up his image before him in every city" reveals a familiarity with the Book of Revelation (13:14) that declares that Satan will "deceive them . . . that dwell on the earth, that they should make an image to the beast, which had the wound by a sword, and did live."

As we embark on a new millennium, people throughout the world are desperate for honest and competent political figures. We need leaders who will solve global problems involving the world economy, environmental degradation, and the growing threat of terrorist weapons of mass destruction. Yet everywhere we look we see corruption, moral weakness, abdication of responsibility, and blind ambition. We are suffering a famine of true leadership. Our generation urgently needs true leaders such as Abraham Lincoln, Winston Churchill, or Franklin Roosevelt.

Our world is desperate for a new "Caesar" — someone who will emerge to take leadership at a time when political and economic problems seem beyond repair. The cry for real leadership, rather than politicians with sound bites and media consultants, is arising in nations around the globe. Throughout the world there is a vacuum of leadership that is waiting to be filled. This "caesar" for a new millennium will appear eventually. He will arise in Europe according to the prophecies of the Bible and have innovative solutions for many of our problems; he will be acclaimed as a global leader that all will willingly follow.

In light of the growing dangers facing society in the opening years of this new millennium, it is not surprising that there is a profound longing for a genuine messianic leader who will hold the answers to the world's problems. Jesus Christ warned His disciples that the generation when He would return would witness an explosion of false christs and false prophets. Both Jesus and the prophet John warned that the diabolic deception of the Antichrist and the False Prophet would be extremely effective, and that many would be deceived. When the time finally arrives for the Holy Spirit's restraining power to be removed in order to allow "the Wicked One" to manifest his satanic power, the Devil's counterfeit Messiah will be brought forth. The world's population will be desperate for strong and determined leadership.

A public comment by Aurelio Peccei, the President of the Club Of Rome, provided an example of this desire for a new Caesar.

> A charismatic leader — scientific, political, or religious —
> would be the world's only salvation from the social and

economic upheavals that threaten to destroy civilization. Such a leader would have to override national and international interests as well as political and economic structures in order to lead humanity away from the maladies that afflict it.[6]

Jesus warned, "For there shall arise false Christs, and false prophets, and shall show great signs and wonders; insomuch that, if it were possible, they shall deceive the very elect" (Matthew 24:24.) The nations will be so awed by "the prince of the power of the air" that they will accept Satan's candidate rather than worship the true Messiah. The great Christian writer, C. S. Lewis, recorded his thoughts and concerns about the dangers surrounding the coming world government and its powerful leader in the following statement:

> I believe that no man or group of men is good enough to be trusted with uncontrolled power over others. And the higher the pretensions of such power, the more dangerous I think it is, both to the rulers and to the subjects.

Former World Empires

Every one of the four world empires described by Daniel in his interpretation of King Nebuchadnezzar's dream was ruled by a single all-powerful king or dictator. The king of Babylon, Nebuchadnezzar, built the greatest city of the ancient world and extended his empire to rule most of the Middle East including Israel. Only seventy years later King Cyrus led the armies of the second world empire, Media-Persia, to victory over Babylon. Cyrus released all of the enslaved people throughout his empire, and allowed the return of the Jewish exiles to the Promised Land. Documentation of this is provided by archeologists who discovered the clay seal of Cyrus near ancient Babylon, and by the decree of Cyrus recorded in Ezra 1:2–3: "Thus saith Cyrus king of Persia . . . Who is there among you of all his people? his God be with him, and let him go up to Jerusalem, which is in Judah, and build the house of the Lord God of Israel, (he is the God,) which is in Jerusalem."

The next world empire was led by Alexander the Great, who ascended to the throne of the Macedonian Kingdom at the age of 23 and quickly conquered all of the remaining Greek city states. Then Alexander led his army of only 32,000 men in the greatest military expedition in ancient history. Within ten years Alexander's army conquered every nation and territory within the known world from Italy to India. After only a few centuries, Alexander's empire was replaced by a new Roman empire with Julius Caesar and the emperors who followed him, expanding this Roman empire and conquering every nation they touched. Rome was the greatest empire in history.

The Rise of Antichrist

The prophets of the Bible spoke of the revival of the ancient power of imperial Rome that would encompass the nations of Western Europe and the coastal Mediterranean states in the last days. Therefore, the reunification of Europe in the last days is a necessary prerequisite for the rise of the Antichrist. In Daniel 9:26, Daniel warns that the "people of the prince that shall come" will arise from the Roman Empire and will destroy Jerusalem and the Temple. This strange prophecy was fulfilled in AD 70 when the legions of Rome conquered the beautiful city of Jerusalem, killing over one and a quarter million of its inhabitants.

Daniel also foretold that in the last days the Roman Empire would arise again, dividing into ten independent nations. As this occurs, Daniel indicated that "another" horn, representing the future Antichrist, "shall rise after them; and he shall be diverse from the first, and he shall subdue three kings." This means the Antichrist will arrive on the scene after the creation of the ten-nation super-state confederacy. He will start to build his power base with the first three nations that he will conquer. The other seven nations that arise from the territory of the ancient Roman Empire will recognize and submit to his brilliant leadership and satanic power. "And he shall speak great words against the most High, and shall wear out the saints of the most High, and think to change times and laws: and they shall be given into his hand until a time and times and the dividing of time" (Daniel 7:25).

The prophet John also describes the world's first multiple nation super-state composed of ten future nations that will form the power base of the future world dictator. Specifically, John says, "And the ten horns which thou sawest are ten kings, which have received no kingdom as yet; but receive power as kings one hour with the beast. These have one mind, and shall give their power and strength unto the beast" (Revelation 17:12–13). The phrase "one-hour" suggests that this alliance will be only for a short time.

The coming prince of darkness will utilize the economic, political, and military power of these ten nations to conquer every other nation throughout the entire world. John reveals that the Antichrist will take full control of the ten nations. "And I stood upon the sand of the sea, and saw a beast rise up out of the sea, having seven heads and ten horns, and upon his horns ten crowns, and upon his heads the name of blasphemy" (Revelation 13:1). The "seven heads" in John's vision seem to refer to the remaining seven subsidiary kings of the original ten nations who remain alive after the Antichrist has destroyed the first three kings.

Daniel prophesied about the character of this future world dictator who will arise in the last days before the return of the Messiah and establish a totalitarian worldwide government:

> And in the latter time of their kingdom, when the transgressors are come to the full, a king of fierce countenance, and understanding dark sentences, shall stand up. And his power shall be mighty, but not by his own power: and he shall destroy wonderfully, and shall prosper, and practice, and shall destroy the mighty and the holy people. (Daniel 8:23–24)

He will be strong and have striking features. He will understand "dark sentences" (this indicates his involvement in occult and satanic religion). His power will be given to him directly by Satan.

The very first prophecy in the Bible refers to the Antichrist as "the seed of Satan." God addressed Satan saying, "And I will put enmity between thee and the woman, and between thy seed and her seed; it shall bruise thy head, and thou shalt bruise his heel"(Genesis 3:15). This phrase "thy seed" suggests that in some spiritual way, the Antichrist will be the "seed" of Satan. As a result, he will be an incredibly evil man motivated by wicked thoughts and satanic powers from his birth until his destruction by Jesus Christ at Armageddon. However, he will not fully become the "son of Perdition" until the major crisis of his career when he will be killed and then resurrected through the satanic power of the Devil.

At the mid-point of the seven-year tribulation, Satan will be cast out of Heaven by the Archangel Michael and his holy angels and will descend to earth with great wrath, determined to destroy humanity (Revelation 12:1–17). From that moment on, Satan will possess the spirit of the wicked man who will become the Antichrist. While this man was the "seed" of Satan from his birth, and lived as a wicked man throughout his earlier life, from the moment of his assassination and satanic resurrection he will completely sell his soul to the Devil.

John warns that such supernatural power will allow the "Wicked One" to "prosper and thrive" in his activities, increasing his power over mankind. During the last three and one-half years following his defiling of the rebuilt Temple, leading to the Battle of Armageddon, the Antichrist will do everything in his power to destroy the righteous Jews who will resist him. The prophet Daniel warned, "And his power shall be mighty, but not by his own power: and he shall destroy wonderfully, and shall prosper, and practice, and shall destroy the mighty and the holy people" (Daniel 8:24). The book of Revelation promises that God will provide supernatural protection to the faithful Jews of Israel who will flee to the wilderness to escape the religious persecution of the Antichrist's forces.

The coming prince of darkness will constantly blaspheme against God during the final three and one-half years of his power over mankind. The prophets Daniel and John both comment on this blasphemy. John said, "And there was given unto him a mouth speaking great things and blasphemies; and power was given unto him to continue forty and two months"(Revelation 13:5). Centuries ago, William Shakespeare, the greatest English playwright in history, wrote a few lines to describe the character and powerful influence of the great Roman general and popular consul, Julius Caesar. His astonishing military successes in Gaul (France) and Britain produced tremendous victories for the growing power of Rome against the barbarians in northern Europe. Later, Caesar's defeat of the numerous legions of his great rival, Pompey the Great, ended the Civil War that threatened to destroy Rome's unity and power at a time when Rome's many enemies would have loved to be free of Rome's tyranny. Julius Caesar's great political and military abilities intimidated even his friends, to the point that they felt compelled to assassinate him in order to prevent him from establishing a dictatorship or monarchy over the existing Roman republic. Shakespeare's description of the great general Caesar who created the Roman Empire through his military victories provides an excellent preview of the character and power of the future political leader known as the "Antichrist," the "Wicked One," the "Son of Perdition" and the "First Beast."

> Why man, he doth bestride the narrow world
> Like a colossus; and we petty men
> Walk under his huge legs, and peep about
> to find ourselves dishonourable graves.
>
> William Shakespeare, *Julius Caesar*

The Scriptural Titles of Antichrist

Throughout the Bible we find repeated descriptions of this end-time world dictator who will oppose Jesus Christ. The Bible addresses him under a number of descriptive titles.

Antichrist

The general title "antichrist" is used in the New Testament Scriptures to describe anyone who denies that "Jesus is the Christ," that Jesus has "come in the flesh," or that denies Jesus as both "the Father and the Son." According to the Scriptures, anyone who denies that Jesus as God was incarnated in the flesh as Jesus Christ, is operating in the spirit of Antichrist. John recorded the following prophetic visions about the coming Antichrist in the following verses from his epistles.

> And every spirit that confesseth not that Jesus Christ is come in the flesh is not of God: and this is that spirit of antichrist, whereof ye have heard that it should come; and even now already is it in the world. (1 John 4:3)

> Little children, it is the last time: and as ye have heard that antichrist shall come, even now are there many antichrists; whereby we know that it is the last time. (1 John 2:18)

> Who is a liar but he that denieth that Jesus is the Christ? He is antichrist, that denieth the Father and the Son. (1 John 2:22)

> And every spirit that confesseth not that Jesus Christ is come in the flesh is not of God: and this is that spirit of antichrist, whereof ye have heard that it should come; and even now already is it in the world. (1 John 4:3)

> For many deceivers are entered into the world, who confess not that Jesus Christ is come in the flesh. This is a deceiver and an antichrist. (2 John 7)

The title "the Assyrian" is found in the prophecy of Isaiah. It appears to refer to the Antichrist's exercise of political and military power over the area of the world that was formerly under the control of the armies of ancient Assyria. "Therefore thus saith the Lord God of hosts, O my people that dwellest in Zion, be not afraid of the Assyrian: he shall smite thee with a rod, and shall lift up his staff against thee, after the manner of Egypt" (Isaiah 10:20–27). Intriguingly, the Antichrist is also called "the king of Babylon," in reference to the scriptural revelation that ancient Babylon will be one of the centers of his political and economic power in the last days. "That thou shalt take up this proverb against the king of Babylon, and say, How hath the oppressor ceased! the golden city ceased!" (Isaiah 14:4).

The Bible describes the Antichrist as "the Son of Perdition." The prophecy of the Apostle Paul states, "Let no man deceive you by any means: for that day shall not come, except there come a falling away first, and that man of sin be revealed, the son of perdition" (2 Thessalonians 2:3). This curious title is used only of one other person in all of the Scriptures, namely Judas Iscariot. "While I was with them in the world, I kept them in thy name: those that thou gavest me I have kept, and none of them is lost, but the son of perdition; that the scripture might be fulfilled" (John 17:12). The title "son of perdition" is likely given to the Antichrist because he, like Judas Iscariot, is destined to eternal perdition or punishment in Hell, because of his total rebellion against Jesus Christ. Some writers have suggested that the Antichrist is in some strange sense a revival of the spirit of Judas Iscariot because the title "son of perdition" is used only of these two individuals.

Some have argued that the curious statement in Acts 1:25, that Judas "might go to his own place," suggests that Judas and the Antichrist are connected. The book of Revelation describes the "beast" as ascending out of the "bottomless pit" and the prophet John refers to "perdition" as his ultimate place of judgment. The prophet John wrote, "the beast that ascendeth out of the bottomless pit shall make war against them, and shall overcome them, and kill them" (Revelation 1:7). John also declared, "And the beast that was, and is not, even he is the eighth, and is of the seven, and goeth into perdition" (Revelation 17:11). Jesus Himself provides a strong hint that the satanic possession of His disciple Judas will be identical to the satanic possession of the future Antichrist in the last days. He says, "Have not I chosen you twelve, and one of you is a devil?" (John 6:70).

While these verses suggest a similar spiritual identity and final judgment for both Judas Iscariot and the future Antichrist, we cannot assuredly declare more than what the Scriptures have clearly revealed about the identity of both of these enemies of Jesus Christ.

Satan set himself on a course of eternal conflict to the will of God from the moment of his rebellion in the dateless past. He led a group of angels to join in his rebellion (possibly one-third of the angels) and desired to set himself up as a god. Isaiah wrote about this ancient rebellion, and the ultimate judgment of Satan.

How art thou fallen from heaven, O Lucifer, son of the morning! how art thou cut down to the ground, which didst weaken the nations! For thou hast said in thine heart, I will ascend into heaven, I will exalt my throne above the stars of God: I will sit also upon the mount of the congregation, in the sides of the north: I will ascend above the heights of the clouds; I will be like the most High. Yet thou shalt be brought down to hell, to the sides of the pit. (Isaiah 14:14–15)

Over seven hundred years later the apostle Paul was given a specific vision of this future enemy of Christ being "revealed" in the last days and finally destroyed supernaturally when Jesus Christ returns to the earth in glory at the Second Coming. Paul wrote, "And then shall that Wicked be revealed, whom the Lord shall consume with the spirit of his mouth, and shall destroy with the brightness of his coming" (2 Thessalonians 2:8).

Antichrist — The Man of Sin

In another passage, Paul described the Antichrist as "the man of sin." This reveals that from the moment of his birth he will be totally surrendered to Satan's spirit of rebellion and evil opposition to the will of God. "Let no man deceive you by any means: for that day shall not come, except there come a falling away first, and that man of sin be revealed, the son of perdition" (2 Thessalonians 2:3).

The prophet Daniel refers to the fact that "the man of sin" will seek to change the laws of mankind regarding the times and seasons. Daniel wrote, "And he shall speak great words against the most High, and shall wear out the saints of the most High, and think to change times and laws: and they shall be given into his hand until a time and times and the dividing of time" (Daniel 7:25). This prophecy about changing "times and laws" may suggest that the Antichrist will seek to change the present calendar used throughout most of the world (i.e., AD 2000). AD refers to Anno Domini, or "year of the Lord," and offends those who hate Jesus Christ. In other words, although the Western calendar acknowledges the birth of Jesus Christ approximately two thousand years ago, it is possible that the Antichrist may even attempt to introduce a new worldwide calendar to replace the present calendar. This coming "prince of darkness" will despise all existing laws and seek to change them because he hates the laws of man as well as the laws of God. He will then present to the world his credentials as "God."

The Origin of the Antichrist

Many biblical scholars have pondered the question of the origin of the coming Antichrist. Unfortunately, some writers have claimed that those who believe that the Antichrist will be Jewish must be anti-Semites. There is no passage in the Scriptures that states specifically that the Antichrist will be either a Jew or a Gentile. However, the burden of evidence from the Scriptures suggests that he will be a Jew. The question of his identity should be answered by an interpretation of the relevant prophecies found in both the Old and New Testament.

The Scriptures teach that the Antichrist will rule the greatest gentile world-empire in human history, the revived Roman Empire. However, this fact does not require that the end-time dictator be a gentile. There are several historical examples of a Jew rising to political power within a gentile nation. The Bible itself records the remarkable careers of Joseph, as second in command to Pharoah in Egypt, and Daniel who rose to become prime minister in Babylon. History provides other examples — British Prime Minister Disraeli, Henry Kissinger, and even Madeline Albright. In light of these historical examples it is not inconceivable that a person of the Jewish race might rise to rule the revived Roman Empire in the last days.

The first indication that the Antichrist might be Jewish is in Daniel. Daniel records that the Antichrist will "speak marvelous things against the God of gods," and not "regard the God of his fathers" (Daniel 11:36–37).

> And the king shall do according to his will; and he shall exalt himself, and magnify himself above every god, and

shall speak marvelous things against the God of gods, and shall prosper till the indignation be accomplished: for that that is determined shall be done. Neither shall he regard the God of his fathers, nor the desire of women, nor regard any god: for he shall magnify himself above all. (Daniel 11:36–37)

Significantly, the phrase "god of his fathers" appears seven times in the Old and New Testament. In every single case, with not a single exception, this phrase was used exclusively in reference to Jews. It is never used to indicate a gentile. For example, in reference to the evil Jewish King Amon, the Bible records, "And he forsook the Lord God of his fathers, and walked not in the way of the Lord" (2 Kings 21:22). Why would God have His prophet even comment upon the fact that a pagan gentile rejected the pagan "god of his fathers" for another equally false god? However, if the final great enemy of God was a Jew who rejected the one, true God, "the god of his fathers," it would be logical for the Lord to cause His prophet Daniel to record this important fact. Jesus specifically warned against "false messiahs" in the last days. He prophesied, "For there shall arise false Christs, and false prophets, and shall show great signs and wonders; insomuch that, if it were possible, they shall deceive the very elect" (Matthew 24:24; Mark 13:22). The Scriptures repeatedly warn against Israel accepting the false messiah who presents himself to the Jews as the legitimate messiah in the last days. It is illogical and virtually impossible that any gentile could possibly present himself to the Jewish people of Israel as a credible candidate. I have discussed this question with several orthodox Jewish rabbis in Israel and they laughed in derision at the very notion.

Jesus Christ prophesied, "I am come in my Father's name, and ye receive me not: if another shall come in his own name, him ye will receive" (John 5:43). Jesus used the Greek word "allos" when He described the Antichrist. This word translates as "another," clearly meaning "another of the same genus or kind." He did not use the Greek word "heteros," meaning "another of a different order." In other words, Jesus declared that He, as the Jewish

Messiah and Son of David, presented Himself to Israel but was rejected. Yet in the last days "another" of the same background would be accepted as the promised messiah. Another reason the Antichrist may be Jewish relates to the very name that the Scriptures assign to him. The name "Antichrist" indicates that this individual will be opposed to Jesus Christ, but will imitate or impersonate Jesus Christ by posing as a messianic figure. The prophecies describe the coming Messiah as being descended from the tribe of Judah (Genesis 49:10), and being born in Bethlehem (Micah 5:2).

Another indication of the Antichrist's origin is found in the prophecy of Ezekiel:

> And thou, profane wicked prince of Israel, whose day is come, when iniquity shall have an end, Thus saith the Lord God; Remove the diadem, and take off the crown: this shall not be the same: exalt him that is low, and abase him that is high. I will overturn, overturn, overturn, it: and it shall be no more, until he come whose right it is; and I will give it him. (Ezekiel 21:25–27)

Notice that this unusual prophecy refers to the Antichrist as the "profane wicked prince of Israel." This seems to indicate that he must be Jewish. It is almost inconceivable that a "wicked prince of Israel" would be a gentile. Ezekiel's prophecy also warns that the temporary triumph of the "wicked prince of Israel" would end upon the return of Christ, "whose right it is" (Revelation 19:19–21).

The final indication that the Antichrist will arise from the Jewish race is again found in the book of Ezekiel. The prophet Ezekiel was given a vision of the future world dictator being killed as a Jew. He foretold this event as follows: "but thou shalt be a man, and no God, in the hand of him that slayeth thee. Thou shalt die the deaths of the uncircumcised by the hand of strangers: for I have spoken it, saith the Lord God." (Ezekiel 28:9–10). Ezekiel declared that the Antichrist would "die the deaths of the uncircumcised." If the Antichrist is a Jew and is killed and buried in a manner consistent with the gentiles, then this prophecy makes sense.

However, if the Antichrist is a gentile, then this prediction makes no sense at all. Why would the Jewish prophet Ezekiel describe the death of the uncircumcised gentile Antichrist as dying "the deaths of the uncircumcised?" It seems logical that Ezekiel is referring to a Jewish Antichrist, dying "the death of the uncircumcised."

Antichrist's Military Career

The ancient biblical prophets Daniel and John commented upon the military success of the Antichrist during the early years of his career. The Antichrist will be totally victorious until he confronts Jesus Christ at the conclusion of the Battle of Armageddon. His initial victories will be so great that the people of the world will acclaim him the promised Messiah.

> And they worshipped the dragon which gave power unto the beast: and they worshipped the beast, saying, Who is like unto the beast? who is able to make war with him? And there was given unto him a mouth speaking great things and blasphemies; and power was given unto him to continue forty and two months. (Revelation 13:4–5)

The prophet John warns that the unrepentant sinners living in those tumultuous days will worship Satan with the knowledge that Satan alone is the true source of the Antichrist's power. This prophetic passage in the book of Revelation helps to explain the reason for God's wrath. During the tribulation period, the vast majority of the earth's population will enthusiastically join in the open worship of Satan and his Antichrist, destroying any who worship God. "And they worshipped the dragon which gave power unto the beast: and they worshipped the beast, saying, Who is like unto the beast? who is able to make war with him?" (Revelation 13:4). His followers will rejoice at the Antichrist's military victories over all of his enemies. Despite his initial successes, Jesus Christ will utterly defeat the armies of Antichrist in the last great conflict of this age called the Battle of Armageddon in the Valley of Jezreel near the ancient Israeli city of Megiddo.

Antichrist's Peace Treaties

The ancient prophets reveal that the Antichrist will use false peace treaties to deceive the nations that face him. Daniel wrote, "And through his policy also he shall cause craft to prosper in his hand; and he shall magnify himself in his heart, and by peace shall destroy many: he shall also stand up against the Prince of princes; but he shall be broken without hand" (Daniel 8:25). The Antichrist will deceive many by evil powers.

The Scriptures' prophesies reveal that the coming "prince of darkness" will subvert the world's natural desire for peace, enabling him to conquer and destroy all enemy states that stand in his path. The future world peace conferences, and the growing desire for peace throughout the population of the world, will create a unique opportunity for the Antichrist to use satanic deception against his opponents. His political and military treachery will destroy one ally after another until he achieves his objective of world power.

The book of Revelation declares that He will create a convenient political alliance with the growing false world church — "the Great Whore of Babylon." This description alludes to its spiritual unfaithfulness to God. During the first three and one-half years, he will coordinate his actions with the worldwide religious ecumenical group in his rise to supreme power. However, once he attains his satanic power, and defiles the rebuilt Temple in Jerusalem, he will instruct the ten kings of his kingdom to turn and destroy the false church with fire (Revelation 17:16–18). Satan will not be willing to share his evil worship with anyone, not even a corrupt false church. Satan will possess the soul and body of the man called the Antichrist, and will demand that all of humanity worship him as God.

The Economic System of the Antichrist

The rise in wealth of the nations of the West and the Pacific Rim continues, while the Third World nations become poorer each year. The book of Revelation contains John's prophetic vision of the terrible disparity between the rich and the poor in the last days.

> And when he had opened the third seal, I heard the third beast say, Come and see. And I beheld, and lo a black horse; and he that sat on him had a pair of balances in his hand. And I heard a voice in the midst of the four beasts say, A measure of wheat for a penny, and three measures of barley for a penny; and see thou hurt not the oil and the wine. (Revelation 6:5–6)

This vision of the third horseman of the Apocalypse indicated famine during the tribulation period. The phrase "a measure of wheat for a penny, and three measures of barley for a penny" reveals a devastating situation where the entire daily wage of a worker (normally a Roman denarius) would only be sufficient to buy a quart of wheat — one day's supply of food. However, the statement "see thou hurt not the oil and the wine" suggests that "the oil and the wine" — the normal luxuries of the rich — will still be available to those who are wealthy.

Treasure Laid Up for the Last Days

James, the brother of Jesus Christ, warned that one of the characteristics of the last days would be a disruption in the normal economic order; abundant riches will contrast abject poverty. James wrote the following prophecy two thousand years ago:

> Go to now, ye rich men, weep and howl for your miseries that shall come upon you. Your riches are corrupted, and your garments are motheaten. Your gold and silver is cankered; and the rust of them shall be a witness against you, and shall eat your flesh as it were fire. Ye have heaped treasure together for the last days. (James 5:1–3)

The old proverb "The rich get richer and the poor get poorer" is being proven to be the truth in our generation more than at any other time in history. The rise in wealth is very unbalanced. The richest Americans continue to grow richer each year, and the poorest have had their net after-tax income drop every year for the last decade.

When Will the Antichrist Be Revealed?

There are many mysteries concerning the nature, background, and timing of the appearances of the "man of sin." For example, the apostle Paul wrote, "Let no man deceive you by any means: for that day shall not come, except there come a falling away first, and that man of sin be revealed, the son of perdition, He will oppose and exalt himself to be worshipped as God" (2 Thessalonians 2:3). Paul intimates that the Antichrist cannot come into his full power until the "falling away" occurs. This "falling away" will happen only after God removes the Holy Spirit's restraining power. Then, and only then, will Satan be able to empower his seed — possessing him as no one else in history has ever been possessed.

The prophet Daniel described the Antichrist's future warfare against God and His saints until the final battle of Armageddon. "Thus shall he do in the most strong holds with a strange god, whom he shall acknowledge and increase with glory: and he shall cause them to rule over many, and shall divide the land for gain" (Daniel 11:39). In another passage the prophet wrote, "And the king shall do according to his will; and he shall exalt himself, and magnify himself above every god, and shall speak marvelous things against the God of gods, and shall prosper till the indignation be accomplished: for that that is determined shall be done" (Daniel 11:36).

The apostle Paul wrote about the activities of the coming Antichrist, "Who opposeth and exalteth himself above all that is called God, or that is worshipped; so that he as God sitteth in the temple of God, showing himself that he is God"(2 Thessalonians 2:4). The prophet Ezekiel was given a supernatural revelation of the overwhelming spiritual pride of Satan that motivates his representative, the Antichrist. Ezekiel wrote about Satan under the prophetic title "Prince of Tyrus."

> Son of man, say unto the prince of Tyrus, Thus saith the Lord God; Because thine heart is lifted up, and thou hast

said, I am a God, I sit in the seat of God, in the midst of the seas; yet thou art a man, and not God, though thou set thine heart as the heart of God" (Ezekiel 28:2).

Daniel warned that the Antichrist would worship a pagan god unknown to his followers or to the rest of the Jewish people. "But in his estate shall he honor the God of forces: and a god whom his fathers knew not shall he honor with gold, and silver, and with precious stones, and pleasant things" (Daniel 11:38).

The Antichrist Will Be Worshipped as God

The Antichrist will rise through the ranks of political, religious, or military organizations, and arrive at a position where he can seize power in a future crisis. Few will notice this ambitious nature until the moment when Satan empowers him to dominate the ten nations of the revived Roman Empire. Paul describes him as one "Who opposeth and exalteth himself above all that is called God, or that is worshipped; so that he as God sitteth in the temple of God, showing himself that he is God" (2 Thessalonians 2:4). Daniel foresaw that Satan, indwelling the body of the Antichrist, would enter the Temple and set himself up to be worshipped by mankind as god. Daniel prophesied:

> And he shall confirm the covenant with many for one week: and in the midst of the week he shall cause the sacrifice and the oblation to cease, and for the overspreading of abominations he shall make it desolate, even until the consummation, and that determined shall be poured upon the desolate. (Daniel 9:27)

This prophecy was confirmed by the words of Jesus Christ in His address to His disciples prior to His death and resurrection:

> When ye therefore shall see the abomination of desolation, spoken of by Daniel the prophet, stand in the holy place, (whoso readeth, let him understand). Then let them which be in Judaea flee into the mountains: Let him which is on the house top not come down to take any thing out of his house: Neither let him which is in the field return back to

take his clothes. And woe unto them that are with child, and to them that give suck in those days! But pray ye that your flight be not in the winter, neither on the sabbath day (Matthew 24:15–20).

The book of Revelation definitely describes the Antichrist as receiving his evil power from Satan, "And the beast which I saw was like unto a leopard, and his feet were as the feet of a bear, and his mouth as the mouth of a lion: and the dragon gave him his power, and his seat, and great authority" (Revelation 13:2).

The Antichrist Will Defile the Rebuilt Temple

And he shall confirm the covenant with many for one week: and in the midst of the week he shall cause the sacrifice and the oblation to cease, and for the overspreading of abominations he shall make it desolate, even until the consummation, and that determined shall be poured upon the desolate. (Daniel 9:27)

Who opposeth and exalteth himself above all that is called God, or that is worshipped; so that he as God sitteth in the temple of God, showing himself that he is God. (2 Thessalonians 2:4)

These prophecies warn that the Antichrist will defile the Holy of Holies of the rebuilt Temple in Jerusalem. He will enter the rebuilt Temple and possibly defile the Ark of the Covenant by touching or sitting on the Mercy Seat. This would certainly qualify as the famous "abomination of desolation" described by both Daniel (Daniel 9:27) and Jesus Christ (Matthew 24:15). This will set the stage for Satan to present his Antichrist as a "god in the Temple" to both Israel and the world.

An "abomination" is an act that is spiritually disgusting or defiling to something that is holy and sanctified. This act of defilement by the Antichrist will be so awful the prophet Daniel could barely describe it. It will be so abominable that the wrath of God will be poured out from heaven upon Jerusalem. All hell will break loose on earth at that very moment, commencing the final three-and-one-half-year period that is called the Great Tribulation that ends with the Battle of Armageddon. Jesus Christ specifically warned His disciples to flee to the mountains when this event occurred: "When ye therefore shall see the abomination of desolation, spoken of by Daniel the prophet, stand in the holy place, (whoso readeth, let him understand:) Then let them which be in Judaea flee into the mountains: Let him which is on the house top not come down to take any thing out of his house" (Matthew 24:15–17). Christ warns the righteous Jews living in Jerusalem in those desperate days to literally run for the hills when the prophesied abomination by the Wicked One occurs. Christ declared, "For then shall be great tribulation, such as was not since the beginning of the world to this time, no, nor ever shall be" (Matthew 24:21).

Jewish Rebellion Against Antichrist

When the Antichrist comes to Jerusalem, and stops the daily sacrifice, and defiles the sacred Temple of God, many Jews will recognize him as the prophesied anti-messiah, Satan's prince of darkness. When the Jews begin to rebel against his false claims to be God, Satan will supernaturally empower the Antichrist and attack the "holy people." The Antichrist will utilize all of Satan's powers in his evil attempt to destroy the woman — Israel — when she flees into the Judean wilderness to the east of Jerusalem. The Temple itself will likely become the first battleground between the forces of the Antichrist and the righteous Jewish priests and worshippers. These righteous Jews will fight to the death against the supporters of the Antichrist. The book of Revelation promised, "The woman [righteous Israelites] fled into the wilderness, where she hath a place prepared of God, that they should feed her there a thousand two hundred and threescore days" (Revelation 12:6).

John warned that "when the dragon [Satan] saw that he was cast unto the earth, he persecuted the woman [righteous Israelites] which brought forth the man child. And to the woman were given two wings of a great eagle, that she might fly into the wilderness, into her place, where she is nourished for a time, and times, and half a time [three and one-half years] ..." (Revelation 12:13–14). The prophet added, "the dragon [Satan] was wroth with the woman, and went to make war with the remnant of her seed, which [kept] the commandments of God, and [had] the testimony of Jesus Christ" (Revelation 12:17).

Assassination and Resurrection of the Antichrist

The Antichrist will be assassinated after he stops the sacrifice in the Jewish Temple. "And he shall confirm the covenant with many for one week: and in the midst of the week he shall cause the sacrifice and the oblation to cease, and for the overspreading of abominations he shall make it desolate, even until the consummation, and that determined shall be poured upon the desolate" (Daniel 9:27).

The assassin will succeed in killing the Antichrist with a sword wound to the head or neck. The prophet John describes the assassination: "And I saw one of his heads as it were wounded to death; and his deadly wound was healed: and all the world wondered after the beast" (Revelation 13:3). John also refers to this deadly wound being healed when he warns that the False Prophet "exerciseth all the power of the first beast before him, and causeth the earth and them which dwell therein to worship the first beast, whose deadly wound was healed" (Revelation 13:12).

Once the Antichrist is satanically resurrected, his evil partner the False Prophet will use the astonishing event to convince the world that the Antichrist is truly their long-awaited Messiah. Revelation warns that the False Prophet uses satanic power, "And deceiveth them that dwell on the earth by the means of those miracles which he had power to do in the sight of the beast; saying to them that dwell on the earth, that they should make an image to the beast, which had the wound by a sword, and did live" (Revelation 13:14). Once he is resurrected from death, the Antichrist will be totally possessed by the spirit of Satan as the true "son of perdition."

After the western-based military forces of Satan establish their military headquarters near Jerusalem, the False Prophet will force everyone under the jurisdiction of his totalitarian world government to worship the Antichrist as God. From the time of the Antichrist's resuscitation from his death wound, the world will experience unprecedented spiritual and physical warfare between the forces of the Antichrist and those righteous Jews and gentiles for the remaining three and one-half years of the Great Tribulation. In the next chapter we will explore the prophecies of the dreaded Mark of the Beast system that the Antichrist will introduce to control the world's population during the final three and a half years leading to the Battle of Armageddon when he will be destroyed by Christ at His return.

Notes

1. The Apocalypse of Peter, *New Testament Apocrapha*, Vol. 2 (Philadelphia: The Westminster Press, 1964).

2. Didache (section 16), *New Testament Apocrapha*, Vol. 2 (Philadelphia: The Westminster Press, 1964).

3. Apocalypse of Baruch, *New Testament Apocrapha*, Vol. 2 (Philadelphia: The Westminster Press, 1964).

4. Ascension of Isaiah, *New Testament Apocrapha*, Vol. 2 (Philadelphia: The Westminster Press, 1964).

5. Ascension of Isaiah, *New Testament Apocrapha*, Vol. 2 (Philadelphia: The Westminster Press, 1964).

6. "Club of Rome Says: 'Messiah Needed,'" *Calgary Albertan*, 18 April 1980.

11

Antichrist and the Mark of the Beast

And he shall confirm the covenant with many for one week: and in the midst of the week he shall cause the sacrifice and the oblation to cease, and for the overspreading of abominations he shall make it desolate, even until the consummation, and that determined shall be poured upon the desolate. (Daniel 9:27)

A Peace Treaty With Israel

The Lord promised the Holy Land of Israel to Abraham and his descendents forever. For thousands of years millions of Jews have fought and died defending this sacred land from a series of invaders. In 1948 after almost two thousand years of exile since the destruction of Jerusalem the Jews have returned to their Promised Land to establish their own nation in fulfillment of the many prophecies in the Scriptures. "And I will make them one nation in the land upon the mountains of Israel" (Ezekiel 37:22).

However, as foretold by the ancient prophecies of Isaiah and Daniel, the future leaders of Israel will surrender their independent sovereignty to the rising European superpower and its brilliant leader, the Antichrist. After his spectacular rise to power over the new super state in Europe, the Antichrist will consolidate his rule over the nations through a strategic series of peace treaties. The prophet John described the coming Antichrist in these words: "And I looked, and behold, a white horse. And he who sat on it had a bow; and a crown was given to him, and he went out conquering and to conquer" (Revelation 6:2).

The prophet Daniel wrote the following description of the Antichrist's rule: "he shall magnify himself in his heart and by peace shall destroy many" (Daniel 8:25). After conquering many nations by deceptive peace treaties (as did Adolph Hitler and Joseph Stalin), the Man of Sin will unleash his great military power against the remaining nations. His military attacks on the nations that resist his rule will be victorious due to his demonic power. As Revelation 13:4 states, "they worshiped the beast, saying, 'Who is like the beast? Who is able to make war with him?'" The extent of his military victories is described in Revelation 13:7: "And it was granted to him to make war with the saints and to overcome them. And authority was given him over every tribe, tongue, and nation."

Recently some critics of the pre-millennial and pre-tribulation resurrection of Christians have falsely attributed the concept of a future Antichrist and the seven-year treaty period as a relatively new doctrine that was invented in the last two hundred years. However, the truth is that a number of Christian writers from the earliest centuries of the Christian era clearly taught about these matters. This ancient manuscript known as *Pseudo-Titus Epistle* confirms that the early Christians understood Daniel 9:24–27 as a prophecy of a final seven-year tribulation period under the rule of the Antichrist at the end of this age. The manuscript carries the name Titus, yet virtually no scholars believe that the Titus of the New Testament wrote it. A writer in the following centuries likely wrote this scroll and affixed the name Titus to it in honor of the disciple. He writes about the future Antichrist under the prophetic title of "Nebuchadnezzar" as he sees a parallel to the ancient king of Babylon in the common satanic opposition to the Jews and God.

> In the end you also will be delivered up to the wicked king of Nebuchadnezzar, as he says, i.e. to the devil who will fall upon you. And as they [the Jews], after they had spent seventy years in anguish, returned to their own place of abode, so a period of seven years is appointed under Antichrist. But the pain of the seven years presents eternal anguish.[1]

The writer refers to the duration of the Antichrist's power over the Jewish tribulation saints as being "a period of seven years appointed under Antichrist." Daniel the prophet said, "And he shall confirm the covenant with many for one week: and in the midst of the week he shall cause the sacrifice and the oblation to cease" (Daniel 9:27).

One of the most important early Church writers was Jerome. In his commentary on Daniel's prophecy (9:24–27), he quotes the writer Hippolytus, one of the most brilliant of the early Christian scholars. Jerome wrote:

> Moreover Hippolytus places the final week at the end of the world and divides it into the period of Elias (Elijah) and the period of Antichrist, so that during the first three and a half years of the last week the knowledge of God is established. And as for the statement, 'He shall establish a compact with many for a week,' during the other three years under the Antichrist the sacrifice and offering shall cease. But when Christ shall come and shall slay the wicked one by the breath of His mouth, desolation shall hold sway till the end.

The Jews have a curious tradition that "all things which are denominated by sevens are always beloved of God including the seventh of days, of portions of lands, and of generations." (Genesis 5:24; Jude v. 14).[2] This optimistic view will fully be understood when their long-awaited Messiah returns at the end of the seven years of tribulation to conquer their enemies and establish His millennial kingdom forever.

Satan in the Temple

Since the creation of humanity Satan has attempted to achieve his diabolical goal of replacing God in the hearts of men and women. In the beginning "God created man in his own image, in the image of God created he him; male and female created he them" (Genesis 1:27). Since humanity was created "in the image of God," Satan's greatest triumph would be to deceive mankind to worship and follow him as "God."

The Antichrist will be content with his supreme political power as the absolute messianic leader until the mid-point of the seven-year Tribulation period. During the first three and one-half years of the Tribulation period the Antichrist will use his alliance with the New World Religion to consolidate his growing power through the vast religious propaganda power of the world's first global faith community. Any religious groups on earth who wish to survive will be forced to join the ecumenical New World Religion and acknowledge the supremacy of the new neopagan faith over any previous religious traditions or doctrines. Only those doctrines consistent with the ancient Mystery Babylonian faith will be approved. Any other manifestation of spiritual activity or faith in God will be ruthlessly suppressed by the religious censors and the police forces of the Antichrist. However, during this same period the ancient Temple animal sacrifice system of the Jews will be allowed to continue in Jerusalem under the protection of the seven-year Covenant between the Antichrist and the Jewish state.

After tolerating this resumption of Israel's ancient Temple worship for several years, the Antichrist will finally attack and "make war with the saints" during the balance of his evil rule. The book of Daniel warns about this crisis at the mid-point of the seven years when he will order the cessation of the daily sacrifice of lambs on the altar in front of the rebuilt Temple.

> And from the time that the daily sacrifice shall be taken away, and the abomination that maketh desolate set up,

there shall be a thousand two hundred and ninety days. (Daniel 12:11)

Daniel's prophecy indicates that the world dictator will stop the daily sacrifice 1290 days (three and one-half years) before the Tribulation period ends at the Battle of Armageddon.

The Mark of the Beast

And he causeth all, both small and great, rich and poor, free and bond, to receive a mark in their right hand, or in their foreheads: And that no man might buy or sell, save he that had the mark, or the name of the beast, or the number of his name. Here is wisdom. Let him that hath understanding count the number of the beast: for it is the number of a man; and his number is six hundred threescore and six. (Revelation 13:16–18)

There is something mysterious and fascinating about the Mark of the Beast that has held a unique place in the minds of men for many centuries. The mark will be a physical, probably visible, mark that the False Prophet will demand every man and woman receive on their right hand or forehead. The Mark will be related to both the "name of the beast" and the "number of his name" — "666." It will indicate that the individual willingly worships the "beast" the satanic Antichrist. If someone does not possess this Mark, they will not be able to buy or sell during the Great Tribulation. The universal application of this system was technically impossible until the last few years, yet now the introduction of laser scans, implantable computer chips, and computerized financial systems makes it feasible.

The introduction of this diabolical Mark of the Beast system will place humanity in an invisible economic prison. The worldwide economic and political system of the last days will be under the control of the Antichrist and his False Prophet. The Mark will enforce worldwide worship of the Antichrist. During the final three and one-half years leading up to the Battle of Armageddon, the Antichrist and False Prophet will rule with the supernatural power of Satan. This terrible time will be far worse than any other tyranny in human history. It will be characterized by the introduction of the totalitarian secret police control system of the Beast. Previously, no matter how horrible the totalitarian control, it was occasionally possible to bribe a border guard with gold or to buy some food with silver coins. However, the Mark of the Beast system will eliminate money in all its previous physical forms and force men to buy and sell through a system that will require the possession of your own individual Mark as the key to your ability to "buy and sell."

For two thousand years the number 666 has been particularly ominous, especially in the minds of Christians. This number 666 has formed the basis of countless speculations about its meaning and connection to the identity and name of the mysterious man who will be the Antichrist. A recent news article from Russia revealed that many members and priests of the Russian Orthodox Church were protesting participation in their government's introduction of a new tax identification number for each citizen. These tax ID numbers are used with bar-code readers that scan the bars on the tax ID application forms. Some Russians believe that the three sets of parallel lines in each bar code that stand for the number six means that the bar-code is tied into the prophesied 666 system. They fear that the bar code numbers including the three sixes will someday replace their Christian names.[3]

666 and the Beast

Here is wisdom. Let him that hath understanding count the number of the beast: for it is the number of a man; and his number is Six hundred threescore and six. (Revelation 13:18)

John instructs the reader who has "understanding" to "count the number of the beast." Over the centuries some students of the Bible have attempted to "count the number" and discern the true meaning of this mysterious verse. John wrote the book of Revelation in the Greek language. This was the commonly used language throughout the Roman world in the days of Christ. Although the Romans and their legal system usually used

Latin, most educated people, even in Rome, wrote and discussed intellectual matters in the Greek language.

Greek was introduced when Alexander the Great conquered the known world from Italy to India in 320 BC and established Greek culture and language everywhere. Centuries later, most educated men still wrote in Greek. One of the curious features of the Greek and Hebrew language is that they do not use the Arabic numerals (1, 2, 3). They express numbers by assigning a letter from their alphabet. In other words, each letter of the Greek and Hebrew alphabet serves a dual purpose as both a letter and a number. This is somewhat similar to the Roman numerals where X stood for 10, and M for 1000. Yet, the Greeks used every letter of their alphabet. For example, the letter a stands for the number 1 and the letter b stands for 2. Thus, when John recorded the number of the beast in Revelation 13:18, he wrote it in the original manuscript using the three Greek letters that represent the number 666. The letters χξς were translated in the English version of Revelation 13:18 as "six hundred and sixty six." Using this Greek numeric-language system, every name or word in the Greek language contains individual letters that also represent individual numbers.

If you were to add up the six letters that compose the name Jesus in the Greek tongue, you would arrive at 888. The value of the letters in the Greek word "Christos" is equal to 1480. Each variation of the name of Jesus — Christ, Savior, Lord, Emmanuel, and Messiah — contains letters that totals equal a number divisible by eight. This fascinating fact suggests that God designed these names to demonstrate a pattern. The number 666 indicates that the letters in the Greek name of the Antichrist will add up to 666. There is a slim possibility that his name will equal 666 in the Hebrew language, since the Antichrist will probably be Jewish. The numeric system does not work in any other language so it is useless to consider names in other languages.

God's Warning to the Tribulation Saints

The purpose of Revelation's prediction that the future Antichrist will possess a name that has a numeric value equal to 666 is to provide the Jewish and Gentile believers living in the Great

Tribulation with a means to determine the Antichrist's true identity. The Antichrist will deceptively present himself as the Messiah by "signs and wonders," supernatural satanic power and satanic deception. The "second beast," the False Prophet, will appear to all men as Elijah the Prophet by way of his miraculous power of bringing fire down from heaven. "And he doeth great wonders, so that he maketh fire come down from heaven on the earth in the sight of men (Revelation 13:13). The False Prophet can only perform his satanic miracles when he is "in his [Antichrist] presence." Unlike God who is omnipresent (simultaneously everywhere at once) Satan, as a fallen angel, can only exert his satanic supernatural power in one place. Since Satan will possess the body of the Antichrist he can only empower his partner, the False Prophet, when he is close to him.

The False Prophet will point to the Antichrist as Israel's long-awaited Messiah. Without the knowledge that the Antichrist's name will be equal to 666, the tribulation saints would be deceived into worshipping this messianic impostor. Jesus warned: "For there shall arise false Christs, and false prophets, and shall show great signs and wonders; insomuch that, if it were possible, they shall deceive the very elect" (Matthew 24:24).

Technology May Lead to the Mark

The introduction of automatic teller machines and laser scanning technology (such as we see in grocery stores) gives you some idea of the ease with which such a control system could be implemented. Scanning devices, including high-speed, long distance optical readers, as well as radio-frequency scanners, are now used regularly at government buildings, universities, industrial plants and custom border stations to read the license plate of your car.

Revolutionary new technology is making it feasible for microscopic-sized ID computer chips to be implanted beneath the skin to enable us to prove our identity, complete financial transactions, or communicate wirelessly with our computer or other electrical devices. Dr. Kevin Warwick, a professor and superintendent of the Cybernetics Department at the University of

Reading in England, claims to be the first person in the world to be implanted with a sophisticated computer chip that allows him to communicate remotely with his computer. According to an article in the *Toronto Star* on August 27, 1998, Dr. Warwick experimented on himself by implanting a special highly sophisticated computer chip allowing him to communicate with the university's communications system in order to receive e-mails and other communications by radio transmission to the computer chip surgically implanted beneath the skin of his arm. The device contains a tiny antenna circuit inside a glass capsule that is less than one inch long and one-tenth of an inch wide that communicates to transceivers through radio signals. After being alerted by the computer communications chip implanted in his arm, he walked into his lab and was greeted by the computerized voice of the university communications system that announced: "Good morning, Professor Warwick. You have five new e-mails."[4] Warwick stated, "The potential for implants is enormous. Implants could one day replace credit and bank cards. And businesses could use them like time clocks." Despite their obvious advantages, the professor warns, "One day, you may not even be able to go to the rest room without a machine knowing about it."[5]

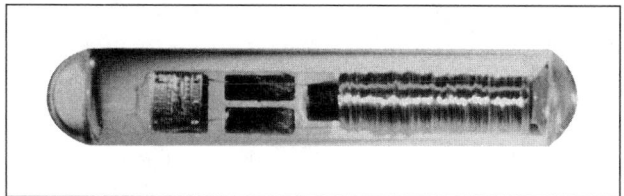

Implantable ID Chip Used in Products or in Humans.

Another astonishing development is called Digital Angel. This new technology involves implanting a radio-frequency computer micro chip beneath the skin that both identifies the carrier and instantly locates them anywhere on the planet through the Global Position Satellite system. Applied Digital Solutions in Palm Beach, Florida is in the telecommunications business and has developed and patented the Digital Angel device (US Patent Num. 5,629,678) as a "personal tracking and recovery system" to assist in locating missing children and prisoners in house arrest programs. It can also monitor the heart rate or other data of medical patients while they are out of the hospital. The company spokesperson says Digital Angel can track lost children, patients, hikers, or other abductees or "military, diplomatic, and other essential government personnel." When implanted, the transceiver is powered electromechanically through the movement of the body's muscles. The device can be powered with micro batteries when used to track valuable objects. The company is looking for further applications of the device in the areas of law enforcement, medical programs, or security. They expect the global market could exceed $100 billion. Marc Rotenberg, director of the Electronic Privacy Information Center in Washington, D.C., warned of the dangers to our privacy and freedom from such Big Brother technology: "It sounds dreadful. That's about as bad as it gets."[6]

The Mark, the Name, and 666

The totalitarian control will involve "the mark, or the name of the beast, or the number of his name." All three of these identifying marks may be used either simultaneously or at different times to identify the worshippers of the Antichrist from those who reject his claims to be god. The mark will be applied to the right hand or forehead of the individual who accepts the Antichrist. One of the reasons for having this "Mark of the Beast" on the forehead instead of on the right hand may be that some individuals may not have a right hand, due to an accident. In addition, if electronic scanners are used to detect the Mark at a distance, a right hand might be out of sight. The forehead will almost always be in plain view. This mark must be something different from the name or the number 666 because scriptures, including Revelation 13:18, mention all three as separate items. We are not told the exact nature of the Mark, but it may be a physical brand on the surface of the skin including either the actual name of the Antichrist or the number 666.

The Mark may also be implanted as a miniature computer micro chip beneath the skin of the right hand or forehead. A powerful electronic scanner could detect the chip and read the vital identification data unobtrusively. While the micro chip and its information would be visible to the scanner, its action and presence will be invisible to the human eye. It is also possible that the different locations of the right hand and forehead may depend on the status of the follower of the Antichrist. Perhaps high-level officials would not have to wear the Mark on their forehead, but would choose rather to wear it on the right hand.

It is possible that the Antichrist might change his birth name to a new name that will become the "name of the beast." The Scriptures record that God changed many of the biblical personalities' names at moments of supreme crisis to reflect their new spiritual condition. Abram was changed to Abraham, Jacob to Israel, and Saul to Paul. For this reason, in addition to the Bible's silence regarding his name, it is futile and worthless to speculate about the name or identify of the Antichrist before he appears. Where God has drawn a veil over a matter in the Scriptures, it is arrogance for a Christian to attempt to reveal it. Those who live through the terrible Great Tribulation will recognize the Antichrist based on his fulfillment of the Bible's prophecies.

It is inevitable that many Greek or Hebrew names will, by chance alone, contain the numeric value 666. In my library of books on prophecy, archeology, and theology, I once compiled a list of over eighty-five different individuals who have been identified over the centuries by Bible scholars and students as the Antichrist. Some have thought the Antichrist will be a reincarnated leader from the past, such as Nimrod, King Ahab, Judas Iscariot, Julius Caesar, Nero, Vespasian, Titus, or Emperor Hadrian. In recent centuries prophetic speculators have identified candidates including Napoleon, various Popes, Kaiser Wilhelm, Adolph Hitler, Mussolini, Henry Kissinger, President Carter, President Reagan, President Bush, President Clinton, President Mikhail Gorbachev, Premier Mao of China, King Juan Carlos, the Hapsburgs, Saddam Hussein, and David Rockefeller. Obviously, these speculations proved to be incorrect. Attempting to identify the Antichrist before he appears is as futile as trying to pick the date for the return of Jesus Christ. The 666 identification will only be relevant for the people living during the Great Tribulation.

Consequences of Receiving the Mark of the Beast

And I heard a great voice out of the temple saying to the seven angels, Go your ways, and pour out the vials of the wrath of God upon the earth. And the first went, and poured out his vial upon the earth; and there fell a noisome and grievous sore upon the men which had the mark of the beast, and upon them which worshipped his image. (Revelation 16:1,2)

The Scriptures record that God hates the Mark of the Beast because He created humans to live in spiritual harmony with Him. Someday God will place His own seal on the forehead of every believer in Heaven, signifying His unbreakable covenant with those who accept Christ as the eternal Lord of their soul. If a man accepts the Antichrist's Mark, his soul will be lost forever. During the Tribulation, horrible skin infections will break out on the people who accept the Mark and worship the Beast. Perhaps these sores will be physically related to the technique used to implant or brand the Mark on their forehead or right hand. More likely, these sores will be the result of the direct supernatural judgment of God upon sinners who worship the Antichrist.

And the third angel followed them, saying with a loud voice, If any man worship the beast and his image, and receive his mark in his forehead, or in his hand, The same shall drink of the wine of the wrath of God, which is poured out without mixture into the cup of his indignation; and he shall be tormented with fire and brimstone in the presence of the holy angels, and in the presence of the Lamb: And the smoke of their torment ascendeth up for ever and ever: and they have no rest day nor night, who worship the beast and his image, and whosoever receiveth the mark of his name. (Revelation 14:9–11)

In addition to the terrible earthly consequences of worshipping the Antichrist, the Scriptures warn that the worst punishment will follow the death of those who choose to wear the Mark. The eternal "wrath of God" will be poured out on those who reject Christ and willingly accept Satan and his Antichrist as their "god."

The Victory of the Martyrs

And I saw thrones, and they sat upon them, and judgment was given unto them: and I saw the souls of them that were beheaded for the witness of Jesus, and for the word of God, and which had not worshipped the beast, neither his image, neither had received his mark upon their foreheads, or in their hands; and they lived and reigned with Christ a thousand years. (Revelation 20:4).

Whoever believes the Word of God and courageously resists the Mark of the Beast during the Great Tribulation will receive the eternal reward of God in Heaven. It will take tremendous courage for the tribulation saints living in that period to reject the Mark when they know it will mean the death of themselves and their families by beheading. However, their choice is ultimately the same as that faced by generations of Christian martyrs for the last two thousand years. Christ commanded, "And fear not them which kill the body, but are not able to kill the soul: but rather fear him which is able to destroy both soul and body in hell"(Matthew 10:28). God's warning to believers to remain faithful has never changed: "But whosoever shall deny me before men, him will I also deny before my Father which is in heaven"(Matthew 10:33). Even today, before the prophesied Great Tribulation begins, hundreds of thousands of Christians die as martyrs for their faith in Jesus every year. These brave tribulation saints of the Tribulation are promised a special position in God's Millennial government of earth. The promise of God is recorded by the prophet John as follows:

I saw the souls of them that were beheaded for the witness of Jesus, and for the word of God, and which had not worshipped the beast, neither his image, neither had received his mark upon their foreheads, or in their hands; and they lived and reigned with Christ a thousand years. (Revelation 20:4)

In the next chapter we will examine the numerous prophecies found in the Scriptures that describe the final cataclysmic Battle of Armageddon. This war will involve all of the armies of every nation on earth and will end with Jesus Christ's total victory over His enemies. Christ will destroy the armies of Satan together with the Antichrist and the False Prophet. Then He will establish His Kingdom of God on earth forever.

Notes

1. Pseudo-Titus Epistle, *New Testament Apocrapha*, Vol. 2 (Philadelphia: The Westminster Press, 1964).

2. *Vajikra Rabba*, Section 29, 1st vol.

3. Andrei Zolotoy, "Tax Numbers Linked to 'Sign of the Beast,'" *National Post*, 12 April 2000.

4. "Computer Chip Implant," *Toronto Star*, 27 August 1998.

5. "Silicon Implants," *Machine Design,* 22 April 1999.

6. Richard Stenger, *"Tiny human-borne monitoring device sparks privacy fears,"* CNN, Washington, 20 Dec. 1999. Internet site http://www.cnn.com/1999/TECH/ptech/12/20/implant.device/index.html

12

The Battle of Armageddon

For thousands of years the word "Armageddon" has instilled fears yet inspired the imagination of millions. While the word itself only appears once in the entire Bible there are hundreds of passages throughout the Scriptures that refer to this cataclysmic battle between the forces of the East and the West. The prophet John wrote, "And he gathered them together into a place called in the Hebrew tongue Armageddon" (Revelation 16:16). The great Battle of Armageddon will occur in northern Israel and extend down the great Valley of Jezreel, below Mt. Carmel and the ancient city of Megiddo. The name Armageddon comes from the Hebrew word *har* for "mountain" and "Megiddo," the name of the ancient city built by King Solomon 3,000 years ago that overlooks this enormous plain. It is also known as the Valley of Jehoshaphat meaning "the Valley of God's judgement." According to Revelation 16:16, this ancient battleground will be the scene of the most devastating military confrontation in human history. While this horrendous world war will involve intense conflict between the armies in Europe, Africa, and Asia, the final battle will occur in the north of Israel.

The final battle between the armies of the Eastern alliance from Asia against the western armies of the nations still loyal to the Antichrist will be focused on a two-hundred-mile-long valley that extends southward from the ancient ruins of Megiddo toward Jerusalem. The battle carnage will be so terrible that horses will sink into the resulting mire of blood, bodies, and mud until the blood reaches "to the horses' bridles" (Revelation 14:19–20). If you have ever seen some of the terrible war photos of soldiers sinking to their chest in the quagmire of blood and mud produced by artillery and modern conventional weapons, you can imagine how this whole fertile valley could turn into a veritable blood bath when the 200-million-man army of the "Kings of the East" attacks the combined armies of the Western nations under the military command of the Antichrist.

Russia will not likely be a major military force at the Battle of Armageddon, due to the fact that its armies will be destroyed in the earlier battle of Gog and Magog, which is prophesied in detail in Ezekiel Chapter 38 and 39. America will probably tend to be somewhat isolationist following the destruction of Russia's military power in their war against Israel. This situation may allow the creation of a political-military power vacuum that would then be filled by a resurgent European superpower under the brilliant leadership of the Antichrist.

The only other major political-military superpower still capable of waging a war to win freedom from the totalitarian government of the Antichrist will be a combination of the vast populations and industrial-military capabilities of China, Southeast Asia, and India, added by the technological and economic leadership of a remilitarized Japan. China and Japan signed a thirty-year treaty of cooperation several years ago. In this new situation, the Antichrist and the revived Roman Empire will have guaranteed Israel's security and her ability to control the flow of oil supplies from the Middle East. From a geopolitical standpoint, Israel's strategic position on the land bridge linking Europe, Africa, and Asia has always made the control of this vital territory essential for a world empire. Whatever power, East or West, that controls Israel and the Middle East oil will ultimately determine the destiny of the world.

The Antichrist will visit his headquarters in Jerusalem at some point in the final years of his rule as world dictator. At that point an alliance of Muslim, African, and Arab nations led by a "King of the South" (Egypt) and another group of rebel nations led by a "King of the North" (probably Syria) will attack the Antichrist's armies. When his forces quickly defeat these initial attacks, his armies will invade and conquer Egypt, Libya, and Ethiopia (Daniel 11:40–43). However, the nations of Asia that deeply resent his totalitarian dictatorship will finally decide that this is the time to attack the Antichrist's armies in Israel in order to win their independence. As these nations in the Far East (China, India, Japan, etc.) and the North (the remaining parts of Russia and the former USSR) begin to mobilize their vast armies for this final battle, the Antichrist will gather all the remaining nations of the West that are still under his dictatorial control, and transport them to Israel to attack the approaching armies of the "Kings of the East" (Daniel 11:44–45). The great river Euphrates will dry up to make it possible for the enormous 200-million-man army to cross over the river to approach northern Israel (Revelation 16:12–16).

John's prophecy that the army of the Asian nations of "the kings of the East" would contain 200 million men was naturally shocking to him (Revelation 9:13–16). The entire population of the Roman Empire in the first century was only approximately 100 million men, women, and children. It was difficult for John, and for many Bible commentators over the centuries, to believe that the Scriptures "literally" meant that one side alone in this titanic Battle of Armageddon would include such an enormous number of soldiers. Until World War II, only twelve battles in human history were fought with more than 50,000 soldiers on both sides. It is only in this century that we have seen the total mobilization of a nation's population and economic resources for war. According to *The War Atlas*, the worldwide arms buildup has now created armies that can field 570 million soldiers when all reserves are called up.[1]

Some writers have mistakenly concluded that the Bible referred to 200 million horsemen. There are less than thirty-five million horses throughout the world. However, a careful reading of Revelation 9:16 reveals that John's use of the word "horsemen" refers to the four horsemen of the Apocalypse, not to the number of actual horsemen in the armies at Armageddon (Revelation 6:1–8). Therefore the prophet John was indicating that the total size of the future army of the four horsemen of the apocalypse will include two hundred million soldiers.

My wife, Kaye, and I visited China in 1986, and had the opportunity to visit Tian'anmen Square, the largest public square in the world, in China's capital, Beijing. We were shocked to find that the reports of the one-child policy in China were true. Out of hundreds of thousands of families out for a Sunday walk, very few young Chinese girls were in sight. At least nine or ten young boys were present for every girl we could see. The result of the rigorously enforced one-child policy in China since 1978 is that up to nine males are born for every female in some of China's provinces. I questioned Chinese officials about the accuracy of these reports. The travel guides, as well as communist officials, confirmed that the 9:1 ratio of boys to girls is a documented fact.

The Chinese population-control authorities have developed several reliable methods to determine the sex of the fetus during the first few months of a pregnancy. Due to the fact that the Chinese couples are only allowed to give birth to one child, many choose to abort a female fetus. Then they attempt to conceive a baby again in the hope that it will be male. If a woman becomes pregnant after having one child, she will be forced to abort it. If she becomes pregnant a third time, she will be forced to undergo abortion and sterilization. Whenever a Chinese couple has a second child, an enormous fine, equal to one year's income, is charged, and other social and employment penalties are applied. Chinese couples want their family name to continue, and naturally desire to benefit from a son's future income to support them in their retirement. A girl will not continue the family name, and will eventually support her husband's parents economically. These reasons motivate Chinese couples to abort female fetuses in favor of a male child.

For thousands of years the male-female balance of human

populations has remained virtually equal. For the first time in history, political decrees, prenatal exams, and economic selfishness have combined to produce an extreme sexual imbalance in the population of the largest nation on earth (China has one-quarter of the world's population). The social, political, and military ramifications of an excess of tens of millions of young men, without any hope of finding wives or the stability of a home, are causing grave concern to the communist political planners in China.

A recent article from Beijing in the *International Herald Tribune*, May 15, 2000, reported that Chinese officials acknowledged China was fighting an unprecedented wave of kidnappings and abductions of woman and girls throughout China. The article announced that security agencies and army troops had rescued over 10,000 women and girls kidnapped during in a five-week campaign between April 1 and May 5, 2000. The Chinese officials admitted that the abductions of women were "skyrocketing" because of "a shortage of women and the desire of many farmers to have sons." The article concluded: "Demographic experts estimate that there are 70 million more men than women in China."[2]

The officials I spoke with in China in 1986 admitted that the one-child policy was essential to avoid potential famines in China. However, this unexpected inequality between boys and girls was already acknowledged in communist party meetings as potentially the greatest social problem that China would face in the new millennium. Today China has an existing population of 1.3 billion people. The growing imbalance of boys to girls will produce a situation unprecedented in human history. By the year 2005, it is estimated that China will have an excess of one hundred million Chinese boys and young men, with no girls or young women for them to marry and no prospects of their ever having a family of their own. This same phenomenon is now being reported in India, Korea, and other Asian countries. When these young men are of military age, and are added to the standing armies and military reserves that these populous countries already possess, the biblical prophecy of a 200-million-man army from the "Kings of the East" is not only literally possible, it is virtually certain to become a military factor facing the nations of the West.

At the conclusion of the climactic Battle of Armageddon, Jesus Christ will return from Heaven with His heavenly army (the millions of saints described in Jude 14-15) and His angels and will destroy the armies of the nations that have joined in an alliance to destroy Israel and each other. Christ will destroy the Antichrist, the False Prophet, and their armies as well as the military forces of the Kings of the East. The Lord will defend Jerusalem and rescue all those who repent and call upon His Name for protection (Zechariah 12:1–9). Jesus Christ will visibly return in glory at Armageddon as the "King of Kings and Lord of Lords" and will set up His Kingdom on earth forever (Revelation 19:11–16).

Wars and Rumors of Wars

In the prophecy given to His disciples on the Mount of Olives, Jesus Christ warned, "And ye shall hear of wars and rumours of wars: see that ye be not troubled: for all these things must come to pass, but the end is not yet. For nation shall rise against nation, and kingdom against kingdom. . . ." (Matthew 24:6–7). Twenty-five centuries ago, the prophet Joel received a divine vision concerning this final conflict. He prophesied the following ominous message: "Proclaim ye this among the Gentiles; Prepare war, wake up the mighty men, let all the men of war draw near; let them come up. Beat your plow shares into swords, and your pruning hooks into spears: let the weak say, 'I am strong'" (Joel 3:9–10). Throughout history mankind has endured thirteen years of war for every single year of peace. However, since 1945 the number of wars has increased tremendously. As dozens of new nations demanded independence and old empires disintegrated, more than three hundred and fifty wars were fought since World War II.

The War Atlas, a military study, concluded that the world has not known a single day since World War II without some nation waging war or conflict somewhere on earth. Despite thousands of negotiations and signed peace treaties, the past century was truly "the century of war." As a result of the obvious dangers to national security, most nations throughout the world have joined global military alliances to protect themselves. Far more sobering than the increasing frequency of war is the fact that modern scientific weapons research and enormous military budgets have combined to produce new devastating weapons of mass destruction that have the potential to totally destroy humanity. Despite the repeated proclamations of the politicians about their desire for peace, weapons labs and defense industries are producing enormous amounts of sophisticated new nuclear, chemical, and biological weapons, as well as staggering numbers of conventional weapons in virtually every nation on earth. The standing armies of the world today contain hundreds of millions of soldiers. The major powers could mobilize and quickly train hundreds of millions of additional troops from national guard divisions and military reserves if needed for world war.

According to the report *Reshaping International Order* issued by the Club of Rome, almost 50 percent (some 500,000) of all of the scientists on earth today are working on advanced weapons research. Almost 40 percent of all scientific research funding throughout the world is now focused on advanced weapons research. The international arms trade now exceeds *one trillion dollars annually*. If only a small fraction of this enormous investment was redirected "from swords into plowshares" we could permanently solve the Third World's food, sanitation, and health problems within a few years.[3]

The huge armament factories of Russia, China, and the Western nations are producing sophisticated weaponry at a truly awesome rate. China has now become the world's fifth-largest weapons supplier — after Russia, the United States, Britain, and France — selling some $3 billion annually. Chinese-manufactured weapons are often direct copies of either Western or Russian arms, but they are much cheaper. China is now fueling a massive arms race in the Middle East, with enormous sales of sophisticated tactical missiles, advanced warheads, and low-cost "knock-off" copies of more expensive but still efficient Russian rifles, tanks, and planes.

China has recently sold more tanks to poor African nations than all western countries combined. A poor African nation can buy four Chinese T-59 tanks for the price of one American M-1 tank. China and Korea are also selling intermediate-range missile systems to many Arab regimes that are preparing for war with Israel. Iraq,

Iran, Syria, and Libya now possess long-range missiles capable of destroying Paris or London with biological or chemical warheads. Unlike America or the European arms suppliers, China makes no demands on how the purchasers use their weapons. For the first time since the Middle Ages, Europe faces a formidable and immediate military threat from the Muslim Arab world. Unfortunately, many of these leaders are absolutely committed to the destruction of Jews, Christians, or Muslims.

Despite dozens of years of peace negotiations between the PLO, the Arab states, and Israel, none of the fundamental underlying reasons for war have been eliminated by the peace process and agreements that have been agreed to so far. These tensions in the Middle East may soon develop into a devastating war. This coming war may well include the use of nuclear, chemical, and biological weapons. To put the strategic military situation in perspective, the twenty-one Arab nations surrounding Israel have accumulated more than three times the number of artillery pieces and tanks possessed by the combined European armies of NATO. The United States has sold staggering amounts of sophisticated Abram's M1 tanks, advanced anti-tank missiles, advanced communications systems, and the most effective F-16 fighter planes in the American arsenal to the Arab states who remain publicly dedicated to the total destruction of population of the Jewish state. The Arab nations have no significant military enemies other than the tiny state of Israel. The territory of the Arab nations is more than five hundred times larger than the land of the Jewish state.

Since World War II, NATO built the largest and most sophisticated military alliance in history in order to confront the millions of soldiers, tanks, planes, missiles and artillery of the massive Warsaw Pact armies of Russia, the fourteen nations of the former Soviet Union, and the occupied nations of eastern Europe. However, the Arab nations, confronting the tiny nation of Israel (with a population of only six million), have amassed huge armies that exceed NATO's military forces by more than a million soldiers. The only rational reason for the Arab states to devote such huge economic, technical, and human resources to their military forces is their fundamental commitment to annihilate the Jews of Israel.

Israel now faces combined Arab armies far larger than the present combined armies of North America and Europe, who make up the forces of the NATO alliance.

Israel cannot agree to surrender the military control of the strategically vital high mountains in the West Bank. If the armies of the PLO and the surrounding Arab nations ever control the high mountainous region of the West Bank of Israel in a future war, they could easily launch an invasion across the remaining narrow band of land along the Mediterranean Sea connecting northern and southern Israel. The narrow strip of flat coastal land connecting northern and southern Israel at its most narrow point, is only nine miles wide between the West Bank and the Mediterranean Sea. Israel's military control of the strategic depth of the West Bank is therefore essential to absorb and withstand the combined Arab tank and infantry force assault. Several military studies by the US Joint Chiefs of Staff have concluded that if Israel ever surrenders military control of the West Bank, the Arab armies would be able to cut Israel in two within a few hours using their overwhelming armored tank forces. If Israel surrenders the military control of the West Bank to Arafat and the PLO, and allows the creation of a Palestinian state, Israel will not survive the coming war with the combined Arab armies. UN Security Resolution 242, the resolution that governs the continuing peace negotiations, guaranteed that Israel would retain "recognized and secure borders." If Israel loses military control of the West Bank, she cannot survive the next war. Without the strategic control of the West Bank and the Golan Heights in the north, Israel may be forced to resort to its nuclear weapons almost immediately, following a powerful Arab attack.

Today the Middle East is awash in imported armaments. Even the poorest of the Third World countries borrow hundreds of millions of dollars annually to buy huge supplies of modern, sophisticated weapons. As a result of this cycle of weapons build-up, there is now more than one military weapon and the equivalent of thousands of pounds of explosives for every man, woman, and child worldwide. Consider the destructive power possessed by the thirty Trident submarines representing only one-third of the US triad of sea–land–air-based nuclear arsenal. At a cost of $3 billion each, every one of these powerful submarines can fire twenty-four missiles with up to fourteen individually targeted D5 warheads per missile. These incredibly sophisticated and super-accurate missiles can deliver their thermonuclear warheads from a submerged ocean location up to ten thousand miles away. They have the ability to detonate within one hundred yards of their designated target. Every Trident D5 nuclear warhead is at least five times more powerful than the atomic bomb that devastated Hiroshima. Every one of these thirty Trident submarines has the capability to destroy 408 separate enemy cities or military bases within any enemy nation. Russia, China, the United Kingdom, France, India, Pakistan, and Israel all have nuclear capabilities that are devastating although they are much less powerful than America.

It is hard to comprehend, but one single Trident submarine can deliver more devastation than all of the combined weapons used by both the Allied forces and Germany during five years of warfare during World War II. The tragic history of thousands of years of warfare suggests that these nuclear weapons will ultimately be used in a future conflict. For thousands of years mankind has engaged in deadly warfare. However, throughout the last five thousand years of recorded history, most battles involved only a few thousand participants. Formerly, nations lacked the means of totally destroying the enemy nation. However, our century has perfected the art of total warfare by which all nations unite with allies and commit the total resources of the country to annihilate the opponent and obtain unconditional surrender.

The total military spending of all nations combined now exceeds one trillion dollars every year, according to the US Arms Control and Disarmament Agency. It is difficult to comprehend the true magnitude of one trillion dollars that humanity now invests annually in preparation for total war. To put this in perspective, the cost of a single Exocet air-to-ship missile exceeds the combined annual income of more than ten thousand people in most Third World countries. Massive military spending has distorted our economic priorities. For example, most Western developed countries are spending less than one-half of one percent of their annual military budgets on foreign aid to help the poorest people on earth. More than 200 million people have died as a result of warfare in the last century. Since 1945, ten nations, including Israel, have accumulated more than sixty thousand atomic warheads in their growing nuclear arsenals.

In the book of Revelation Jesus Christ prophesied that the Antichrist's armies, represented by the red horseman of the Apocalypse, will ride forth to destroy many nations during the Great Tribulation (Revelation 6:3–4). Surely, even now, we can hear his approaching hoof beats.

In the Gospel of Matthew, Jesus Christ warned His followers, "For then shall be great tribulation, such as was not since the beginning of the world to this time, no, nor ever shall be. And except those days should be shortened, there should no flesh be saved: but for the elect's sake those days shall be shortened" (Matthew 24: 21–22). When you consider the enormous problems facing humanity — disease, famine, ecological disaster, and millions of homeless people — we must recognize the terrible moral vacuum at the core of the leadership of our modern western and eastern nations. Despite the overwhelming problems facing the billions of people in deep poverty throughout the world, the leadership of our nation continue to choose to spend billions of dollars annually on the tools of war, rather than solve the serious problems facing humanity.

Billions of people throughout the world are crying out for real peace, but no rational nation dares to disarm before its enemy does the same. Jesus Christ described the final conflict that faces mankind in these words: "Upon the earth distress of nations, with perplexity; . . . men's hearts failing them for fear, and for looking after those things which are coming on the earth: for the powers of heaven shall be shaken" (Luke 21: 25–26).

Since the breakup of the communist-controlled Soviet Union in 1991, the Russians and American military have engaged in a complex series of disarmament treaties that have produced a wave of euphoria among millions of people worldwide. These people hope that true peace is finally at hand. According to the historical research of author Sidney Lens, there have been more than six thousand disarmament negotiating sessions since 1945. Despite these thousands of treaties, very few nuclear bombs were ever actually destroyed. Unfortunately, most arms treaties allowed each super power to take the older nuclear warheads and simply reuse them as warheads of new, more accurate missiles, much more destructive than the original weapon.

The Scriptures prophesy that the world will experience a devastating world war involving all nations during the last days. The second red horseman of the Apocalypse represents this terrible world war during the final years of the seven-year Tribulation period. "And when he had opened the second seal, I heard the second beast say, Come and see. And there went our another horse that was red; and power was given to him that sat thereon to take peace from the earth, and that they should kill one another; and there was given unto him a great sword" (Revelation 6: 3–4). Daniel and John both predicted that the nations of the world would ultimately surrender their sovereignty to the Antichrist in the hope that he would provide security and true peace.

A large number of politicians of key nations throughout the world have abandoned belief in their nation's sovereignty and now believe that the only way to prevent a devastating world war is for every nation to surrender its sovereignty to a future world government. The Scriptures warn that the earth will never know true peace until the Prince of Peace comes. Although men are desperately seeking peace, the Antichrist will only be able to produce a short period of false peace. The prophet John revealed that the First Horseman of the Apocalypse would be a rider on a white horse with a bow, but no arrows. This symbol represents the Antichrist impersonating the true Prince of Peace, Jesus Christ, who will appear riding on a white horse during His triumphant return to earth (Revelation 19). John prophesied: "I looked, and behold, a white horse. And he who sat on it had a bow; and a crown was given to him, and he went out conquering and to conquer." The Antichrist will use men's deep longing for peace "to conquer" the nations of the world and force them to join his growing world government.

In his speech to the University of Georgia forum on terrorism, US Defense Secretary William Cohen warned that the Internet is now providing a medium for terrorists to widely distribute both instructions for building bombs and racist propaganda. He called for increased vigilance against terrorist use of unconventional chemical and biological weapons (including the deadly Ebola River Virus) that are now available to these terrorist groups. In addition, he warned ominously about the dangers presented by new electromagnetic weapons that might be used by terrorists or rogue Islamic nations to "punch holes in the ozone layer or trigger earthquakes or volcanoes" (*Toronto Star*, April 29, 1997).

The 1972 Biological Weapons Convention absolutely prohibited the developing, producing, and stockpiling of biological and chemical weapons by any nation. However, many Third World countries are now spending enormous sums to acquire deadly chemical and biological weapons (CBW). Most of the world's nations, including Russia and the United States, have ratified this peace agreement. However, many nations are secretly developing deadly biological and chemical weapons that will devastate unprotected populations in a future conflict. Some future dictator may be tempted to use these deadly CBW weapons because of their low cost and their ability to be used secretly. These chemical and biological weapons are a tempting alternative for a Third World nation, compared to the enormous cost of developing a huge conventional army or producing a sophisticated nuclear capability. Some researchers have described biological and chemical weapons as the "poor man's nuclear bomb."

Syria, Iraq, Egypt, and Iran are rapidly developing their own advanced chemical weapons programs. Libya recently built two huge chemical and biological weapons plants located deep within the mountains at the edge of the southern Libyan desert. Over sixty German and Swiss companies have provided extensive chemical engineering services and the sophisticated laboratory equipment required to modify Libya's Russian-built SCUD missiles to carry chemical warheads. Many of these same European companies built Iraq's chemical weapons facilities before and after the Gulf

War and are still willing to sell their technological soul to the highest bidder.

During the War in the Gulf, President Saddam Hussein of Iraq threatened to "burn half of Israel" with his advanced chemical weapons supplied by European countries. Despite his defeat in the war in the Gulf, and the continued UN sanctions, Saddam Hussein has now totally rebuilt his army. Over ten thousand Russian nuclear scientists and technicians continue to develop Iraq's secret nuclear arsenal despite the presence of UN arms inspectors. Chemical weapons were seldom employed in past wars, partly because of the universal repugnance against their use. Unfortunately, chemical weapons have proven to be both effective and deadly. In World War I chemical weapons killed almost one hundred thousand soldiers in Europe. In the Vietnam War, America unleashed hundreds of tons of chemical weapons, including herbicides such as Agent Orange, on Viet Cong areas in an attempt to defoliate the jungle cover. President Saddam Hussein repeatedly used massive amounts of chemical weapons against Iranian soldiers in the eight-year Iran–Iraq War.

President Hussein launched a devastating chemical attack against the Kurdish minority living in the north of Iraq. His troops killed over 13,000 villagers in the northern provinces of his country. The American soldiers occupying southern Iraq after the end of the Gulf War discovered over one hundred thousand Iraqi chemical artillery shells that were ready for immediate use. Tragically, tens of thousands of American troops were exposed to these exploding chemical weapons when US soldiers blew up Iraqi chemical warheads following the western allied victory. In addition, recent medical evidence suggests that all American troops were vaccinated with new and complex vaccines to protect them against the possibility of chemical and biological warfare from Iraq. Unfortunately, numerous reports suggest that hundreds of thousands of troops were adversely affected by exposure to vaccines given to US troops.

In addition, many intelligence reports from Afghanistan and Cambodia confirm that chemical and biological weapons were used under Russian control during those conflicts. Despite the 1925

Geneva Protocol against chemical and biological warfare, many nations have stockpiled enormous quantities of these biological and chemical doomsday weapons in case they are needed in a future conflict. Virtually every nation in the West has also developed its own stockpile of these deadly biological and chemical weapons munitions to protect themselves against their enemies.

Russia's military laboratories have developed a dangerous new variant of the deadly anthrax toxin that is impervious to previous antibiotics. A report from *Jane's Land Based Air Defence 1997–1998* revealed that there is a growing danger from the biological and chemical weapons buildup from numerous nations that are involved in conflicts that are likely to break out into open warfare at some future point of time. Historically, anthrax has been a fatal disease affecting primarily sheep and cows. However, if anthrax infects humans, they will die an agonizing death characterized by festering boils and severe pain. In addition, the report claims that Russian defectors admitted that three new nerve gases were recently developed that can be made easily from commonly available chemicals. The authoritative Jane's report entitled *Jane's Land Based Air Defence 1997–1998* clearly declared: "It only needs this, or the new chemical nerve agents, to be independently discovered by an ostracized nation's scientists and then developed for missile delivery for an Armageddon situation to occur whereby the only reliable retribution may well be overwhelming nuclear response" (*Toronto Star*, April 4, 1997).

All of these nations conduct their chemical-weapons research based on the clause in the 1925 Geneva Protocol agreement that allows a country limited research for "defensive" purposes. However, it is impossible to verify whether research on a new chemical or biological weapon in a secret research laboratory is truly defensive or offensive. Israel has developed over three hundred nuclear weapons over the last few decades, including sophisticated neutron bombs that are capable of destroying their targets with powerful nuclear radiation that would destroy all biological life without creating a large explosion. Today Israel is surrounded by twenty-one powerfully armed Arab states with virtually unlimited military budgets and over two hundred million people. Naturally Israel prefers to rely on her own control of her nuclear arms rather than trust that the United States would ever risk its own national survival against a credible threat to destroy the Jewish state with nuclear, chemical, or biological weapons in a future military confrontation in the Middle East.

The continued acquisition of Russian and North Korean nuclear, biological, and chemical scientists by the nations of the Middle East that are committed to an absolute war to the death with the Jewish population of Israel represents an unprecedented threat to the existence of the Promised Land in these last days.

Over fifteen Third World countries (including Cuba, Libya, North Korea, Iraq, and Iran) will soon join the exclusive nuclear club by the year 2000. Each of these nations will possess its own nuclear armed ballistic missiles capable of using nuclear, biological, and chemical weapons within a few years, in addition to the 20,000 remaining nuclear warheads in Russia that are still aimed at the cities of the West. Many of the militant Islamic leaders openly declare their goal to achieve the destruction of both Israel and America, who they identify as the "great Satan."

For the last fifteen years these Muslim states, including Libya, Iran, Syria, and Iraq, have spent untold billions of dollars in a desperate attempt to acquire the nuclear warheads that would allow them to destroy both Israel and her strongest ally, America. Despite these well-known threats, the president and Congress have refused to fund a realistic strategic defense against incoming missiles. Intelligence sources in Europe confirm that the Russians have sold advanced nuclear missile technology to North Korea, enabling them to produce their own nuclear weapons. North Korea has already sold this nuclear technology to Iraq, Iran, Syria, and Libya. Many of the nations of the fifteen-nation Arab alliance facing Israel are now desperately trying to develop or purchase nuclear warheads from the nations of the former Soviet Union. The tragedy we face today is that every single arms race in history ultimately resulted in the use of these weapons, regardless of the devastating consequences. The continued arms buildup in America involves every nation in the national web-sites including Russia, the United Kingdom, Canada, India, Pakistan, Japan, China, the Middle

East, and the Third World. The world's nations are setting the stage for the final Battle of Armageddon that will drench the world in blood.

The Armies of Armageddon

An enormous number of biblical prophecies that deal with the Antichrist and the climactic Battle of Armageddon will soon be fulfilled. At the end of this age, Christ will defeat the Antichrist's armies and establish His eternal kingdom. The Antichrist will establish his kingdom on earth forever; Jesus Christ will establish His kingdom on earth forever. The prophet John described the ultimate location of the final battle in this final war between the western armies of the Antichrist and the eastern armies of the Kings of the East.

A Military Highway Across Southern Asia

In the book of Revelation the prophet John foretold his prophetic vision about the future details of the Battle of Armageddon and the involvement of the many nations of the East. "And the sixth angel poured out his vial upon the great river Euphrates; and the water thereof was dried up, that the way of the kings of the east might be prepared" (Revelation 16:12).

John foretold in Revelation that the gentile nations would build a future military highway across Asia, from East to West, to make it possible for this army to march toward the final battle in Israel. John appears to refer to the building of this highway in these words: "The way of the kings of the east might be prepared" (Revelation 16:12). The Chinese government has spent enormous sums and expended the lives of many thousands of construction workers to build a military super-highway across Asia, heading directly toward Israel. This highway has no economic purpose, and no foreigners are allowed anywhere near this road. The highway has been built at a staggering cost in money and lives through the extremely rugged terrain across the southwestern provinces of China and through Tibet, Pakistan, and Afghanistan. This unusual prophecy about "the way of the kings of the east" is being fulfilled in our day. It is one of the essential requirements for the final battle of this age.

The Drying Up of the Euphrates River

In the book of Revelation John prophesied that the Euphrates River would dry up, enabling the enormous army of two hundred million soldiers to cross from Asia into the Middle East to invade Israel. The Euphrates River has been an almost impenetrable military barrier between East and West. However, the government of Turkey recently constructed the huge Ataturk Dam that can now block the headwaters of the Euphrates River for the first time. For thousands of years the river Euphrates has stood as a great military barrier between East and West. It runs for over a thousand miles from its source in the mountains of Turkey until it runs into the sea at the Persian Gulf. Its width varies from a few hundred feet to over a mile in various places.

The prophets foretold that the great river Euphrates, which has run continuously since man's creation, will someday dry up to allow the army of "the Kings of the East" to cross it on their march toward northern Israel. John prophesied, "Then the sixth angel poured out his bowl on the great river Euphrates, and its water was dried up, so that the way of the kings from the east might be prepared"(Revelation 16:12). Several years ago a mammoth construction project, the Ataturk Dan, was completed in Turkey. When the President of Turkey pressed a button, the dam closed and the flow of water in the great Euphrates River dropped more than 75 percent. For the first time in history, the Euphrates River can be blocked exactly as this ancient prophecy of Revelation foretold almost two thousand years ago.

The prophet John warned: "Loose the four angels which are bound in the great river Euphrates. And the four angels were loosed, which were prepared for an hour, and a day, and a month, and a year, for to slay the third part of men. And the number of the army of the horsemen were two hundred thousand thousand: and I heard the number of them" (Revelation 9:14–16).

The Scriptures reveal that when the terrible Battle of Armageddon is over Jesus Christ will defeat the forces of Satan and will save

Israel from the threat of destruction. Christ will then establish His righteous kingdom over the world forever.

The prophet John described the final victory of Jesus Christ over all of His enemies:

> And I saw heaven opened, and behold a white horse; and he that sat upon him was called Faithful and True, and in righteousness he doth judge and make war. His eyes were as a flame of fire, and on his head were many crowns; and he had a name written, that no man knew, but he himself. And he was clothed with a vesture dipped in blood: and his name is called The Word of God. And the armies which were in heaven followed him upon white horses, clothed in fine linen, white and clean. And out of his mouth goeth a sharp sword, that with it he should smite the nations: and he shall rule them with a rod of iron: and he treadeth the wine press of the fierceness and wrath of Almighty God. And he hath on his vesture and on his thigh a name written, King of Kings and Lord of Lords. (Revelation 19:11–20)

Notes

1. Michael Kidron and Dan Smith, *The War Atlas* (London: Pan Books Ltd., 1983).

2. "China Foils Kidnappers," *International Herald Tribune*, 15 May 2000.

3. Antony J. Dolman, ed., *Reshaping International Order* (New York: New American Library, 1976).

13

Humanity at the Crossroads

The evidence presented in *Surveillance Society* reveals that thousands of years ago the Scriptures prophesied that the nations would join into a world government in the last days. Furthermore, the prophets predicted that the ancient Roman Empire would be revived in the end times in a super state composed of ten nations. Finally, the Bible foretold the rise of a world dictator who would somehow be able to control the actions and allegiance of everyone on earth, whether "small and great, rich and poor, free and bond." For the first time in human history these prophecies are about to be fulfilled as the new surveillance technologies allow totalitarian governments to monitor the actions and economic activities of each citizen. Humanity stands today at a crossroads. The decisions made by individuals and government leaders will determine whether the astonishing new technologies will be used to improve the lot of mankind or whether these remarkable devices will be used to enslave us in a totalitarian nightmare that will only end when the Lord Jesus Christ returns from Heaven to defeat the forces of the coming Antichrist. Those who love their freedom and privacy need to become aware of the growing dangers and alert their democratic representatives to the potential of these technologies and policies to destroy our precious freedom and privacy.

Jesus Christ warned His disciples: "When ye shall see all these things, know that it is near, even at the doors. Verily I say unto you, This generation shall not pass, till all these things be fulfilled" (Matthew 24: 33–34). In the preceding pages, attention has been focused on the remarkable technology of surveillance, and the economic, political, and military trends that are rushing us toward the world government described in the Word of God. As we turn to examine our personal future, we can see that these same incredibly accurate Scriptures prophesied that every one of us will face our personal appointment with God. The writer of the book of Hebrews wrote about our personal destiny: "It is appointed unto men once to die, but after this the judgment" (Hebrews 9:27).

The apostle Paul said that God "Now commandeth all men every where to repent:

> because he hath appointed a day, in the which he will judge the world in righteousness by that man whom he hath ordained; whereof he hath given assurance unto all men, in that he hath raised him from the dead" (Acts 17: 30–31).

Every one of us will someday come face to face with Jesus Christ to give an account of what decision we have made regarding our relationship with Him. Every one of us has rebelled against God and sinned throughout our lives. The apostle Paul wrote, "For all have sinned, and come short of the glory of God" (Romans 3:23). The consequences of our choice to sinfully rebel against God is that we have become unfit to enter Heaven. God's Word declares, "For the wages of sin is death; but the gift of God is eternal life through Jesus Christ our Lord" (Romans 6:23). The Scriptures declare that our sinful rebellion has alienated each of us from the holiness of God. Continued rebellion and rejection of Christ will prevent us from ever entering Heaven until our sins are forgiven by God.

The sacrificial death of Jesus Christ on the cross is the key to bringing us to a place of true peace in our hearts. The death of our old sinful nature, as we identify with Christ's death on the cross, is the key to finding true peace with God. Jesus asked His disciples this vital question, "'Who do you say that I am?' Simon Peter answered, 'You are the Christ, the Son of the living God'" (Matthew 16:15–16). Every one of us must answer that same question for ourselves. If the Bible truly is the Word of God, your answer to that question will determine your eternal destiny. Each of us must answer that question. We cannot evade it. If we refuse to answer, we have already rejected Christ's claims to be our Savior.

According to God's Word, the choices we make in this life will have eternal consequences in the next. The apostle Paul wrote: "For it is written, As I live, saith the Lord, every knee shall bow to me, and every tongue shall confess to God. So then every one of us shall give account of himself to God" (Romans 14:11–12). Someday every human will bow their knee to Jesus Christ and acknowledge Him as Almighty God. The question is: Will you choose to repent of your sins now and bow your knee willingly to your Savior and Lord? Or, will you reject His offer of salvation today and finally be forced by His majesty to bow your knee before your final Judge as you are sent to an eternity in Hell?

When we meet Jesus Christ on Judgment Day, everyone will know whether we accepted or rejected His precious gift of salvation. When Jesus was crucified on the Cross, He paid the complete price of our sins. His final statement before His death was: "It is finished." As the sinless Lamb of God, Jesus allowed Himself to be offered as a perfect sacrifice to pay the price of our sins and to reconcile each of us to God. However, in a manner similar to a pardon offered to a prisoner awaiting execution, each of us must repent of our sins and personally accept Christ's pardon for His salvation to become effective. The New Testament declared, "We shall all stand before the judgment seat of Christ" (Romans 14:10). The basis of God's judgment following our death will be our personal relationship with Jesus Christ — not whether we were better or worse than most other people — this alone will determine our eternal destiny.

One of the righteous religious leaders of Israel, Nicodemus, came to Jesus and asked Him about how he could be certain of his future salvation. Jesus answered in these words, "Verily, verily, I say unto thee, Except a man be born again, he cannot see the kingdom of God" (John 3:3). It isn't simply a matter of intellectually accepting the facts about Christ and salvation. To be "born again" you must sincerely repent of your sinful life, asking Christ to forgive you and to wholeheartedly trust in Him for the rest of your life. This decision will transform your life forever. God will give you new purpose and meaning. The Lord promises believers eternal life in Heaven: "This is the will of Him who sent Me, that everyone who sees the Son and believes in Him may have everlasting life; and I will raise him up at the last day" (John 6:40). The moment a person commits his life to Christ, he receives eternal life. Though your body will die, you will live forever with Christ in heaven. Jesus explained to Nicodemus, "For God so loved the world, that he gave his only begotten Son, that whosoever believeth in him should not perish, but have everlasting life" (John 3:16).

Jesus said, "He that believeth in him is not condemned: but he that believeth not is condemned already, because he hath not believed in the name of the only begotten Son of God" (John 3:18). After thirty-five years of studying the accuracy of fulfilled prophecy in the Bible, I am convinced that the Bible is the inspired Word of God. Therefore, I believe the words of Jesus Christ, "I am the way, the truth, and the life. No one comes to the Father except through Me" (John 14:6). God declares in these inspired words that there is no other road to salvation than accepting the "way," the "truth," and the "life" of Jesus Christ.

God demands perfect holiness and righteousness. However, it is obvious that no one can meet these requirements on their own merit. Since God could never ignore the fact that we have all sinned against Him, it was necessary that someone who was perfect and sinless should pay the penalty of physical and spiritual death as a substitute for us. The only person who could qualify was Jesus Christ, the Holy Son of God.

Christ's sacrificial gift of His life on the cross paid the price for our sins. Every one of us, by accepting His pardon, can now stand before the judgment seat of God clothed in Christ's righteousness: "For he hath made him [Jesus] to be sin for us, who knew no sin; that we might be made the righteousness of God in Him" (2 Corinthians 5:21). This fact of Christ's atonement is perhaps the greatest mystery in creation. Jesus is the only one in history who, by His sinless life, was qualified to enter Heaven. Yet He loved each one of us so much that He chose to die upon that cross to purchase our salvation. In a marvelous act of God's mercy, the righteousness of Jesus is placed to our account with God.

It will cost you a great deal to live as a committed Christian today. Many people will challenge your faith in the Bible and in Christ. The Lord Jesus Christ asks His disciples to "follow Me." Your decision and commitment to Jesus Christ will change your life forever. However, your commitment to Christ will release His supernatural grace and power to transform your life into one of joy and peace beyond anything you have ever experienced. While the decision to follow Christ will cost you much, it will cost you far more if you do not accept Him as your Savior before you die. Jesus challenges us with these words, "For what shall it profit a man, if he shall gain the whole world, and lose his own soul?" (Mark 8:36).

All those who have accepted Christ are called to be "witnesses" of Christ's message to our world. To be a faithful witness to Christ demands an active, not passive, involvement in the life of our Christian brothers and sisters. It requires a willingness to pay the price of a personal commitment to our coming Messiah. Our belief in the imminent Second Coming of Christ should motivate us to witness to our unsaved brothers and sisters about His salvation. This belief in the Second Coming will purify our walk before the Lord. The apostle John wrote, "And everyone who has this hope in Him purifies himself, just as He is pure" (1 John 3:3). If you are a Christian, I challenge you to share the evidence in this book to witness to your friends and family about your faith in Jesus Christ.

As the prophetic clock ticks on toward the final midnight hour, the invitation of Christ is still open:

> Behold, I stand at the door, and knock: If any man hear my voice, and open the door, I will come in to him, and will sup with him and he with me. (Revelation 3:20).

Many of the readers of this book have already chosen to follow the Lord; I encourage you to obey the Great Commission of our Lord and Savior. In Matthew 28:19–20, Jesus commanded, "Go therefore and make disciples of all the nations, baptizing them in the name of the Father and of the Son and of the Holy Spirit, teaching them to observe all things that I have commanded you; and lo, I am with you always, even to the end of the age." Our knowledge of the nearness of the return of Jesus Christ should awaken a renewed love of Christ and a passion to witness to those around us while there is still time. I have written this book, and my previous books, to introduce non-believers to faith in Christ and to encourage Christians in their faith. In addition, my goal is to provide believers with books that they can give to their friends and neighbors who do not yet have a personal faith in Christ. The incredible events of the last decade are causing many to ask what lies ahead for the earth. There is a growing fascination in North America with Bible prophecies regarding the last days. This tremendous interest in prophecy presents us with a great opportunity to witness to those around us who do not yet know Christ as their personal Savior.

Selected Bibliography

Adams, James. *Secret Armies*. London: Pan Books, 1988.

Algosaibi, Ghazi A. *The Gulf Crisis*. London: Kegan Paul International, 1993.

Anderson, Robert. *The Coming Prince*. London: Hodder & Stroughton, 1894.

Arendt, Hannah. *The Origins of Totalitarianism*. Cleveland: The Word Publishing Company, 1969.

Armerding, Carl Edwin, and W. Ward Gasque. *Dreams, Visions and Oracles*. Grand Rapids: Baker Book House, 1977.

Attali, Jacques. *Millennium*. Trans. Leila Conners and Nathan Gardels. New York: Times Books, 1990.

Auerbach, Leo. *The Babylonian Talmud*. New York: Philosophical Library, 1944.

Bamford, James. *The Puzzle Place*. Middlesex: Penguin Books, 1987.

Barnes, Albert. *Notes on the Book of Daniel*. New York: Leavitt & Allen, 1855.

Baylee, Rev. Joseph. *The Times of the Gentiles*. London: James Nisbet & Co., 1871.

Begich, Nick, and James Roderick. *Earth Rising — The Revolution.* Anchorage: Earthpulse Press, 2000.

Bernstein, Richard, and Ross H. Munro. *The Coming Conflict with China.* New York: Alfred A. Knopf, 1997.

Besant, Walter, and E. H. Palmer. *Jerusalem.* London: Chatto & Windus, 1908.

Blackstone, Wm. E. *Jesus is Coming.* London: Fleming H. Revell Co., 1908.

Blackstone, Wm. E. *The Millennium.* New York: Revell Publishing Co., 1918.

Boutflower, Charles. *In and Around the Book of Daniel.* Grand Rapids: Kregel Publications, 1977.

Bowen, William M., Jr. *Globalism: America's Demise.* Shreveport: Huntington House Inc., 1984.

Bradley, John. *World War III — Strategies, Tactics and Weapons.* New York: Cresent Books, 1982.

Bresler, Fenton. *Interpol.* Toronto: Penguin Books, 1992.

Brown, Lester R., et al. *State of the World.* New York: W. W. Norton & Company, 1997.

Brown, Rebecca. *Prepare for War.* New Kensington: Whitaker House, 1992.

Bullinger, E. W. *The Apocalypse.* London: Eyre & Spottiswoode, 1909.

Bultema, Harry. *Commentary on Daniel.* Grand Rapids: Kregel Publications, 1988.

Burkett, Larry. *The Coming Economic Earthquake.* Chicago: Moody Press, 1991.

Burstein, Daniel. *Euroquake.* New York: Simon & Schuster, 1991.

Calder, Nigel. *Unless Peace Comes.* Victoria: Penguin Books, 1968.

Cantelon, Willard. *Money Master of the World.* Plainfield: Logos International, 1976.

Cetron, Marvin, and Owen Davies. *Crystal Globe*. New York: St. Martin's Press, 1991.

Childers, Erskine, and Brian Urquhart. *Renewing the United Nations System*. Uppsala: Dag Hammarskjold Foundation, 1994.

Cook, Terry L. *The Mark of the New World Order*. Indianapolis: Virtue International Publishing, 1996.

Cuddy, Dennis Laurence. *Now is the Dawning of the New Age New World Order*. Oklahoma City: Hearthstone Publishing Ltd., 1991.

Culver, Robert Duncan. *Daniel and the Latter Days*. Chicago: Moody Press, 1977.

Davidson, John. *Discourses on Prophecy*. London: John Murray & Co., 1825.

de Marenches, Count, and Christine Ockrent. *The Evil Empire*. London: Sidgwick and Jackson, 1988.

de Marenches, Count, and David A. Andelman. *The Fourth World War*. New York: William Morrow and Company, Inc., 1992.

Dreifus, Henry, and J. Thomas Monk. *Smart Cards*. New York: Wiley Computer Publishing, 1998.

Dunnigan, James F. *How to Make War*. New York: William Morrow and Company, Inc., 1982.

Elliott, E. E. *Horae Apocalyptic*. London: Seeley, Burnside, & Seeley, 1846.

Epperson, A. Ralph. *The New World Order*. Tucson: Publius Press, 1990.

Fabun, Don. *The Dynamics of Change*. Englewood Cliffs: Prentice-Hall, Inc., 1967.

Fialka, John J. *War By Other Means*. New York: W. W. Norton & Company, 1997.

Fruchtenbaum, Arnold, G. *The Footsteps of the Messiah*. Tustin: Ariel Press, 1982.

Gill, Stephen. *American Hegemony and the Trilateral Commission*. Cambridge: Cambridge University Press, 1991.

Goetz, William. *The Economy to Come*. Beaverlodge: Horizon House Publishers, 1984.

Gorbachev, Mikhail. *Perestroika*. New York: Harper & Row, Publishers, 1987.

Graham, Billy. *Approaching Hoofbeats: The Four Horsemen of The Apocalypse*. Waco: Word Books, Inc., 1983.

Graham, Daniel. *High Frontier*. New York: TOR, 1983.

Guinness, H. Grattan. *The Approaching End of the Age*. 8th ed. London: Hodder & Stoughton, 1882.

Haldeman, I. M. *The Signs of the Times*. New York: Charles C. Cook, 1911.

Hersh, Seymour M. *The Samson Option*. New York: Random House, 1991.

Hindson, Ed. *Approaching Armageddon*. Eugene: Harvest House Publishers, 1997.

Hindson, Ed. *The New World Order*. Wheaton: Victor Books, 1991.

Hoy, Claire, and Victor Ostrovsky. *By Way of Deception*. Toronto: Stoddart, 1990.

Hunt, Dave. *Global Peace*. Eugene: Harvest House Publishers, 1990.

Jensen, Carl. *Censored*. Chapel Hill: Shelburne Press, Inc., 1993.

Josephus, Flavius. *Wars of the Jews*. Kingston: N.G.Ellis, 1844.

Kah, Gary H. *En Route to Global Occupation*. Lafayette: Huntington House Publishers, 1992.

Kahn, Herman. *Thinking about the Unthinkable in the* 1980s. New York: Simon and Shuster, 1984.

Kalafian, Michael. *The Prophecy of the Seventy Weeks of the Book of Daniel*. Lanham: University Press of America, 1991.

Keegan, John, and Andrew Wheatcroft. *Zones of Conflict: An Atlas of Future Wars*. New York: Simon and Schuster, 1986.

Kidron, Michael, and Ronald Segal. *The New State of the World*. New York: Simon & Schuster, 1991.

Kidron, Michael, and Ronald Segal. *The New State of the World Atlas*. London: Pan Books, 1987.

Kidron, Michael, and Dan Smith. *The New State of War and Peace*. Hammersmith: Grafton Books, 1991.

Kidron, Michael, and Dan Smith. *The War Atlas*. London: Pan Books Ltd., 1983.

Kincaid, Cliff. *Global Bondage*. Lafayette: Huntington House Publishers, 1995.

King, Alexander, and Bertrand Schneider. *The First Global Revolution*. New York: Pantheon Books, 1991.

Kirban, Salem. *Before it Happens*. Huntingdon Valley: Second Coming Inc., 1993.

Kurtzman, Joel. *The Death of Money*. Boston: Little, Brown and Company, 1993.

LaHaye, Tim. *No Fear of The Storm*. Sisters: Multnomah Press Books, 1992.

Larkin, Clarence. *The Book of Daniel*. Philadelphia: Clarence Larkin, 1929.

LaSor, William Sanford. *The Truth about Armageddon*. Grand Rapids: Baker Book House, 1982.

Levine, Herbert M. *World Politics Debated*. New York: McGraw-Hill Inc., 1992.

Lindsay, Hal. *The Final Battle*. Palos Verdes: Western Front Ltd., 1995.

Livingstone, Neil C. *The Cult of Counterterrorism*. Lexington: Lexington Books, 1990.

Lockyer, Herbert. *All the Messianic Prophecies of the Bible*. Grand Rapids: Zondervan Publishing House, 1973.

Lowth, William. *A Commentary Upon the Prophet Ezekiel*. London: W. Mears, 1773.

Ludwigson, R. *A Survey of Bible Prophecy.* Grand Rapids: Zondervan Publishing House, 1951.

McAlvany, Donald, S. *Toward a New World Order.* Oklahoma City: Hearthstone Publishing, 1990.

McGinn, Bernard. *Anti-Christ.* New York: HarperSanFrancisco, 1994.

McGinn, Bernard. *Visions of the End.* New York: Columbia University Press, 1979.

Malachi, Martin. *The Keys of this Blood.* New York: Simon and Schuster, 1990.

Marshall, Paul, and Lela Gilbert. *Their Blood Cries Out.* Dallas: Word Publishing, 1997.

Miller, Charles W. *Today's Technology.* Lansing: Tip, 1990.

Newton, Bishop Thomas. *Dissertations on the Prophecies.* 2 vol. London: R & R Gilbert, 1817.

Nigel, H. *Unless Peace Comes.* Victoria: Penguin Books, 1968.

Pacepa, Ion. *Red Horizons.* Washington: Regnery Gateway, 1987.

Patai, Raphael. *The Messiah Texts.* Detroit: Wayne State University Press, 1988.

Payne, J. Barton. *Encyclopedia of Biblical Prophecy.* Grand Rapids: Baker Book House, 1980.

Peccei, Aurelio. *One Hundred Pages for the Future.* New York: New American Library, 1981.

Pentecost, Dwight. *Things to Come.* Grand Rapids: Dunham, 1958.

Peters, George. *The Theocratic Kingdom.* Grand Rapids: Kregel Publications, 1957.

Pink, Arthur W. *The Antichrist.* Grand Rapids: Kregel Publications, 1988.

Pusey, E. B. *Daniel the Prophet.* Plymouth: The Devonport Society, 1864.

Randal, Jonathan C. *Going All the Way.* New York: Vintage Books, 1984.

Reagan, David. *The Master Plan*. Eugene: Harvest House Publishers, 1993.

Ritchie, David. *Space War*. New York: New American Library, 1982.

Robertson, Pat. *The New World Order*. Dallas: Word Publishing, 1991.

Saleem, Musa. *The Muslims and the New World Order*. London: ISDS Books, 1993.

Schell, Johnathan. *The Fate of the Earth*. New York: Avon Books, 1982.

Scherman, Nosson, and Meir Zlotowitz, eds. *Daniel*. Trans. Hersh Goldwurm. Brooklyn: Mesorah Publications, 1980.

Scherman, Nosson, and Meir Zlotowitz, eds. *Ezekiel*. Trans. Hersh Goldwurm. Brooklyn: Mesorah Publications, 1980.

Schmitt, Gary. *Silent Warfare*. Washington: Brassey's, 1993.

Schneier, Bruce, and David Banisar. *The Electronic Privacy Papers*. New York: Wiley Computer Publishing, 1997.

Schwartau, Winn. *Information Warfare*. New York: Thunder's Mouth Press, 1994.

Seiss, Joseph. *The Apocalypse*. Philadelphia: Approved Books, 1865.

Sklar, Holly, ed. *Trilateralism*. Montreal: Black Rose Books, 1980.

Smith, Barry R. *Final Notice*. Singapore: Barry Smith Family Evangelism, 1985.

Smith, Jack Russell. *The Unknown CIA*. New York: Berkley Books, 1992.

Smith, Wilbur M. *Israeli/Arab Conflict . . . and the Bible*. Glendale: Regal Books, 1967.

Suborov, Victor. *Inside the Soviet Army*. London: Granada Publishing Ltd., 1984.

Swenson, Richard A. *Hurtling Toward Oblivion*. Colorado Springs: NavPress, 1999.

Tapscott, Don. *The Digital Economy*. New York: McGraw-Hill, 1996.

Taylor, Gordon R. *The Biological Time Bomb*. London: Thames and Hudson, 1968.

Tinbergen, Jan. *Reshaping the International Order: A Report to the Club of Rome*. Scarborough: The New American Library of Canada, 1976.

The Ante-Nicene Fathers. Grand Rapids: Eerdmans Publishing Co., 1986.

Toffler, Alvin. *Power Shift*. New York: Bantam Books, 1990.

Toffler, Alvin, and Heidi Toffler. *War and Anti-War*. Boston: Little, Brown and Company, 1993.

Tregelles, S. P. *Remarks on the Prophetic Visions in the Book of Daniel*. Guilford: Billing and Sons, 1965.

Van Impe, Jack. 2001: *On the Edge of Eternity*. Dallas: Word Publishing, 1996.

Walvoord, John F. *Daniel: The Key to Prophetic Revelation*. Chicago: Moody Press, 1989.

Walvoord, John F. *The Nations in Prophecy*. Grand Rapids: Zondervan Publishing House, 1976.

Weber, Timothy P. *Living in the Shadow of the Second Coming*. New York: Oxford University Press, 1979.

White, John Wesley. *World War III*. Grand Rapids: Zondervan Publishing House, 1977.

Wright, Susan, ed. *Preventing a Biological Arms Race*. Cambridge: The MIT Press, 1990.

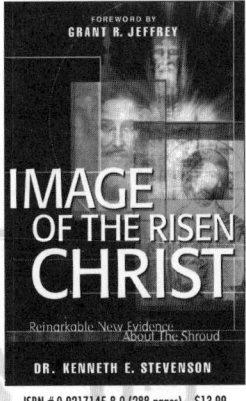

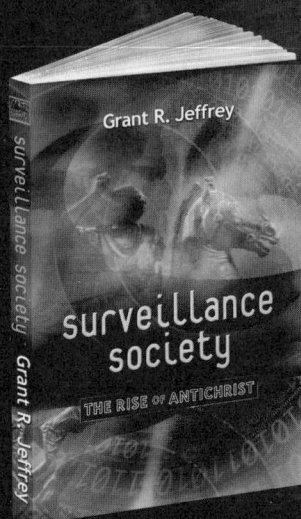

JESUS THE GREAT DEBATE
Video Documentary

This fascinating video documentary explores the powerful historical, archeological, and scientific evidence that proves the Gospel record about Jesus Christ is authentic. An excellent teaching and evangelism resource for study by families, small groups, and churches.

VIDEO: Retail: $19.99 • ISBN: 0-921714-39-4 • (Running Time: 60 Minutes)   *Also Available* AUDIO: Retail: $15.99 • ISBN: 0-921714-41-6

AVAILABLE IN CHRISTIAN BOOKSTORES EVERYWHERE
(OR BY CALLING) IN USA: 1-800-883-1812 IN CANADA: 1-800-853-1423
www.grantjeffrey.com

(Prices may vary in Canada)

Frontier Research Publications

Grant Jeffrey Ministries

Available in Christian bookstores everywhere

Quantity	Code	Description		Price	Total
		Softback Books			
	BK-3	Messiah – War in the Middle East & The Road to Armageddon		$12.99	
	BK-4	Apocalypse – The Coming Judgment of the Nations		$12.99	
	BK-5	Prince of Darkness – Antichrist and the New World Order		$13.99	
	BK-6	Final Warning – Economic Collapse and Coming World Government		$13.99	
	BK-7	Heaven – The Mystery of Angels		$12.99	
	BK-8	The Signature of God – Astonishing Biblical Discoveries		$13.99	
	BK-9	Yeshua – The Name of Jesus Revealed in the Old Testament (Yacov Rambsel)		$11.99	
	BK-10	Armageddon – Appointment With Destiny		$12.99	
	BK-11	His Name is Jesus – The Mysterious Yeshua Codes (Yacov Rambsel)		$12.99	
	BK-12	The Handwriting of God – Sacred Mysteries of the Bible		$13.99	
	BK-14	The New World Religion (Gary H. Kah)		$12.99	
	BK-16	Jesus, The Great Debate		$13.99	
	BK-17	Image of the Risen Christ (Dr. Kenneth E. Stevenson)		$13.99	
	BK-18	Surveillance Society – The Rise of Antichrist		$13.99	
	BK-19	Journey Into Eternity – Search for Immortality		$13.99	
		ANY THREE BOOKS OR MORE	**EACH**	**$11.00**	
		Hardcover Books			
	HC-H	Heaven – The Mystery of Angels		$15.99	
	W-50	Mysterious Bible Codes		$19.99	
	W-51	Flee The Darkness (Grant R. Jeffrey and Angela Hunt)	*Fiction*	$17.99	
	W-52	By Dawn's Early Light (Grant R. Jeffrey and Angela Hunt)	*Fiction*	$18.99	
	W-53	The Spear of Tyranny (Grant R. Jeffrey and Angela Hunt)	*Fiction*	$18.99	
		Videos			
	V-5	The Rebirth of Israel and The Messiah		$19.99	
	V-6	The Antichrist and The Mark of The Beast		$19.99	
	V-7	The Rapture and Heaven's Glory		$19.99	
	V-8	The Coming Millennial Kingdom		$19.99	
	V-9	The Search for The Messiah		$19.99	
	V-13	Archeological Discoveries: Exploring Beneath the Temple Mount		$19.99	
	V-14	Prince of Darkness and The Final Inquisition		$19.99	
	V-15	Secret Agenda of The New World Order and The Tribulation		$19.99	
	V-16	Rush to Armageddon		$19.99	
		ANY TWO VIDEOS OR MORE	**EACH**	**$17.00**	
	V-20	Jesus, The Great Debate		$19.99	
		Total this page (to be carried forward)			

continued overleaf

Quantity	Code	Description	Price	Total
		Total from previous page		
		Double-length Videos		
	V-17	The Signature of God – Astonishing Biblical Discoveries	$29.99	
	V-18	Mysterious Bible Codes	$29.99	
	VP-1	Final Warning, Big Brother Government	$29.99	
		Audio Cassettes		
	AB-14	The Signature of God (2 tapes)	$15.99	
	AB-15	Mysterious Bible Codes (2 tapes)	$15.99	
	AB-17	Jesus, The Great Debate (2 tapes)	$15.99	
		Computer Programs		
	BC	Unlocking the Bible Codes (on CD-ROM; for IBM-compatible computers only) (*shipping and handling included*)	$69.99	
	PIB	**Product Brochure**	No charge	
		One low shipping and handling fee for the above (per order)	$4.95	$4.95
		Zondervan Prophecy Marked Reference Study Bible Grant R. Jeffrey, General Editor		
	KJV	Hardcover	$34.99	
	KJV	Bonded Leather: Black	$59.99	
	KJV	Bonded Leather: Burgundy	$59.99	
	KJV	Top Grain Leather: Black	$69.99	
	NIV	Hardcover	$34.99	
	NIV	Bonded Leather: Black	$59.99	
	NIV	Bonded Leather: Burgundy	$59.99	
		Shipping and handling fee for Bibles (per order)	$5.95	$5.95
		Oklahoma residents add 7.5% sales tax		

Additional shipping charges will apply to orders outside North America.

All prices are in U.S. dollars

Grand Total

PLEASE PRINT

Name _____

Address _____

City _____ State _____ Zip _____

Phone _____ Fax _____

Credit card number _____

Expiry date _____

U.S. orders: mail along with your check or money order to:
Frontier Research Publications
P.O. Box 470470
Tulsa, OK 74147-0470
U.S. credit card orders: call 1-800-883-1812

Canadian orders: call or write for pricing to:
Frontier Research Publications
P.O. Box 129, Station "U"
Toronto, Ontario M8Z 5M4
Canadian VISA/MC card orders: call 1-800-853-1423

Prices effective July 1, 2000